THE REGENCY
CRISIS AND THE
WHIGS
1788–9

THE REGENCY
CRISIS AND THE
WHIGS
1788–9

BY

JOHN W. DERRY
M.A., Ph.D.

*Assistant Lecturer in Political Science at the
London School of Economics, and formerly
Research Fellow of Emmanuel College
Cambridge*

CAMBRIDGE
AT THE UNIVERSITY PRESS
1963

PUBLISHED BY

THE SYNDICS OF THE CAMBRIDGE UNIVERSITY PRESS

Bentley House, 200 Euston Road, London, N.W.1
American Branch: 32 East 57th Street, New York 22, N.Y.

CAMBRIDGE UNIVERSITY PRESS

1963

Printed in Great Britain by
Spottiswoode, Ballantyne & Co. Ltd.
London and Colchester

CONTENTS

PREFACE

Like all young historians I owe a considerable debt to those whose kindness and courtesy have done much to facilitate my research. I should first like to acknowledge the assistance so freely given by the Librarian and Staff of the Sheffield Central Library; of the University Library, Cambridge; and of the Royal College of Physicians Library; and by the Superintendent and Staff of the Reading and Students' Rooms of the British Museum; of the Search Rooms of the Public Record Office; and of the Prior's Kitchen, Durham. Professor G. R. Potter and Dr John Woods did much to aid my work in Sheffield, whilst Professor A. Aspinall, of Reading University, answered queries about the Rosslyn MSS. and the correspondence of George, Prince of Wales. The University Librarian at Nottingham and Miss M. Holmes, the County Archivist of Dorset, also replied to my inquiries in a prompt and helpful fashion. I must also acknowledge the permission of Earl Fitzwilliam and the Trustees of the Wentworth Settled Estates in using the Wentworth Woodhouse MSS. now deposited in the Central Library, Sheffield. Professor Elliott Perkins was originally responsible for making me aware of the Baker diaries, and I must also thank Sir Randle Baker Wilbraham, of Rode Hall, Stoke-on-Trent, for permission to consult the typescript and facsimiles now in the Library of the Royal College of Physicians. Colonel White, of the Historical Manuscripts Commission, was most co-operative in telling me of the present whereabouts of the Baker diaries.

I also wish to thank Professor Herbert Butterfield, Master of Peterhouse, who first suggested the Regency Crisis to me as a subject for research, and Mr R. J. White, of Downing College, for their unfailing encouragement, helpful criticism, and sympathetic understanding, during the years in which they supervised my work as a research student. I have also profited from the criticisms made by Dr J. H. Plumb and Dr Lucy Sutherland, who examined this study in its earlier form as a Ph.D. dissertation. I should also like to express my gratitude to the Master and Fellows of Emmanuel College, who by electing me, first into a Bachelor Scholarship and then into a Research Fellowship, made it possible for me to undertake this piece of historical research. During the course of revision Mr David Newsome pointed out several awkwardnesses of style and expression, and I should like to thank my friends, Mr and Mrs T. A. Neal and Mr J. W. Garbutt, whose hospitality, at various times, made my task so much easier.

Finally, I owe a great debt to the Syndics of the University Press, Cambridge; to the Master and Fellows of Emmanuel College; and to the Cambridge University Board of Research Studies, all of whom generously voted subsidies towards the publication of this book.

J.W.D.

LONDON
January 1963

> *Superior figures in the text refer to notes, which begin on p. 202*

INTRODUCTION

The Regency Crisis of 1788 is frequently regarded as a barren and futile episode in party warfare, complicated perhaps by wearisome discussions on constitutional technicalities, but essentially sterile nevertheless. Yet, over twenty years later, the precedents of 1788 were followed when George III went mad for the last time, and it is reasonable to suggest that whatever the political situation a genuine predicament was created by the incapacity of the King. Although Pitt is often depicted as the defender of Parliamentary privilege, and Fox as the apologist of hereditary right, these attitudes were adopted only after a prolonged period of uncertainty on both sides. Amongst the Opposition there was never general agreement, either on the constitutional significance of the crisis, or on the political tactics most appropriate in a confused and perplexing situation. So much turned on the condition of the King, that the opinions of the doctors were throughout a major factor governing political conduct. The mingling of constitutional interpretations and party motives forms one of the most fascinating aspects of the contest between Pitt and Fox, and, if Lecky could speak in terms of the inversion of roles by Tory and Whig in 1788, that inversion was characterised by doubts, differences of opinion and changes of plan, abortive negotiations and daily anxiety. With the exception of Thurlow, the Cabinet presents a united front, at least from the beginning of December 1788, but the devious twists of policy on the part of the Opposition, heightened as they were by personal feuds, thwarted ambitions, and critical differences of opinion between Fox and Burke, Loughborough and Sheridan, foreshadow the break-up of the party in the 1790's. To follow the conduct of the Opposition from day to day, in the light of popular rumour, Parliamentary debate, and schemes of negotiation, is to experience something of the uncertainty, excitement, and tension, which, for Government and Opposition alike, made the winter of 1788–9 a time of scarcely relieved and almost unbearable strain. Until a very late stage in the crisis expectations were high, and yet subject to constant fluctuation as the latest bulletins arrived from Kew.

Much of the controversy seems petty, distressingly capricious, and irritatingly wilful, but few courtesies can be expected in a struggle for power. Both Pitt and Fox knew they were fighting for their future; and for the Whig party, living as they were on myths and memories from the past, it seemed as if their very existence as a party was at stake. In circumstances of peculiar difficulty they sought to recover their cohesion and sense of purpose, and if they failed in this task they did so because the outcome of the contest depended on technicalities of constitutional law and practice which, with two notable exceptions, they underestimated and misunderstood throughout the crisis. The poverty of their ideas intensified their constant and embarrassing contradictions in debate, their suspicion of each other's motives, their neurotic preoccupation with the satisfaction of their own desires and private ambitions. They were unprepared for the demands which the King's illness laid upon them, and it was no accident that confident hopes and gleeful anticipations of office should wither—that they should be replaced by recrimination, bitterness, and distrust.

It is possible, therefore, to see the crisis of 1788 principally in terms of the decline of the Whig party; a party which even in its moments of degradation appealed to memories of Rockingham and the American War—to an era which became progressively more glorious as the present became more frustrating. It was cruelly ironic that no one anticipated, when the disturbing rumours of the King's behaviour at Windsor inspired amateur prophets to discern the signs of the times, that the result of

George III's lunacy would be the discomforture rather than the triumph of the Whigs. And, since the King's illness thrust both the Ministry and the Opposition into a situation fraught with dilemmas and bristling with problems, it is necessary to give some account of the onset and course of the indisposition of the King.

CHAPTER I

THE KING'S ILLNESS AND
THE CRISIS TO 10 DECEMBER

(i)

In the autumn of 1788 the health of King George III was the subject for persistent speculation on the part of the public. Curiosity was heightened by uncertainty, and when, on the last day of October, the King failed to come to town as expected, gossip gave way to anxiety, despite assurances that the King's disorder, which was said to be of a dropsical tendency, was 'by no means of the alarming kind'.[1] Soon it became impossible to disguise the unpleasant facts any longer, even if a combination of discretion and ignorance distorted them in confusion and contradiction. Some called the royal malady water on the brain; others an ossification of the membrane; but by 7 November it was common knowledge that the King was dangerously ill, and Mr Crawford, writing to the Duchess of Devonshire, told her of his own suspicions: 'My opinion, from all the different accounts I have heard, is that the humour to which his whole family is subject has fallen upon his brain, and that nothing will save him except an eruption upon his skin.'[2]

On the same day Payne asked Lord Loughborough for advice, on behalf of the Prince of Wales, describing the situation at Windsor as 'very alarming', and holding out the most gloomy prospect for the King:

. . . I fear his dissolution is almost the best that can be hoped. He has at present, with a more considerable degree of wandering, a most violent heat, accompanied at the same time with a great chillness: every moment we fear something dreadful.[3]

The next day the illness was diagnosed as an 'absolute mania, distinct from and wholly unconnected with fever', and for several

4

days the city was full of rumours that the King was dead or dying, the stocks falling by two per cent as a result.[1] These fears were finally dispelled, but the ugly truth could not be denied. The King was mad, and a mad King meant a Regency:

The malady with which his Majesty is afflicted is of such a nature—that the Medical Gentlemen have their doubts as to future consequences, and if the King continues a few days longer in his present Situation a Regency will be *if situation worsens* appointed; at the head of which will be his Royal Highness the Prince of Wales.[2]

The King had foreseen the onset of his illness. On 3 November he had confessed his fears to the Duke of York, exclaiming 'I wish to God I might die, for I am going to be mad!', and within the next few days his behaviour became more disturbing, confirming his premonitions. He complained of being 'all at once' an old man, and on another occasion attacked the Prince of Wales without provocation, battering his head against the wall. It was said that he had descended from his coach in Windsor Great Park, only to shake hands with an oak tree, under the delusion that he was addressing the King of Prussia.[3] His sleep was disturbed and he suffered from intermittent fever. He had little thirst and no appetite, and complained of giddiness and confused vision. Even when his fever abated he remained in a state of mental incoherence. Sometimes he talked quietly to himself in an apparently contented fashion; at other times he was abusive and violent. Though he was capable of acuteness and precision, for the most part he babbled away to his pages in vigorous confusion, and on most occasions his conversation was desultory.[4]

Contemporaries were shocked and surprised, but the catastrophe had been approaching throughout the summer. The King had suffered from persistent bilious attacks from the middle of June, and, whilst taking the waters at Cheltenham, he had dieted on mutton, potatoes, and port, as well as going out riding for exercise. Some improvement had resulted, but distressing symptoms reappeared in October. On the 20th, George wrote to Pitt, excusing his delay in answering correspondence on grounds of poor health, and confessing that he was 'not quite in a situation to write at present'. He meandered on about the American War—'that most justifiable war any country ever waged'—and mingled references to Don Quixote and his early life with miscellaneous political reflections.[1] His letter bore clear indications of his disturbed state. Sir George Baker, his physician, attended him daily, and the King complained to him of acute pains in the pit of his stomach. He was also troubled with rheumatism in his limbs, and cramp in the muscles of his legs. On successive days both his feet were swollen, and he had also been afflicted with a rash.[2] When these symptoms eased others took their place. It was necessary to give the King doses of purgative, and when Baker visited his patient on the afternoon of 22 October, he was received 'in a most unusual manner':

> The look of his eyes, the tone of his voice, every gesture and his whole deportment represented a person in the most furious passion of anger. 'One medicine had been too powerful; another had only teazed him without effect. The importation of Senna ought to be prohibited, and he would give orders that in future it shall never be given to any of the royal family.'[3]

Baker was detained for three and a half hours by the frequent repetition of similar language, and on his return to London he wrote a hasty note to Pitt, telling him that he had left the King in a condition 'nearly bordering on delirium'. In the evening Pitt called on Baker and received a full description of the King's condition.[4]

During the following two days there was some improvement. The King seemed calm, composed, and free from fever, and though he slept badly on the night of 23 October his pulse remained quiet. He was, however, languid, weak, slightly lame, and troubled at the thought of the levee at St James's on 24 October; yet, with characteristic courage and devotion to what he considered his duty, he attended the function, in an attempt, so he told Pitt, 'to stop further lies and any fall of the stocks'.[5] But his appearance only heightened the rumours. Sir Gilbert Elliot told his wife that the King was 'certainly in a bad state of health', though he himself did not think it anything 'material'.[1] No one really knew what the trouble was. It had been suggested that the King was suffering from unformed gout, but on 29 October Burke revealed to Elliot that he had been in extreme danger during his illness, spasms in his stomach being of so violent a nature as to leave him speechless for an hour and a half. He also claimed that the secrecy which had surrounded the King's retreat to Cheltenham during the summer confirmed that the illness had been much more serious than had been disclosed. Although he neglected to give Elliot the authority on which he had his information, Burke left him under no doubt of his own conviction that it was authentic.[2]

What transformed a series of bilious and muscular disorders into madness remains a mystery. Contemporaries sought an explanation for the King's collapse in chills, carelessness, and an unfortunate combination of minor ailments. He had committed the 'great imprudence' of remaining for a whole day in wet stockings. By drinking cold water and eating a pear he had accentuated his indigestion, driving the humour which had first showed itself in his legs into his bowels. The necessary medicines had expelled the disorder into the King's brain and the doctors were later to attempt to lure the humour back into his legs by the use of warm baths and the application of poultices. Other suggestions were that the King's breakdown had been precipitated by his annoyance at the endeavour of the Duke of York to introduce Turkish instruments into the Band of Guards, and by a discussion over the dinner table on 5 November on the subject of murder.[3] All this seems inadequate.

In his life George III was attacked by insanity on five occasions —in 1765, 1788, 1801, 1804, and 1810—and it is possible to discern a weakness in his heredity on his mother's side. An uncle was suspected of suicide, and two cousins were probably

schizophrenic. George himself was a manic-depressive, a form of
madness which, though primarily a disturbance in mood rather
than mentation, has a strong tendency to recur. The constant
changes in temper which were so characteristic of the King's
illness, and which puzzled his doctors and baffled his contemporaries, would seem to indicate that form of insanity. At
times the King was sunk in listless depression, only to exchange
that attitude for excited vehemence. Although he could display
sound sense and wit, as when he reminded Willis that if Christ
went about healing the sick he did not get £700 a year for doing
so, there were other days when the King was incapable of focusing
his thoughts, when he imagined that London was under water,
and when he busied himself with writing letters to foreign courts
on fictitious issues. Stories were told of him showing his backside
to his attendants to prove that he was not suffering from gout;
of him pulling off Baker's wig, and thrusting the doctor to his
knees to look at the stars. It was even claimed that the King had
hoodwinked Baker into releasing him from his strait-jacket, only
to fell him with a savage buffet on the ear, the contents of the
royal chamber pot being emptied over the prostrate physician.
Other accounts had George lavishing dignities on pages and
gentlemen of the bedchamber, neglecting to shave, and raving
against the Queen. Alleged incidents at Cheltenham were cited
as evidence of the approaching breakdown: the King had run a
race with a horse, and had asked a Mr Clements if he was the man
who ran away with Lady Sarah Bunbury when he was in love
with her.[1]

Disillusionment and overwork also helped to bring about the
King's collapse. George III was an intensely conscientious
monarch, applying himself to his duties with unrelenting
diligence. By toil and application he had made himself master
of the intricacies of government, and conscious as he was of the
immense responsibilities laid upon him by Providence, and of his
own unworthiness to bear them, he strove to supply through

painstaking and devoted labour what he lacked in genius and imagination. But the years had taken their toll. Filled with a high conviction of his calling, and inspired by lofty ideals concerning the privileges and duties of kingship, he had seen his dreams shattered and his ideals mutilated in the cruel world of politics. Deficient in human sympathy and understanding, and seeing the world exclusively in terms of his own fervently held values, his disillusionment was all the more bitter and hard to sustain. Honest, industrious, and upright, but narrow and self-righteous, he blamed others for the inner frustration which clouded his life. He came to pride himself on his virtues, thanking heaven that his morals and way of life 'but little resembled those too prevalent in the present age'.[1] The age was profligate, depraved, characterised by knavery, indolence, and cowardice. And, as his children grew up, their conduct added the raw pangs of paternal disappointment to the anxieties of public life. George had sought to make his children useful examples, 'worthy of imitation', but, whilst his daughters were (in their father's phrase) 'all Cordelias', his sons were selfish, ungrateful, extravagant in their disobedience, and ostentatious in the irresponsible expression of their whims. The Prince of Wales led a life of elegant dissipation, and by his devotion to Charles James Fox he shocked his father's sense of morality and provoked his deepest political prejudices. Horror at his son's private life was mingled with abhorrence of his political conduct, and Fox became doubly hateful, as the malignant seducer of the Prince, as well as an unscrupulous and ambitious politician. When the Duke of York, the King's favourite son, returned from the Continent in 1787 his father saw his adored Frederick submit to the contagious charms of Carlton House, and in his ravings the cruel agony inflicted by the Duke's desertion found its outlet.[2] As a father the King had been well-meaning but rigid, a perplexing mixture of affection and severity, and he felt his family disappointments keenly. The stresses on his mind were great, and in the absence of any acute political crisis in the autumn of 1788 the behaviour of his sons must be considered one of the decisive factors in precipitating his mental collapse.

Other elements in George's private life were seized on by the public. He had always been frugal, dieting carefully and exercising regularly in an effort to escape the hereditary corpulence which he had seen swamp his uncle, the Duke of Cumberland. One newspaper declared that the King's diet and ferocious devotion to exercise were the real causes of the trouble:

> The abstemious system which his Majesty has invariably pursued, is thought to have occasioned his present complaint. Opposite causes sometimes produce a similar effect; and living too freely is not more prejudicial to health than too abstemious. The King throughout his whole life has used a great deal of exercise both on foot and horseback; but he did not proportion the use of wine to his exercise, which when used to a great degree, must exhaust Nature instead of refreshing her.[1]

(ii)

Bewilderment over the King's illness was paralleled by uncertainty as to its political implications. A mad King posed new problems, and, in English history, regencies were associated with strife, instability, and the worst excesses of faction. The fate of Edward II, the Wars of the Roses, the reigns of Edward V and Edward VI, did not constitute a happy list of precedents, and more recently the inveterate jealousy between Hanoverian father and son had contributed to the distaste which was felt for princely ambition and impatience, except amongst those politicians who saw in the heir to the throne the best hope for their advancement. More serious still the legal position was obscure. Was madness equivalent to any other temporary incapacity? Or to the absence of a monarch? Or to a minority, or even to a demise of the Crown? These difficult and tangled issues were not to be settled in an atmosphere of legal calm and precision. Political interests, long frustrated hopes, repressed ambitions, were all to play their part. The Government of William Pitt was faced with its most severe trial since the defeat of the Fox–North coalition, and there was now a real possibility that the Opposition would take office under the protection and patronage of the Prince of Wales. When the King was thought to be dying it seemed inevitable that Pitt would be dismissed on the accession of George IV, and the exultation of the Whigs at the prospect of a return to the profitable pastures of office was equalled only by the depression of the Ministerialists. The situation was excitingly tense, brimful of possibilities, exhilaratingly transformed; fraught with apprehension and delight.

Yet the alternative to the death of the King—'a continuance of the present derangement of his faculties without any other effect upon his health'—was one which could not be contemplated without horror. That the King should live in his melancholy state was 'most to be feared'.[1] The naive assumption that the Prince would be appointed Regent with kingly power gradually gave way to perplexity and embarrassment as the technical difficulties became more apparent. Grenville touched on one of the most troublesome aspects, when, writing to his brother Buckingham on 8 November, he commented:

> Parliament cannot proceed to business without the session being opened by the King, or by some commission authorised by him. No Regent can be appointed or authorised to exercise acts of royal authority but by act of Parliament, nor can any such act be valid and binding in law without the King's consent.[2]

The *Morning Post* thought it a gross mistake to suppose that the Prince of Wales had a right to take upon himself the administration of affairs:

> Whenever it shall become requisite to take any step in so extraordinary a case, the decision must depend upon the judgment of Parliament; and Parliament certainly will not precipitate in determining upon so nice and critical a point—but when they do decide there can be no doubt but that their determination will be in such a manner as to prove at once their affection and duty for

the Sovereign, and their anxiety to remove every obstacle that may stand in the way of an effectual discharge of the grand business of the State.[1]

Two days later the same newspaper, which remained staunchly loyal to Pitt throughout the crisis, again denied that there was any right to the Regency on the part of the Prince of Wales: 'if such a right exists it must owe its existence to the present or some future Parliament'.[2] Yet there was never any real dispute as to the person of the Regent, even if for a fleeting moment at the beginning of December the Government's thoughts turned to the Queen when it was rumoured that the Prince would refuse a limited Regency. The controversy raged over the terms on which he was to assume office and the powers with which he was to be entrusted.

For the King's illness confronted Pitt with a situation calling for extreme tact and delicacy. The madness of the King was an event for which no obvious provision had been made in law, and constitutional precedent gave no immediate and precise answer. Pitt acted with characteristic caution. He studied both precedents and constitutional theory with care and diligence. On 18 November, when the fate of his Ministry was still undecided and when he was still uncertain of what action to take to preserve it, he was presented with extracts from a manuscript entitled 'Incepta de Juribus Coronae', discussing the natural and political capacities of the King together with means of supplying deficiencies both during the ordinary course of events and in times of infancy, illness, and absence.[3] He also studied a series of notes on various technical issues raised by Regency, and a list of references to the transactions in Parliament and Council during the incapacities of Henry VI in 1454 and 1455. In this Pitt was following the example of Newcastle, who had had a paper prepared in 1751, discussing minorities from the time of Henry III, in connexion with the preliminary business for the Regency Bill of that year.[4]

Precedents drawn from the fifteenth century required interpretation if they were to prove of any value; and yet, remote as they were from the situation in 1788, they had affirmed certain principles. Claims to the Regency on grounds of kinship had been subjected to Parliamentary scrutiny, and a clear distinction had been made between the position and responsibilities of a Regent and a King. No succession to the Regency was recognised. Each case was settled on its merits, and, if this implied that principles had to be deduced from several instances, it also meant that Parliamentary discussion and adjudication were indispensable. The provisions which had been made for the King's minority and insanity emphasised, in Sir William Holdsworth's words, 'that elective principle in the descent of the Crown which took permanent shape in the power of Parliament to regulate the succession to the throne'.[1] This is not to credit the magnates of the fifteenth century with any conception of liberal democracy. They were preoccupied with their own influence and their own power. Their motives were selfish and their aims simple: they saw no reason why they should allow a Regent to flaunt his authority as if he was King. They had a chance to safeguard their own rights and to assert their own importance, and they took it. The real power during a minority was to remain in their hands. In the pursuit of their own interests, and with no altruistic intent, they made any hereditary Regency impossible. For Fox and his friends this was inconvenient, irritating, and exasperating; and, in the last resort, it was also to prove undeniable.

At his accession Henry VI was only nine months old, and in providing for the minority Parliament successfully asserted its right to make provision for the government of the country, and to decide not only who was to exercise the executive power during the King's infancy, but also the powers to be granted to him. The Duke of Gloucester, who was in England at the time of his brother's death, had received the Great Seal from Bishop Longley on 28 September 1422 but he was not empowered until 6 November to open Parliament. He could not act without the advice of the Council, from whom he derived his authority to open, carry on, and dissolve Parliament. His commission contained a clause insisting on the assent of the Council, and Gloucester, who was ambitious and impatient, was dissatisfied. He objected to the clause but the magnates replied they could not agree to its removal, claiming that it was as necessary for the Duke's security as their own. The Duke was compelled to give way. On 9 November 1422 he opened Parliament, acting by virtue of his relationship to the infant King, and also of the commission which he had received.[1]

But Gloucester was determined to seek more power. He claimed the Regency under the will of Henry V and as next of kin to the young King. The Lords denied the claim on grounds of kinship, after duly searching for a precedent, and refuted the power of the late King to dispose of the kingdom after his death without the consent of the estates. They also voiced their distaste for the titles of Regent, Tutor, Governor, and Lieutenant, and on 5 December the King, by the assent and advice of the Lords Spiritual and Temporal, and of the Commons, nominated the Duke of Bedford Protector and Defender of the Realm and of the Church and Principal Counsellor to the King, whenever he should be present in England. During Bedford's absence in France, Gloucester was to hold the same posts. He accepted the responsibility, but his claim to the unlimited Regency as of right had been refuted. A Council of Regency was named and specific powers were entrusted to it.[2]

In 1428 Gloucester made another attempt to seize power, asking the Lords to define his powers as 'Protector and Defender of the realm of England and chief Counsellor to the King'. But again he was rebuffed. He was reminded that his claim to the Regency had been denied, and the Lords saw no reason why they should give the Duke further powers. They asked him not to demand any addition to what he had already been granted. In November 1429 Henry VI was formally crowned at Westminster.

The office of Protector lapsed, and on 15 November Glouce renounced the office.[1]

Fox denounced references to the reign of Henry VI as irrelevant to the problems of Regency in 1788, but, even allowing for the development in the country's institutions which had taken place in the intervening period, it remains true to say that a claim to the Regency on grounds of kinship had been formally rejected by Lords and Commons. To suggest that because the Lords were then predominant no parallel could be drawn for 1788 was un- realistic. To assert a right, which ran counter to precedent, was dangerous, and for Fox and his friends ultimately disastrous. In any event more recent proceedings in cases of minority had given further support to the principle of Parliamentary sanction.

Minority had always involved some restriction on the powers of the Regent. In both 1751 and 1765, the Act passed in Anne's reign, providing for the absence of her successor, had been followed when making provision for the accession of minors; the Regent could not consent to a Bill altering the succession, repealing Charles II's Act of Uniformity, or the Scottish Act securing the Presbyterian form of Church government. In 1751 the Princess of Wales was to be made Guardian of the persons of her children, and as Regent she was to be given power to exercise the prerogative. A Council of Regency was named, and this provision was repeated in 1765. All this emphasised Parlia- ment's powers of discretion, and in 1765, when George III had wanted an unrestricted right of nomination to the Regency, his Ministers had prevailed upon him to accept the limitation of his choice to members of the royal family. At the same time no automatic right to the Regency had been recognised as residing in anyone. There was support here for Pitt's distinction between a right and a claim, and it was ironic that the restrictions compel- ling the King to nominate a member of the royal family were of Parliamentary origin.[2]

The action taken in 1454 and 1455, when Henry VI was

incapacitated by madness, gave even less consolation to Fox and his friends. In the first instance the initiative had been taken by the Lords, for when the King's condition had rendered him incapable of carrying out his duties, they had chosen the Duke of York Protector on 27 March 1454 and this resolution was embodied in an Act which received the assent of the Commons—'the King had just sense enough to place the Great Seal in the hands of the Earl of Salisbury, and in this way the royal assent was given'.[1] On the second occasion the formalities of 1454 were repeated, though this time the Commons took the lead in asking for the nomination of a Protector. The Duke of York was to continue in the post until relieved by the King in Parliament, or until the baby Prince of Wales came of age. A Council was appointed, of which the Duke was chief, but, although it was decided that the Council was to 'provide, commeyne, ordain, speed, and conclude all such matters as touch and concern the good and politique rule and governance of this . . . land', the members protested that the sovereignty must always remain vested in the person of the King.[2]

Fox claimed that the clause protecting the rights of the Prince of Wales implied that the existence of a Prince of Wales of full age in 1788 gave him an automatic right to the Regency and that all further discussion was useless and unnecessary. On the other side it was argued that only the specific insistence on the Prince's rights by Parliament gave them any validity, and that Parliament's own right of discretion existed prior to those of the Prince of Wales. It is easy to see how both sides could claim that the precedent of 1455 supported their own case. The action taken by Parliament was no more than a wise precaution. By securing the rights of the Prince against those of the Protector appointed during his father's illness and his own minority, Parliament had not committed themselves to more than a necessary review of the situation should the Prince come of age during his father's in-capacity. Even if recognition was accorded to the pre-eminent claims of a Prince of full age, Parliament had not limited its own right to determine his powers and to settle the matter as and when it arose, according to its own discretion. In so far as the proceedings in the reign of Henry VI proved anything they supported the contention that no automatic right to the Regency existed in any one person, and that Parliament's right to review each case on its merits was confirmed. That the Prince of Wales was of full age in 1788 did not, as Fox maintained, render the precedents of 1454 and 1455 null and void; it merely threw into greater relief the need for their careful study and scrupulous interpretation.

If the parallel between cases of illness and minority was denied, and if the steps taken to supply the deficiency during Henry VI's bouts of insanity were considered too remote to be of practical value, it was still possible to argue that the King's breakdown was analogous to absence. In this case there were no grounds for considering the Prince of Wales the only possible choice as Regent. In the Middle Ages the justiciar had acted for the King during periods when the monarch was absent in his foreign dominions, and when the office of justiciar became extinct Lords Justices were usually appointed to carry on the Government by letters patent from the King. In the seventeenth and early eighteenth centuries the Lords Justices appointed for this purpose were usually members of the Cabinet. In 1689 Parliament had decided that Mary should continue the Government during the absence of William III, but in this instance the parallel is inexact. Mary II was Queen in her own right, and Parliament was therefore recognising her status, rather than making provision for Regency. In 1707 provision had been made for the appointment of Lords Justices to carry on the executive functions of Government between the death of Anne and the arrival of her successor in England. In 1716 the Prince of Wales had been appointed Guardian and Lieutenant of the Realm during his father's absence in Hanover, but his powers were severely curtailed. He could not call Parliament; he lacked the right to make appointments in the Royal Household, the Treasury, and the Admiralty; his right of promotion in the Army was strictly limited; he could take no decision relative to foreign affairs.[1] If the Prince was Regent his powers had been rigorously pruned, and this was to be the solution finally adopted by Pitt in 1788. But whilst George I had brought himself to endow his hated son with a sparse allocation of powers in 1716, the bitter rivalry and corroding jealousy between George II and Frederick, Prince of Wales, meant that on later occasions the King took care not to trust his son with even the starkly rationed powers of a Regent during his own visits to the Continent. In 1732, for example, George II appointed Queen Caroline as caretaker during his absence. But since the King was in no position to indicate in 1788 whom he wished to be entrusted with the executive power, the practice of George II's reign gave little practical help, except in so far as it implied a qualified Regency, not necessarily devolving upon the Prince of Wales. None of the precedents afforded a simple and readily acceptable solution. No set procedure, no order of precedence or line of succession, was acknowledged in cases of Regency.[2]

But even if the distinction between monarch and Regent was accepted, and even if there was general agreement on the person of the Regent and the powers he was to exercise, another difficulty presented itself in the shape of how the Prince was to be invested with whatever powers it was thought proper for him to exercise. In 1688 the Convention Parliament had proceeded by an Address to William of Orange, but on that occasion the throne had been considered vacant.[3] In 1788 a similar assumption could not be made. George III had not fled the country, nor was it possible to construe the King's indiscretions in his sick room at Windsor as parallel to James II's notorious destruction of the Great Seal. A mad King had not abdicated. Even if its occupant was incapable of attending to business the throne was occupied.

Supporters of the Ministry in 1788 claimed that this breach with the precedent of 1688 rendered an Address to the Prince asking him to accept the Regency under certain conditions an inappropriate step. If the throne was occupied then Parliament was a full Parliament, not a Convention, and therefore an Act of Parliament was the most suitable way of effecting a Regency. In many ways an Address would have been the simplest means of supplying the deficiency, but Pitt could not be sure that the Prince would accept the Regency on the understanding that his power was to be limited in certain respects, nor could he be trusted to abide by any promise once he was installed in office. An Act of Parliament would have much greater force and would be much more binding than an Address from the two Houses.[1]

But, if an Act was to be passed constituting the Prince of Wales Regent, whilst defining the scope of his powers, how was the royal assent to be given to the Bill? The King could hardly consent to a Bill which had been necessitated by his inability to conduct business. The answer to the riddle was found in the relationship between the natural and political capacities of the King. The lawyers were convinced that no distinction could be made between the natural and political capacities of the monarch, for any deficiencies in his natural ability were filled by various branches of the constitution.[2] If Henry VI, at nine months of age, could hand over the Great Seal to the Master of the Rolls in order to seal several commissions, including that empowering the Duke of Gloucester to call a Parliament, it was thought that no objection could be raised to a similar use of the Great Seal during the madness of the King. A commission sealed with the Great Seal was indisputable, especially if it was fixed by order of the King and the two Houses.[3] Such a procedure could be criticised as enabling Parliament at any time to eliminate the King by depriving him of his right of withholding consent to legislation, but, in reply, it was maintained that since the expedient was merely a means of supplying a particular necessity it was limited by that necessity. Unwieldy as this process was it was the only way in which the creation of the Regency could be given the full sanction of an Act of Parliament. The assumption that there was no distinction between the natural and political capacities of the King, and the parallel one that a document sealed with the Great Seal was binding, were well-established legal conventions. Once the initiative had been attributed to Parliament by a study of precedents there was little else the Government could do in order to give practical expression to what was considered a legitimate interpretation of constitutional theory and practice. No one could ignore precedent and no one could act without due reverence for legal forms and accepted conventions. A genuine problem existed in deciding the process by which the incapacity of the King was to be provided for. Although a distinction had always been made between the status and powers of a monarch and a Regent, and while the responsibility of Parliament to supply a deficiency had been indicated in a variety of cases, these factors were inextricably tangled with the strife of party. But the bitterness of political conflict should not obscure the technical difficulties which faced William Pitt as he strove to deal with the situation created by the mental collapse of George III.

(iii)

Pitt was still only twenty-nine years of age when the crisis broke, but he had borne the heaviest public responsibilities for almost five years. Though he was popular as Prime Minister he was something of an enigma as a man. He lacked Fox's gift of making friends quickly and easily, and he was inferior to his rival in the arts and graces of carefree companionship. He never lost an aloof reserve which could be mistaken for pride, and his habitual dignity was often interpreted as a cloak for the most inhuman cunning. As a boy he had been trained by his father for the gravest burdens which life could lay upon him, and his natural diligence was intensified by his upbringing. Frail in body he had

been subjected to a Spartan discipline for his mind, and alt'
he never lost the taste for port wine which Dr Addington ,
prescription for youthful fatigue stimulated, he lacked many of
the other colourful extravagances which marked the gay, witty,
cruel, and vicious society of his time. His morals were irreproach-
able. He kept no mistress, and, despite the chaotic state of his
private finances, he was not a gambling man. Yet his purity
caused as many gibes, taunts, and titters as Fox's devotion to
games of chance and Mrs Armistead. He was not given to displays
of emotion in the House, and when towards the end of his life
he wept at the disgrace of his friend Dundas, he pulled his hat
over his eyes to disguise his grief. His appeal was to the intellect,
not the heart, yet he had no taste for the hypnotic delights of
abstract thinking, and he was the least likely to succumb to what
Burke later described as the French fashion in politics. He saw
government in terms of sound finance and efficient administration, rather than in grandiose projects for the salvation of mankind. Yet, while he was too intelligent to be deceived by the
brave slogans of the French Revolution, he was sufficiently unimaginative to underestimate its power, its appeal, its dynamic
assault on all the old securities of Europe.

There were moments when he could unbend in the company
of relatives, or with several close friends. With his face blackened
with cork he played on the floor with the Stanhope and Napier
children, but, when the romp was interrupted by the arrival of
Hawkesbury and Castlereagh, one of his young companions
never forgot the change which came over Pitt's demeanour in an
instant. The Prime Minister's 'tall, ungainly, bony, figure'
seemed to grow to the ceiling, the Secretaries of State bowing
like willows before their master.

Enemies often accused him of hypocrisy, and ambition was
frequently alleged to be the inspiration and explanation of his
conduct. His scrupulous sense of decorum and his frigid behaviour
in the House made it easy for these charges to be hurled about.

That he was ambitious is undeniable. Most able men in politics are, and Pitt, inheriting as he did a confident esteem for his own abilities from his father, knew that he was able. But to suggest that he was interested solely in remaining in office is a gross exaggeration. In his relationship with George III he was a loyal servant, but he was determined to be no second North, and when he deferred to the King's wishes on several important occasions he was doing no more than conform to the conventions of the time. Throughout the crisis of 1788–9 Pitt was concerned to secure the rights of the King, but he was no more a pawn in the hands of the King than he was a lackey of the House of Commons. In 1788, despite his tenure of office, he had only a tiny gathering of personal followers in the Commons, and for support in debate he relied, not so much on those who understood and approved his policies, but on the habitual supporters of any government 'under any Minister not peculiarly unpopular'.[1] Pitt was dependent, in a real sense, on the confidence of the King and on the House of Commons in an age of little party organisation and lax party discipline. With the support of the King he could face a hostile House, as in 1783–4, but on that occasion circumstances had been extraordinary. He was compelled to humour both King and Commons. He could not afford to risk his Ministry on issues for which he had the support of neither, and this, rather than crude egoism, explains his conduct over Parliamentary reform, Hastings, and Ireland. For Pitt was not impressed by the extravagant but vacuous political gesture, and he had little time for that dramatic posturing in the face of events which so frequently passes for political idealism and fortitude. He lacked neither courage nor nobility, but, more than either, he was acutely aware of the need for political responsibility, and he weighed carefully the possible consequences of any course of action when called upon to make any decision.

In debate he was masterly, lucid, persuasive. He could marshal facts in so logical a fashion that even the dryest recital of figures seemed almost eloquent. Although no mere opportunist, no man knew better how to exploit his opponents' errors, putting any tactical miscalculation to decisive use. His gestures were stiff and angular, but he was blessed with a resonant and clear voice, and his early training in the translation of Thucydides had developed his natural command of language. Yet he never allowed a temporary advantage to tempt him into forgetting his primary task. When Rolle introduced the Fitzherbert question into the Regency debates, in much the same manner as he had raised the matter two years before, Pitt refrained from using it as a means of embarrassing the Whigs, and gave Rolle no support in pressing for further information on the vexed topic. He knew how distasteful the affair had been in 1787, and how difficult it would be to prevent the spirit of inquiry from going too far, once it was roused. There was little to be gained by discrediting the Prince of Wales, and it would be better for the Prince to take up the responsibilities of the Regency without any unpleasant investigation into his relationship with Mrs Fitzherbert. Pitt had one constitutional crisis on his hands. He did not want another.[1]

Since the 1784 election Pitt's hold on office had been secure. He had the confidence of the King and the support of a majority in both Houses, and his administration had been both successful and popular. His financial policy, his adjustment of the Customs, the Eden Treaty with France, had all been successful, while more controversial measures on Parliamentary Reform and the Slave Trade had humoured the friends of reform without endangering the Ministry. Despite the frustration which he had experienced over his Irish proposals, the Dutch crisis had added the lustre of a triumphant foreign policy to his already impressive achievements. As an anonymous author of the period asserted:

The minister at this extraordinary period possessed in the highest degree the confidence of the nation. The public prepossession to the name he bears was grown into a great popular regard, from his having conducted himself, according to the general opinion, in a manner which added new honours to it. The nation was recovering under his administration from the ruinous consequences of the late war; the measures of government were almost universally thought to be framed with wisdom and the energies of it employed with spirit and judgment. . . .[1]

Pitt's popularity is borne out by less favourably disposed witnesses. Sir Gilbert Elliot complained that even if the Opposition came into office Pitt would make a very popular—if not initially powerful—Opposition, and Robert Sinclair, writing to Earl Fitzwilliam at the height of the crisis, lamented that Pitt's 'plausibility and hypocrisy have produced him a high degree of popularity that ought to astonish discerning men and which it is not easy to suppress or extinguish. . . .'[2] Yet, despite all this, disaster loomed.

Speculation concerning the political results of the King's indisposition ranged from extreme pessimism to bright optimism. Some contemporaries hoped that the calamity would reconcile the parties and produce 'union'. Others feared that party strife would generate such 'a scene of confusion . . . as would threaten the nation with a still greater calamity'. The dislike which the Prince felt for Pitt was well known, and, though it was suggested that he had been more favourably disposed to Pitt since the affair of his debts in the preceding year, no permanent change of heart had taken place. Nevertheless, it was hoped that the gravity of the crisis would 'lessen the acrimony of the Prince's feelings towards Mr Pitt'.[3] Pleas were made for the Prince to change his mind: 'Ill are you advised when you are persuaded to exclude Mr Pitt in the meridian of his glory. The nation will look back with regret on the happiness of his administration and become clamorous for his return.'[4] But, while the same author cried 'The national acclamations already echo the name of Pitt! At the very sound—PATRIOTISM rises from her seat to pay the tribute of obeisance . . .',[5] such enthusiasm was not shared by the Heir Apparent, who based his political conduct, not on any national considerations, but on personal convenience and caprice.

Like everyone else Pitt had been taken unawares by the King's
collapse, despite the letters which he had received from George III
in which it is possible to trace a deterioration in the King's mental
condition. Baker gave Pitt a full account of the King's state of
health on 22 October,[1] but there is no evidence to suggest that
at that date the Minister anticipated the seriousness of the crisis
which was to be upon him within such a short space of time.
Initially the Ministry was as bewildered and confused as the
public by the unexpected sequence of events, and however
fervently he advocated the thesis that the Government was
harbouring sinister threats against the succession, Burke was
wide of the mark in his accusations.[2] Only as the crisis unfolded
did Pitt take the stand which was to preserve his hold on office.
We have seen how carefully he studied precedents and constitutional theory, but he was unsure of himself until the end of
November; hesitant in his adoption of the stratagems which were
to prove his principal weapons in the struggle for power, and
uncertain what action would best secure the rights of the King.
He and his colleagues clung to the hope that the King's recovery
would render any action unnecessary, anticipating that the crisis
would vanish as suddenly as it had appeared.[3]

His position was not easy. Within the Cabinet opinion was
divided. Richmond and Camden favoured a coalition, though by
the end of the month it was hoped that any proposal on the
Opposition's part would only serve to gain the Ministry credit
for rejecting it.[4] Throughout the first two months Thurlow's
behaviour was dangerously ambiguous.[5] Pitt faced the prospect
of resuming his legal career, but he was determined to relinquish
his position in as dignified a manner as possible.[6] But as long as
the medical experts' prognosis remained inconclusive he did not
commit himself. Warren, Baker, and Reynolds, the King's
doctors, hesitated to make any public pronouncement, and Pitt,
dissatisfied with the physicians, called in Dr Addington, his own
doctor. Addington had had experience of treating lunatics; the

King's doctors had none. Twenty years before he had kept an asylum at Reading and after seeing the King on 27 November he predicted that a recovery would take place.[1] Just over a week later Dr Willis, a clergyman from Lincolnshire, who had some claim to be a specialist in the treatment of the insane, made the same prediction even more confidently. Only as Willis took over the care and supervision of the King did Pitt's confidence rise and his policy take shape.[2]

(iv)

Meanwhile, though they were jubilant at the unexpected turn of events which had brought office within their grasp, the Opposition were as little prepared as the Ministry to meet the demands which were to be made of them. Their leaders were scattered far and wide. Fox was holidaying in Italy with Mrs Armistead, rambling 'no one knew where on the continent . . . in the arms of faded beauty',[3] and the latest information—that he was at Venice with the intention of going on to Rome—was a fortnight old.[4] Burke was at Beaconsfield. The Duke and Duchess of Devonshire heard of the King's illness at Chesterfield, and it was not until 19 November, after the Duke of Portland had twice begged them to come to town (he had no political friends to consult), that they returned to London.[5]

Nor had the history of the Whigs since their last experience of office been fortunate. The failure of the Fox–North coalition had banished them to the deserts of political futility. For all Fox's eloquence, for all his avowals that his friendships not his enmities were eternal, he and his party never earned forgiveness for allying themselves with the good-natured and indolent victim of their most violent denunciations during the American War. Though Fox could legitimately claim that with the termination of hostilities no public issue separated him from North, it was a simple matter for pamphleteers to seize upon the union as the most damning proof of his restless and unscrupulous ambition:

BURKE and FOX! In that instant are recollected their very pathetic appeals to heaven for the sincerity of their abhorrence of Lord North. . . . We are then led, by an easy transition, to that infamous event, the COALITION, an event which unmasked the hypocrisy of the heart. . . .[1]

Elsewhere Fox's conduct with respect to the 'monstrous coalition' is compared with that of Cataline and Shaftesbury.[2]

Fox had been in politics for almost twenty years[3] when the Regency Crisis seemed to promise that the years of frustration were over and those of fulfilment at hand. Almost his entire career had been spent in opposition, and although he could look back with pardonable pride to the period of the American War, the defeat, and worse still the humiliation, of 1784 had meant that his ejection from power and place seemed irrevocable. He had been impotent in the face of the King's tactics in the House of Lords, and his own folly had contributed as much to his undoing as the subtleties of George III and the cunning of Robinson and Jenkinson. By his conduct since the death of the Marquis of Rockingham he had driven the King to greater lengths to throw off the dominion of unscrupulous politicians. Fox was no longer the young debater of the 'seventies, and it was now impossible to laugh off his indiscretions as the amusing, if occasionally embarrassing, foibles of a gifted but undisciplined boy. In the autumn of 1788 it was rumoured that he would soon retire from politics.[4]

For all his brilliance, his astonishing powers in debate, and the magnetic charm of his personality, Fox lacked maturity in political conduct. He was capable of insight but not stamina, and, driven to dubious extremes by the enervating frustration of opposition when such a role was only haltingly recognised by the constitutional practice of the day, he was often too eager to attack the Government simply because it was the Government, and to object to any proposal put forward by William Pitt. His greatest weakness was a habit of committing indiscretions at the moment most inconvenient for his colleagues. Even when by his conduct of a party he had 'approved himself equal to the conduct of an empire'[1] there had been an element of bravado, of the brilliant impromptu sally, in Fox's behaviour. Confronted as he was by his sovereign's unyielding distaste and distrust he was the victim, not only of his own frailties, but also of the political atmosphere in which he moved. Opposition could be little other than ill-starred in the 1780's, and by his own misjudged attempts to escape from the realities of the situation Fox plunged deeper into the morass.

Yet he could inspire the most devoted and lasting friendship as well as the implacable hostility of George III. By his charm he fascinated those who were irritated and exasperated by his errors of judgment. It was possible for one of his disciples to define his politics as simple loyalty to Mr Fox,[2] and even when he infuriated his associates by some catastrophic blunder he was soon forgiven, even if on occasions he burst into tears at the scolding he received. He ambled through life with a casual good nature which not even the excessive indulgence of his father had destroyed, and to the end he retained an easy good humour which sweetened all his relationships.

He was a man of generous emotions, and unlike his great antagonist he did not shield his deepest joys and sorrows from the keen light of publicity. When the great breach with Burke came in the debate on the Quebec Government Bill in May 1791, Fox found it impossible to control his feelings and broke down in the House.[3] He lived openly and did not scruple to hide his follies. He gambled with the carefree extravagance of the spend-thrift, yet he was as unlucky in play as in politics. For all his love of the races he was dogged by ill-luck, and on one occasion he protested that the Prince of Wales had won by a low cheat. He outraged society by remaining faithful to his mistress when her beauty had faded and by making an honest woman of her after years of illicit bliss. (The initiative to legalise the union came from Fox not Mrs Armistead.) He played cricket with more enthusiasm than skill, being constantly run out because of his huge bulk, and when in his last illness he had to be wheeled about in a chair, he still went out to bat, chair and all.

He was fond of books and fancied himself a man of letters, liking nothing better than to lie under the trees at St Anne's Hill reading one of his favourite authors, dispensing with the book when the inclination came over him. Even idleness exercised a certain charm, and in the heat of political strife he longed to leave it all far behind and spend the rest of his life amidst his books and his garden, and in the company of his 'dearest Liz' and his loyal friends. He could correspond on the role played by the nightingale in poetry from Theocritus to Chaucer, claiming that 'Philomel' had not always been regarded as a melancholy bird. He dabbled in history, planning a narrative of the reign of James II, but though some of the projected account was written he lacked the application necessary to finish it.

He could be magnanimous in politics. In 1791 he pleaded with Burke not to allow political differences to break old friendships, and when Burke lay dying Fox strove, in vain, to see his old companion in order to say good-bye. He was later to warn Napoleon of an intended attempt on his life. Yet his sense of honour could also lead him to adopt attitudes which his con-temporaries often thought petty and vindictive. He refused, for example, to join in the formal tributes to Pitt after the latter's death in 1806.

He had no political or philosophical system. He was no thinker in political abstracts. From his youth he had a devotion to liberty, the product perhaps of his enthusiastic reading in the classics, but he never defined exactly what he meant by liberty. He tended to follow his emotions, his generous impulses, and rationalise afterwards. Liberty was threatened by Hardwicke's marriage act, so as a very young and inexperienced member he introduced a Bill to amend the law. But he was too busy gambling to prepare his own Bill, and though he made a brilliant impromptu speech the effort was unavailing. During the revolutionary wars he saw the dangers in Pitt's repressive legislation, but turned a blind eye to the indiscretions committed in Paris. He had been a bitter opponent of the Eden Treaty in 1787, on the grounds that it would help Britain's hereditary foes, yet during the 'nineties he never flinched in his sympathy for the French people. The constant advocate of peace with Napoleon was to be cruelly disillusioned.

It was no accident that Fox's career was dogged by frustration and futility. Sir Gilbert Elliot and the Duchess of Devonshire both complained in 1788–9 of his limitations as a party leader.[1] There were times when his deeply-felt emotions resulted in a curious obstinacy; there were others when he would wait for events to rescue him from the consequences of his own miscalculations. But he never gave up hope, and would never admit that all was lost. In politics, as in racing, he consoled himself with the assurance that eventually his luck would change, misinterpreting the realities of the situation as a result.

Like Pitt, he was charged with harbouring sinister and ambitious designs—a stock accusation in eighteenth-century political life. His enemies cited his chequered career, with all its twists of fortune, as proof of ruthless unscrupulousness.[2] He was accused of going over to the Rockinghamites out of personal pique rather than conviction. Certainly he was never a true Rockinghamite, for during the American War he remained something of a freelance, and when his fortunes were shattered by Rockingham's death in 1782 the attempt he made to recover his losses only provided his enemies with more material. When in 1788 he defended the Prince's right to the Regency in language which many of his colleagues found extreme and embarrassing the story was given another discreditable turn.

But when in office the gambler could discipline himself to the hard routine of official correspondence and his diligence amazed both friend and foe. He abandoned Brooks's for the severe duties of office. His restless vitality helped him to master the intricacies of his department, and when he died in 1806 George III paid him an unexpected compliment, saying that he had not thought that he would miss Mr Fox so much.

It is not easy to go through life knowing that one's career has been persistently frustrated, that the rich promise of youth has never been fulfilled. Fox contributed to that frustration more than his admirers care to admit, but while he was more than the undeserving victim of George III's hatred and William Pitt's bleak distaste, he was also more than the unreliable braggart of Brooks's and Newmarket. His vices were merely the reverse side of his virtues, and his real weakness lay in his temperament, for which his early training was partly responsible. It is common to compare Pitt's private life with that of Fox, and to allow the latter—in consolation for his political disappointments—the blessing of a fuller private life than that enjoyed by his more successful rival. But Fox would not have been gratified with such a dubious reward. He had no wish to be remembered as an amiable failure, however much he was admired and loved by his acquaintances. His charm should not obscure his ambition, which was voracious and ardent, as well as being less reprehensible than contemporaries realised. It was ironic that Fox's private virtues— his generosity, his warm-heartedness, his stubborn loyalty— contributed as much to his political weakness as his failings. The winter of 1788–9 was saddened by political disappointment which was all the more cruel as the sequel to soaring hopes and great expectations, as well as being aggravated by ill-health. Failure was all the more bitter when it lay so close to success, and for Fox —a man of forty when the Regency Crisis left him impotent and angry—hope long deferred made the heart sick.

The catastrophe of 1784 bequeathed a legacy of mutual suspicion and jealousy to the Whig Opposition. John Nicholls laid the principal responsibility for the India Bill at Burke's door, disclaiming that Fox had any share in it.[1] Sheridan often declared in later life that he had been opposed to the coalition, but forty-six years after that disaster Lord John Townshend assured Lord Holland that at the time Sheridan had been 'one of the most eager and clamorous for it':

His hatred of Pitt, and his anxiety to get into office, were motives sufficient. It is true that he had no hand in carrying the measure into effect for nobody had any sort of trust or confidence in him. Think of his impudence afterwards in boasting that he had always deprecated the coalition, and foretold its disastrous consequences.[2]

While Burke approved of the coalition because it was the party's only chance of office,[3] Townshend maintained that until the India Bill 'and all Burke's folly' the coalition had been popular.[4] The failure of that desperate attempt to secure place and power meant that those who had hoped for the venture's success were only too willing to shift the responsibility for its failure on to other shoulders.

Whilst the 1780's brought increasing prosperity to the country and growing popularity to Pitt, they were years of depression and gloom for the Whigs. In opposition they put up a feeble display, and to an ever increasing extent they were forced to rely on the support and patronage of the Prince of Wales. But if he was their greatest asset he was also their most crippling liability. They found themselves entangled in the devious complications of the Prince's private life. His financial extravagances embarrassed them, and in 1787 the Duke of Portland fell out with the Prince over the problem of his debts.[5] The Fitz-herbert marriage was a still more sinister threat. Fox had warned the Prince of the dangers of such a match on 10 December 1785, only to be told: 'Make yourself easy, my dear friend, believe me the world will now soon be convinced that there not only is, but never was, any ground for these reports which have of late so malevolently been circulated. . . .'[6] Within ten days of this assurance the Prince was secretly married to Mrs Fitzherbert according to the Anglican rite. Rumours continued to gather strength, until in April 1787, Mr Rolle referred in the Commons to the dangers of the suspected marriage. Fox, claiming to speak 'from direct authority', described the inference as a calumny, but when Mrs Fitzherbert heard of what had taken place she was bitterly offended. She was an honest woman and a devout Catholic, and, as she resented a semi-official denial of her position, Sheridan was called upon to defend her honour. Obviously the denials contradicted one another and members of Parliament and the general public drew their own conclusions.[1] Whatever his public pronouncements on the subject Fox knew that he had been deceived, and for about a year after the incident he and the Prince were on less convivial terms. But although their relationship was never to be restored to its pristine warmth it was once again a factor in the political situation by the autumn of 1788. Fox could not afford to antagonise the Heir Apparent as well as the reigning monarch. Nevertheless the Fitzherbert affair was a continual source of anxiety. Fox and his friends could neither affirm nor deny the marriage. If they admitted that it had taken place the Prince would be placed in a position of acute embarrassment, for the marriage was doubly illegal, violating as it did both the Royal Marriages Act and the Act of Settlement; and if they denied it too vehemently, in an attempt to silence the strident inquiries of Rolle and his fellows, they would have to face the hostility of Mrs Fitzherbert and the Prince. All they could do was to hope that the issue would not be reopened. In the meantime pamphleteers such as Horne Tooke and Withers persistently raised the matter in outspoken and often indecent language, and efforts to suppress their forceful assertions failed ignominiously. Scurrilous dialogues between 'Lady Herbert' and 'Prince Henry' appeared, and the author of *The Crisis* could assure his readers 'We have a right to know whether the person who governs us is a Papist, or married to a Papist. . . . Let us insist on having the mysterious connection between the Prince of Wales and Mrs Fitzherbert instantly cleared up.'[1] Though the Whigs clung to the Prince as their only hope, the alliance did not bring them any of the popularity they coveted so dearly. For the Prince of Wales was not popular, and was destined never to enjoy the public's favour until his visits as an ageing King to Ireland and Scotland:

> The great personage, into whose hands the Regency of the Country was about to be delivered, was not, at this time, a popular character in the nation he was about to govern. He is known to possess many amiable qualities and an understanding far above the level of common men; and the errors of royal youth would soon have been forgotten in the contemplation of princely virtues. But it appears that his Royal Highness yielded himself up to the affections of his heart, and left his understanding unconsulted. . . . The generous temper of an unsuspecting young man might easily be worked upon by the arts of interested people to appear at the head of a party. . . .[2]

Whig pamphleteers replied to the criticisms which were frequently made of the Prince's character, and in *The Prospect Before Us* the legend of the 'first gentleman' makes an undeniable appearance: 'There is a kind of practice which the customs of amusement among the European nations require gentlemen to be expert in . . . which this Prince makes an act of nameless elegance and a source even of fame.'[3] The Prince's qualities are enumerated in the most enthusiastic and unqualified language:

> The Prince of Wales is in fact a true genius. Parts more lively and quick, a discernment of characters more acute and keen, and understanding more sharp and comprehensive, no man is blessed with. His conversation is unembarrassed and eloquent; his language pure, without care, and flowing with fluency. . . .[4]

> Variety and versatility of talents he undoubtedly possesses in the first perfection. The gift of accommodating himself to the situation he is placed in—of lowering or exalting conversation to the capacity or inclination of his society, no man can have in a higher degree. . . .[5]

> I pronounce . . . that, taken for all in all, and rank and royalties out of the question, he is himself the first young man in Great Britain![6]

Unhappily, the Prince was far from being this paragon of attainment and virtue. He was a young man with a taste for pleasure, extravagance, and amusement. Though intelligent and witty, and possessing a genuine aesthetic sense, he was selfish, unreliable, indifferent to the feelings of others, and excessively sensitive in any matter concerning himself. He was a brilliant mimic, and he did not hesitate to entertain his companions at dinner by parodying his father's ravings. In politics his loyalty was determined by personal whims, not objective judgment, and—worst of all—he was a practised and inveterate liar. Subjected as a child to the rigorous and stingy discipline which George III and Queen Charlotte mistook for firmness and wisdom, he had developed the habit of turning away wrath, not so much by a soft answer as a dishonest one. By his dissipations he had embittered his relationship with his father, and when he flaunted his friendship for Charles James Fox in the King's face, father and son stood apart as political foes. Irresponsible, with little regard for public opinion, and no sense of decorum, the Prince outraged all but his circle of close friends, and the feckless self-indulgence of the Heir Apparent became as notorious as the indiscretions of Fox.

By adopting tones of ironic flattery the Prince's opponents were able to emphasise the great gulf separating his alleged abilities and his conduct. 'The Man of Kent' entertained the pious hope that one day the Prince would take his seat 'by the side of Alfred', and pleaded with him to cultivate 'manly pleasures and employments', the study of philanthropy, the fine arts, and philosophy. He maintained that 'It is . . . necessary to dismiss such companions as degrade your dignity by their approach. . . . They will teach you to recline in indolence, or to be active in unprincely employment, not to say in vicious excesses.'[1] He warned the Prince 'To take the lead of a despised faction . . . must render you . . . completely unpopular.'[2] The irrepressible Withers took advantage of the crisis to republish his assertions about the Fitzherbert marriage, besides portraying the Prince's partiality for Fox as a dereliction of his duty:

> But in the important question, to whom ought the Prince to entrust the subordinate government of the Kingdom? I find no difficulty in answering Mr Pitt will be the man—if the conservation of the just Prerogatives of the Crown and the sacred Privileges of the People—the extension of commerce, with the glory and happiness of the realm—be of greater estimation with his Highness, than the friendships of the card Table or the attachments of the Turf.[1]

The Prince and the Whigs were inseparably linked in the popular mind, distrust of the one heightening suspicion of the other, and in the circumstances it was impossible for the Prince's 'right' to the Regency to be received with complacency.[2] The pity and sympathy which the public felt for the King intensified the dislike which they entertained for the Prince, whose excesses had helped to bring his father into his unhappy state.

Attacks on the Prince were paralleled by similar onslaughts on Fox, Burke, and Sheridan. The pamphleteers did not lose the many opportunities afforded by Fox's private life:

> His whole life has been one of dissipation, as well as of ambitious struggles; who at this moment lives by the horse course and the gaming table; and who has a paternal example of the impunity with which a man may grow rich at the expense of the nation will not easily induce the nation to love or trust him.[3]

He was 'a desperado, who will have no remorse in tearing up the constitution by the roots to gratify the ravings of his monstrous passions'.[4] Sheridan, likewise, was 'an orator by profession . . . a good actor if you give him time to learn his part', a 'needy adventurer ready to bring his abilities to the best market'.[5] Sheridan and Burke, partly because of their common Irish origin, were often lumped together as 'men of inferior character', possessing 'the insidious faculty of persuading the Prince that the violence of their zeal in hastening the gratification of their interested ambition was nothing more than the ungovernable ardour for his honour and the good of the country'.[1] Burke was distrusted and feared as a particularly sinister, and yet ludicrous, figure. 'Edmund the Jesuit' could be portrayed as one endowed with the 'palm of sagacity' whilst eagerly anticipating the time when he and his companion Falstaff (Fox) could 'attack the Company' and 'riot in the exquisite delights of Insult and Revenge'.[2] Rare indeed was the Man of Kent, who advised the Prince to treat Burke with due consideration:

> Of Mr Burke I reverence the character, and I sincerely hope that you will reward the labours of a long political life with ease and dignity. I venerate him as a man of uncommon genius. I lament that such a man should be driven . . . to the narrow character of a party advocate. Even as an advocate for a party, he seems at present little valued; for he is heard in the House with impatience. Dismiss him, then, to ease; as you would turn out a good old horse to a fertile pasture for life.[3]

For whilst Fox was at the end of his tether in 1788, the position of Burke, both within the party and in public life generally, had been growing more desperate since the death of Rockingham had split the Whigs into two bitterly antagonistic factions. The status he had enjoyed during Rockingham's lifetime, as 'the brain, the voice, and the pen of the Rockingham party'[4] had terminated with the Marquis's frail life. At first Burke had hoped that Fitzwilliam would follow in his uncle's footsteps,[5] but when Portland became the official leader of the party he was no longer the intellectual inspiration of what was now a not very intellectual company of frustrated politicians. The stolid and unimaginative Duke turned to him for advice from time to time, and they were on good terms personally, but the old relationship between Burke and Rockingham was not repeated. As early as 1783 Burke had denied that his influence had ever been as great as had commonly been supposed, and he had admitted that it had 'considerably diminished'.[6] As the failure of the coalition and the subsequent success of Pitt deepened the prevailing gloom, nostalgia became the substitute for action. The 'united opposition' to the American War seemed ever more glorious and attractive, and while the memory of Rockingham was venerated his ghost was frequently invoked as the mentor of the Whigs.

The campaign against Hastings was the only outlet for Burke's frustrated genius, and though the burden of the impeachment was immense he shouldered it manfully. Yet even here his position was not shared by his colleagues on the Opposition front bench. For Burke the impeachment was no mere move in the political charade. He was concerned to protect the lives and property of millions, to affirm justice, to raise up the humble and cast down the proud, and it was his zeal for these ideals which made so much of his behaviour towards Hastings ruthless, intolerant, and bitter. But his enthusiasm was not shared by Fox and Sheridan, who soon wearied of the business in Westminster Hall, especially when they realised that as a move in the party struggle it was unprofitable. Sheridan told the Duchess of Devonshire that he wished Hastings would 'run away, and Burke after him',[1] and Burke found himself almost alone in his conviction that the impeachment was worth while. It is astonishing that during the winter of 1788–9 Burke should rouse himself to renewed political activity and great physical and mental effort. Even during the bustling 'seventies he had been prone to attacks of depression: '. . . sometimes when I am alone, in spite of all my efforts, I fall into a melancholy which is inexpressible, and to which, if I give way, I should not long continue under it, but . . . totally sink. . . .'[2] Only his 'natural good spirits' and 'strong sense of what I ought to do' had enabled him to bear up so well that no stranger could possibly guess what he had endured. A similar fit afflicted him after Rockingham's death, on that occasion linked with a wistful desire for retirement, and in 1789 only the feeling that he was bound in a point of honour by the Indian business prevented him from giving way to his own longings for the sedate joys which a withdrawal from politics would bring.[3] Poor health added its trials to those of political isolation. Burke had been unwell during the summer of 1788[1] and in January 1789, active as he was in the controversies over the Regency, he had again to seek a brief respite at Beaconsfield from ill-health and over-anxiety.[2] Alone amongst the Opposition leaders he saw the crisis as primarily a constitutional one, and the intensity with which he expressed his uncompromising views aroused new suspicions of insanity.

For Burke was an intellectual plunged in the confused and murky perplexities of politics. The admiration which was showered upon him during the revolutionary war had no parallel in the years preceding the French Revolution. Burke was respected by a small group of friends for his intellectual attainments, but, though he was a member of Johnson's Literary Club, he was not universally accepted even within that society. Sir John Hawkins disliked him as an upstart Irishman, and as the son of an Irish attorney he was never accepted as an equal by the Whig aristocrats. He never held a Cabinet post, and had the party been successful in 1788 he would have returned to his old appointment at the Pay Office. Portland and Elliot sought to recognise Burke's services by the award of a pension, not a Cabinet place.

Despite his great gifts—gifts which gave him an intellectual pre-eminence over his political associates—Burke lacked a sense of the possible. He had in full measure the intellectual's impatience with the world of men, and when baulked by folly and stupidity he indulged in passionate denunciations and extravagant accusations. He could be both loyal and vindictive, and once he had taken a stand upon any issue he found it difficult—at times impossible—to withdraw. At the time of the Pay Office scandal in 1783 he added fuel to the flames by his obstinate defence of the men involved. He would follow a line of argument out to its logical conclusion with little thought of how practical such conduct was, and consequently he could be an embarrassing companion. He was incapable of giving way gracefully, and he was guilty of atrocious lapses of taste. The Regency Crisis widened the gap which separated Burke from his political associates, but unlike the debate over the French Revolution it brought him no closer to Pitt and the Ministerialists. In 1791 Pitt was bewildered by Burke's obsession with French affairs, and only the excesses of the Republicans in Paris drove the Government towards a position approximating to that which Burke had adopted from the start, but no two attitudes could be more opposed than those of Pitt and Burke in 1788. Both took their stand on an interpretation of the constitution, and in each case the conclusions drawn were radically different. During the winter months, therefore, Burke was a lonely figure, the object of scorn, astonishment, and dismay, misunderstood by his friends and vilified by his foes; and yet, despite the jibes of the pamphleteers, the amused mockery of opponents, the exasperated incomprehension of his associates, there was—as will be seen—an inner consistency in Burke's conduct. But this consistency was bought at the price of increasing loneliness, cruel misrepresentation, and bitter disgust.

(v)

In the early days of the crisis it seemed as if the Prince of Wales was deeply affected by his father's illness. Only later did his behaviour become notorious. He wept abundantly, and was so distraught that it was necessary to bleed him.[1] Perhaps out of a sense of duty, perhaps out of sheer impatience to exercise some power and influence, he took over command at Windsor—'in consequence of which there is *no command whatsoever*', sneered Lord Bulkeley to Buckingham on 11 November.[2] On the 6th the Prince summoned Lord Thurlow to Windsor, and desired that Fox should be sent for—'which ought to be a secret, but is none, for I heard it at Brooks's', wrote Crawford to the Duchess of Devonshire on the following day.[3] The official purpose of Thurlow's visit was to enable the Prince to consult him as to the most appropriate means of looking after the King, but it is possible that an attempt was made to sound him on the prospects of his

changing sides, particularly as Sheridan and Payne, who were
the Prince's confidants at this time, were eager to come to some
arrangement with the Chancellor.[1] At an early stage in the
negotiation Thurlow made it clear that it would be possible for
him to support the Whigs only if he retained the Great Seal,[2]
but the wily Chancellor was adept at the by-ways of negotiation,
and possibly his skill at withholding his own intentions, while
discovering those of his friends and opponents, explains the
conflicting interpretations and reports of his conduct during the
Regency Crisis. On 6 November the Prince received the Lord
Chancellor with 'marks of the highest consideration', telling
him that he had sought his attendance, not only as his father's
friend, but as his own, and expressing the utmost confidence in
his judgment.[3] Thurlow was to have many more interviews
with the Prince and Opposition politicians during the crisis and
little evidence exists for any of them. At one of his interviews
with the Prince he was alleged to have assured him that

he felt himself strongly devoted to his Royal Highness . . . that he should on
no account unite with Mr Pitt, or enter into any opposition to his Royal
Highness's government, when his dismission, which he saw was at hand,
should take place. He should on the contrary give it every support in his
power; and if at any future day his services should be thought of use he should
be happy to offer them.[4]

He spoke of Pitt as 'a haughty impracticable spirit, with whom it
would be impossible for him ever cordially to unite', and informed the Prince that 'the whole party was split, divided, and
disunited, in a manner which would prevent their ever acting
in opposition with vigour and effect'.[5] Nicholls (on the other
hand) maintained that Thurlow 'studiously sought intercourse
with the Prince of Wales, that he might have an opportunity of
conveying his sentiments on his Royal Highness's situation, and
that the Chancellor

recommended him to lie upon his oars, to show no impatience to assume
the powers of royalty. He pointed out to him, that, if the King's illness

were of any considerable duration, the Regency must necessarily devolve on him.[1]

Nicholls knew that Thurlow was 'much abused for his conduct on this occasion' and that

some members of the Opposition have gone so far as to say that he would have acted against the opinion of Mr Pitt, if the Opposition would have engaged to continue him in the office of Chancellor; but I do not believe this assertion to be true. Trimming was not congenial to the character of Lord Thurlow . . . I believe Lord Thurlow acted with great integrity: he once told me that if it had been ultimately necessary to pass the Regency Bill framed by Mr Pitt, he should have agreed with great reluctance.[2]

Throughout the crisis Thurlow's conduct was ambiguous and his attitude undefined. But there is little doubt that he wanted to continue as Lord Chancellor, whatever changes took place in administration, and that he was unwilling to sell himself—even to the highest bidder—before he was convinced, not only of the willingness of the Whigs to pay his price, but also that events would justify the transaction. Until a definite pronouncement had been made on the King's health, and his chances of recovery, it was only natural that Thurlow should act with great circumspection. It is possible that he was also uncertain as to the most commendable solution to the problems posed by the incapacity of the King. On 9 November, whilst writing to Hawkesbury to tell him that 'the worst of all possible events' was indicated by the medical account, he continued:

Two shapeless Ideas have alone occurred to me. The first is, for the Parliament to address the Prince to take the Custodia Regni upon Him, properly qualified and modified; and actually hold a Parliament which should thereafter ratify His acts, till the King should deal with His Parliament in Person.

The second is, that the Parliament, taking notice of the King's disorder as a temporary one, and that Doubts might possibly be conceived on the propriety of receiving His Majesty's commands for the appointing a Custos Regni under the Great Seal, to resolve that the Chancellor should be at liberty to find the opportunity of receiving such commands, and that no question should hereafter be made of the propriety of His proceeding therein—This perhaps would require an act similar to that of the 8th of Henry the Fifth, Chapter the First, to declare the Regent's capacity of acting with effect, notwithstanding the King remains in the realm.[1]

This would seem to indicate doubt in Thurlow's own mind. The problem was that the technical aspects of the crisis—which were of particular importance to Thurlow—were confused and capable of more than one interpretation. The Lord Chancellor perceived the advantages of proceeding by an Address to the Prince, but he was also aware of the limitations of such a policy. Although he ultimately defended the Government's policy in the House of Lords, his final decision about the means of fulfilling the vacancy in the executive branch of the Government depended on the prospects of the King's recovery. The vacillations which made Thurlow's conduct so infuriating to Ministry and Opposition alike were geared to the daily fluctuations in the King's condition and the opinions of the doctors. Until Willis arrived on the scene at the beginning of December Thurlow thought that the Prince's assumption of the duties of Regent was only a matter of time, but thereafter he sought to insure his position against the King's recovery as well as the Prince's accession.

On the other side, Sheridan was itching to get into office as quickly as possible, but with as little commotion as could conveniently be managed. Yet he was acutely aware of the need for restraint. Writing to the Prince shortly after the adjournment of Parliament on 20 November, he was emphatic in his plea for good sense and moderation:

I take the liberty of repeating my firm conviction that it will greatly advance your Royal Highness's credit, and, in the case of event, lay the strongest grounds to baffle every attempt at opposition to your Royal Highness's just claims and right, that the language of those who may be, in any sort, suspected of knowing your Royal Highness's wishes and feelings, should be of great moderation in disclaiming all party views, and avowing the utmost readiness to acquiesce in any reasonable delay. At the same time I am perfectly aware of the arts which will be practised and the advantages which some people will attempt to gain by time; but I am equally convinced that we should advance their evil views by showing the least impatience or suspicion at present. . . .[1]

Sheridan's conduct bore little resemblance to what one would expect from the drunkard of legend. Sceptical of the advantages which would follow public discussion of the constitutional issues pertinent to the King's incapacity, he was prepared to subordinate everything to the attainment of office. The Prince and Payne were both eager to win Thurlow over, and Sheridan took up the project with enthusiasm. Fox, who was abroad in the early stages of the negotiation, and who was kept in the dark about it until it became necessary to ask him to persuade Loughborough to waive his claims to the Chancellorship, only condoned it with extreme reluctance, assuaging his conscience with the thought that the scheme would fail.[2] Perhaps the abortive character of the discussions with Thurlow explains Fox's neglect of the subject in his conversations with Nicholls on the Regency Crisis during the 1790's. Nevertheless, although the attempt to gain Thurlow for the Whigs finally miscarried, at the beginning of November 1788, it was a grave threat to the stability of the administration. Pitt and Thurlow were on bad terms generally and had disagreed over the impeachment of Hastings; this, combined with Thurlow's obvious distaste at the thought of giving way to Loughborough, gave credible foundations to the Government's fears.[3]

On his return to town after seeing the Prince on 6 November, Thurlow sent a note to Pitt, communicating the Prince's command that he should see his Royal Highness at Windsor at 11 o'clock on the morning of 8 November. Immediately it was suspected that a negotiation was intended but this was not regarded as a welcome development.[4] Grenville was of the opinion that while Pitt could not refuse to negotiate he would be justified in rejecting any proposal which would not leave him as First Lord of the Treasury and Chancellor of the Exchequer. At the same time he believed that the Opposition would turn the Government out 'all at once' on the Prince's accession, either as Regent

44

or King—'which I am sure is the thing we ought most to wish'.[1]

When Pitt visited Windsor on 8 November he had a long conversation with the Prince on the King's condition, but no indication was given of the Prince's intentions if his father died or if he remained in a state of permanent lunacy. Pitt was treated with civility 'but nothing more', and though the physicians did not anticipate any serious deterioration in the King's condition they feared that his insanity would prove incurable. But they still hesitated to make any firm pronouncement on the subject, and this uncertainty in the diagnosis hampered both Government and Opposition. On 8 November applications of James's powder were made without success, for, though the King's fever disappeared, his derangement was unabated.[2] The doctors claimed a fortnight's grace before making up their minds, telling Pitt that brain disorders were the least understood of all maladies. The King's incapacity might last for years, or suddenly leave him, or just as suddenly kill him. In this situation rumours of negotiation flourished, despite Grenville's scepticism, and opinions fluctuated from hour to hour.[3]

Slowly the Ministry was being driven to take a stand. In the opening weeks of November it was thought best to announce that the King was in no condition either to prorogue the two Houses, or to sign a commission opening the session. Parliament could meet on 23 November, when an adjournment would be proposed, and as soon as the physicians had made up their minds about the King's illness they would be examined before the Privy Council, Parliament informed of the situation, and a Bill brought in to make the Prince of Wales Regent. The Ministry gradually perceived their object to be 'the keeping the government in such a state as that if the King's health should be restored he might be, as far as possible, enabled to resume it, and to conduct it in such a manner as he might judge best'.[4] Here political advantage and constitutional rectitude went hand in hand, but Grenville confessed that there was great doubt 'whether any, and what, limitations ought to be proposed'.[1]

Pitt visited Windsor on 10 November and again two days later. There had been some improvement in the King's condition, but, after understanding some questions which had been put to him, he had relapsed into his former state.[2] It was still hoped that either the King's sudden death or his sudden recovery would resolve the crisis one way or the other, but this was merely longing for the need for decision to pass unanswered. Nevertheless the King's uncertain and unpredictable condition and the inability of the doctors to come to any conclusion on the matter, were additional reasons for putting off as long as possible any steps for carrying on the Government in existing circumstances. Opinion had now shifted to convening Parliament on 20 November. Pitt intended to ask the House to adjourn, and since Fox had not yet returned from the Continent it was not anticipated that there would be any objections to the proposal. But the uncertainties of the situation are clearly reflected in Pitt's letter of 10 November to Bishop Pretyman:

> You will have heard enough already of the King's illness to make you very uneasy. The fact is that it has hitherto found little relief from medicine, and, what is worst of all, it is attended with a delirium the causes of which the physicians cannot clearly ascertain. On the whole there is room to apprehend the disorder may produce danger to his life, but there is no immediate symptom of danger at present. The effect to be more dreaded is on the understanding. If this lasts beyond a certain time it will produce the most difficult and delicate crisis imaginable in making provision for the government to go on. It must, however, be yet some weeks before that can require decision, but the interval will be truly an anxious one. . . .[3]

By 13 November, however, Pitt had decided to introduce a Bill declaring the Prince of Wales Regent, or Guardian, with the right to exercise the royal powers in the name of his father during the emergency.[4] But no decision had been reached on the precise powers which were to be conferred on the Prince. The Government did not feel that the Prince should be granted full regal powers, as it was essential not only to preserve the King's legal rights, but also the means for him to exercise those rights on his recovery 'according to the opinions which he entertains both of public men and public measures'.[1] At the same time they realised the need for restraint:

> We must be extremely cautious that we do nothing which shall bear, in the public estimation, the appearance of wishing to establish ourselves under this pretence in the continuance of our power in opposition to the Prince of Wales, in whom we are to propose the supreme authority to be vested.[2]

Political considerations told against the appointment of a Council of Regency, and a better method of controlling the Prince seemed to be to limit his powers: to restrain him from granting any office or pension for life, from creating and promoting peers, and from dissolving Parliament. The Cabinet became more decided on the necessity of restrictions between 9 and 13 November, yet, whatever hopes they harboured for the prolongation of their tenure of office, they were still preoccupied with going out of office on the best possible terms. Pitt was busy studying the precedents, but he and his colleagues knew that a change of Government was inevitable, once the Prince took over as Regent, and they were striving to ensure that on the King's recovery a second reversal of situations would take place.

Hesitation as to the proposals which were to be made was closely linked to ignorance of the intentions of the Opposition. Despite rumour and counter-rumour the Prince of Wales had made no suggestion of negotiation, nor had he informed the Ministry of his policy on becoming Regent. Pitt and his colleagues could only make deductions from his previous conduct and known feelings.[3] Buckingham related to his brother on 11 November a conversation which Anthony St Leger had had with Fitzherbert in August, and another which St Leger had had with Fitzgibbon later in the year. Both of these suggested that the Whigs would try a negotiation. St Leger told Fitzherbert that

the Prince was afraid of Fox, and that his opinion of Pitt was very much altered since the negotiation on the subject of his debts; that he was sure that the Prince would in case of any accident send for them both, and endeavour to make his time quiet by employing them jointly; and that his coolness to Fox was much increased by Mrs Fitzherbert who would never forgive his public declaration on her subject in the House of Commons, and had taken every opportunity of alienating the Prince's mind from him.[1]

On 9 November Fitzgibbon repeated the story which he had from St Leger in September, despite the fact that he was totally ignorant of the other conversation. All this made Buckingham think a negotiation possible. He did not believe that a coalition would take place, but if a negotiation was attempted it would create 'the most unpleasant and difficult of all situations':

for I do not think Mr Pitt can refuse it, if they leave him in his present employment. To this, however, I think Fox will not consent, and upon that question it may turn; but if it should be possible that Mr Pitt should go on I must desire explicitly to renounce all idea of continuing in Ireland or in any public station, unless such a continuance is bona fide an object to him and to his situation.[2]

If the Prince dismissed the administration, or if Pitt tried a coalition and failed, Buckingham assured his brother of his determination 'of steadily supporting you in the object nearest your heart, I mean the support of him out of office, who, I verily believe, is (in office) the honestest minister we ever saw. . . .'[3] On 12 November Buckingham informed Grenville of a conversation he had had with C. F. Sheridan (R. B. Sheridan's elder brother), who had told him that

he had every hope that a negotiation might take place which might include Pitt and Fox; and in the course of the conversation he said he was convinced that the latter had always looked to this idea in such an emergency. I said that I could not see how they were to adjust the very first step of the Treasury, to which he said that he had no idea that there would be a thought of proposing Pitt to quit it. . . .[4]

All this merely added to the prevailing confusion, and still no overture was made to Pitt. Perhaps the Opposition hesitated to act before Fox returned from Italy, and this possibly explains the mounting impatience which Burke, for one, felt over the long-awaited, but agonisingly delayed, home-coming.[1] The Prince was consulting Sheridan in an ostentatious fashion, and it was believed that this had offended the Duke of Portland, who had yet to make up his quarrel with the Prince.[2]

In this confused situation, haunted by the spectre of negotiation and fearful of the threat of dismissal, the Government clung to the hope that the King would recover his sanity. Grenville thought that a bona fide junction with the Whigs was out of the question; any proposals made by the Opposition would have no other purpose than placating the Prince's alleged desire to bring Fox and Pitt together, whilst throwing the blame for any change in administration on to Pitt. It was important for the Government not to involve themselves in 'contradictory obligations', for if the King recovered, only to discover that during his illness his enemies had been installed in office, his mind, as well as his feelings, might reel under the shock.[3]

When Pitt visited Windsor on 14 November, Warren, always the most pessimistic of the doctors, assured him that a 'more rapid amendment' on the King's part would be 'a less pleasing symptom'.[4] The Prince saw Pitt, and they discussed the ordering of prayers for the King's recovery, but although he was polite the Prince was no more communicative than on previous occasions. No proposals were made about a coalition, and from the Prince's behaviour it seemed that the rumours suggesting that he would dismiss Pitt, rather than negotiate with him, were correct.[5] On 15 November Pitt wrote to Buckingham, and his letter demonstrates the indefinite and baffling nature of the predicament in which the Government found themselves:

. . . our last accounts begin to wear a more favourable aspect though there is not yet ground for very confident hope. There is certainly now no danger to his life, but the other alternative, which there was some danger to apprehend, was, if possible, more distressing. It seems now possible that a total recovery may take place, but even on the best supposition there must still be a considerable period of anxiety. . . .[1]

The Prince was reluctant to encounter Pitt—possibly because he had not made up his own mind as to the policy to adopt—and, after submitting his plans for the Regency to Thurlow and Weymouth, Pitt announced to a silent House on 20 November that the King's health prevented a prorogation, moving (on the recommendation of the Lord Chancellor) an adjournment for a fortnight.[2]

But for all their silence in the House the Opposition were busily spreading rumours that the King's illness was incurable. Warren had been indiscreet on the subject, and Grenville complained that 'the indecency of any language held on your side of the water cannot exceed the universal tone of the opposition within the last four or five days'.[3] The day before he had visited Windsor, only to find that the position there had deteriorated. The King talked incessantly for hours on end without any appearance of sense or reason; he did not know the persons about him, and fancied himself engaged in various types of employment. At times he seemed to have 'that sort of consciousness of his situation which lunatics are observed to possess, and to use the same . . . methods for concealing it'. Warren had told Pitt that there was 'every reason to believe that the disorder was no other than a direct lunacy'.[4] When the medical accounts varied so alarmingly from day to day the strain upon all those involved was considerable. The Opposition publicised every report of a pessimistic character, whilst supporters of the Ministry did their best to give prominence to any favourable symptom. Sheffield told Eden that many of these stories, though apparently well authenticated, were in fact untrue:

There is little doubt of its being the general real opinion of the Physicians, that there is as little probability of recovery as in any case of the kind that has come within their knowledge. . . . It seems generally believed that his life is not in immediate danger. The present situation appears to most people as the worst of all. It must present difficulties to all men and to all parties. What set of Men can wish just at this time to form a new Administration with the prospect of a possible recovery. The Present Administration will find a great difference from the support they have hitherto had. Rattism will prevail & I shou'd not be surprised, supposing the present Parliament to continue, if looking towards the rising Sun it shou'd turn out the very Minister that made it. . . .[1]

Whilst Sheffield awaited the downfall of the Ministry with complacent confidence, Philip Yorke interpreted the medical opinions in a very different fashion:

If the King's unfortunate illness shall not have given way to the skill of his Physicians by that time (Monday se'nnight) the situation of publick affairs will be very embarrassing—I do not however yet entirely abandon hope, & in the case of a private friend, no one would in such a case despair of a recovery in so early a period of the disorder. . . .[2]

The strain, bewilderment, and doubt, were proving too much for the Prince of Wales, whose sense of filial duty was being undermined by regal impatience. The self-control which he had shown in the early days of the crisis (at least in his public conduct) was giving way to more characteristic expressions of his feelings. It was said that he had introduced Lord Lothian into the King's room so that he could see his sovereign's ravings at their worst.[3]

When Fox arrived in London in the early hours of 24 November he expected to find the King dead, from the information he had gleaned on his journey.[4] His hasty dash across Italy and France had exhausted him, and on his arrival he found uncertainty and rumour, perplexity and division, awaiting him. His colleagues had not yet formulated any considered policy. Optimism was the order of the day, and there was much jubilation at the prospect of returning to power, but little progress had been made in the more humdrum tasks incumbent on those who daily expected their dreams to come true. Sir Gilbert Elliot confided his misgivings to his wife:

> I do not much relish . . . this triumphant sort of conversation, especially before the battle is won, or even fought; for I remember that just such triumphs preceded by a very few days our utter defeat four years ago. . . .[1]

Elliot was pleased that the Prince had decided not to have anything to do with Pitt, but Sheridan was still wooing Thurlow, and trying to persuade his companions to follow him into the devious subtleties of negotiation, whilst shunning the more spectacular diversions of controversy. The Prince was 'wonderfully of late attached to Thurlow', and it was suspected that the old Rockinghamites were dissatisfied with this touching display of affection, that there was 'a division among them, which . . . a sense of common interest and common danger may rectify before the day of trial'.[2] Sheridan was flitting to and fro, revelling in the opportunities for intrigue which the situation afforded, and the Prince expressed his confidence in him by carrying on secret discussions with him.[3]

One member of the party—Loughborough—viewed the proposed accommodation with Thurlow with nothing less than distaste. If Thurlow came over to the Whigs Loughborough would be deprived of what he regarded as his rightful prize, and he had already on one previous occasion withdrawn in favour of his rival, placing party interests above private ambitions.[4] But he could hardly be expected to make the same concession a second time without a great deal of persuasion, and his views on the Regency were emphatically in favour of the doctrine of hereditary right. He not only thought that the Prince had a right to the Regency, but that he ought to take the initiative in supplying the deficiency. (In this his outlook was similar to that of Burke.) Payne had asked Loughborough for advice on the technical aspects of the problem, and his request had been met by a paper arguing the case in forthright terms, as well as by a declaration to be read by the Prince on assuming the Regency. It was not surprising that Loughborough emphasised the unreliability of the Lord Chancellor, even when he was compelled to allow the negotiation to go forward.[1]

The Opposition was riddled with jealousies and feuds. Burke wisely stayed at Beaconsfield, but, while protesting his faith in Fox and Portland as party leaders, he could not refrain from giving them advice:

> I mean to continue here until you call upon me; and I find myself perfectly easy, from the implicit confidence I have in you and the Duke, and the certainty I am in, that you two will do the best for the general reputation of the cause, and for your own and our common reputation. In that state of mind I feel no desire whatsoever of interfering, especially as the too great infusion of various and heterogenious opinions may embarrass that decision, which it seems necessary you should come to, and for which I do not think a great deal of time is allowed you. . . .[2]

Yet, despite his apparent reluctance to take an active part in the formulation of party policy—a reluctance motivated, perhaps, by the knowledge that he was distrusted within the party itself—Burke made his position clear. It was vital not to allow the Ministry to take the lead in any settlement of the crisis. Though they were in 'legal situations of trust' their responsibility was limited to 'such functions as can be performed in office without resort to the Crown', and in no sense would he recognise the members of the current administration as the King's 'confidential servants'. The country was suffering from an 'interregnum'—though paradoxically Burke did not consider the throne vacant—and those in office were unacceptable as 'persons to whose wisdom the government is to look for its future form'. To permit this was neither reputable nor advantageous. It would be better for the Prince to take the initiative by communicating the King's unhappy situation to the two Houses of Parliament, whilst asking for their advice and support during the exigency. In this way the Prince's stature as a public figure would increase, and he would seem a person 'possessed of the spirit of command'.

This in itself would 'stifle an hundred cabals, both in Parliament and elsewhere, in their very cradle'. Any indecision on the Prince's part would, on the other hand, result in a 'vexatious and disgraceful regency and reign'. At long last the malignant power which had frustrated Fox throughout his career would be overthrown; but Burke warned his friend that the effects of twenty-eight years 'proscription' would not be thrown off easily. If Fox failed this time the situation would be desperate.[1]

Thus, in the opening weeks of the crisis, Burke kept tactfully in the background. Perhaps he knew that his best chance of influencing the party lay behind the scenes, recognising as he did the deep distrust and distaste which was felt for him as an 'Irish adventurer', and (especially after the India Bill fiasco) as a sinister threat to established interests. His campaign against Hastings had brought him much criticism and made him many enemies. But for all his resolutions to stay at Beaconsfield he was in London at the beginning of December, seeking to exercise a decisive influence on the course of events.

Though Portland was the official leader of the party, and the inevitable choice as First Lord of the Treasury in any Whig administration, he was still on bad terms with the Prince of Wales. His wife had advised him not to become Prime Minister unless such a proposal came from the Prince himself, and Portland was insisting on an apology from the Prince for the way he had been treated at the time of the furore over his Royal Highness's debts. When the Prince foolishly drew attention to himself by driving his sisters and Lady Charlotte Finch through the streets of Windsor in a manner wild enough to break several lamps, the Duchess of Portland repeated the story to her friends with no little relish. Such tales could only do the Prince harm, however much his apologists tried to soften his conduct by giving it the name of 'giddiness', and the Duchess of Devonshire strongly disapproved of the way in which the Duchess of Portland had helped to give the story a good airing.[2]

Meanwhile Grey, young, ambitious, and inexperienced, was causing trouble. Shortly before Fox's return Sheridan had attempted to persuade him to moderate his demands in the interests of the party, citing as a worthy example his own withdrawal of his claims to the Chancellorship of the Exchequer, and his ostensible desire to prove himself first in a more humble and unpretentious office. But Grey was adamant. He wanted the Chancellorship. If he could not have it he wanted the Secretaryship at War. But he would only give way to Lord John Cavendish, Fox, or Sheridan himself—not to the Norfolks, Windhams, and Pelhams.[1]

Sheridan was doing his best to mitigate these rivalries. On 26 November the Prince sent a message to the Duke of Portland 'cancelling all former discontents', though he still thought that the Duke had been 'personally unkind to him'.[2] He had asked Fox to 'shake the Duke of Portland by the hand for me, and tell him that I hope everything that is past may be forgot between us'.[3] The Duke was 'properly touched with this conduct' and on 30 November the Prince and the Duke of York visited him, behaving in 'the kindest manner'.[4] But although the Opposition leaders had not yet agreed amongst themselves on the distribution of places in the new Government, the public were being supplied with lists of the new Ministry. On 28 November the *Morning Post* printed a list of those who would hold office in the new administration. Portland was named as First Lord of the Treasury, Fox and Stormont as Secretaries of State, Lord John Cavendish as Chancellor of the Exchequer, Sheridan as Treasurer of the Navy, and Burke as Paymaster of the Forces. Significantly no mention was made of the Lord Chancellor, Loughborough being named as First Commissioner of the Great Seal. It was also claimed that thirty new peers were to be created in order to secure a majority in the Upper House, and that Parliament would be dissolved as soon as current business was completed.[5] But however eager the Whigs were to seize the fruits of power the newspapers

exaggerated the extent of their harmony. Windham was outlining in trenchant language his interpretation of the situation:

... If the King of a country is completely out of his mind, whatever sorrow
may be felt for that event, the extent of the evil is however known: It is, for
the time it lasts, just as if the King were dead. The same person must, upon all
principles of reason, & all views of the constitution, carry on the government,
as if the King were actually dead. Should He again be completely restored to
his senses, the case is then equally clear: He must be restored completely to his
government. Whatever other opinions are broached or thrown out in conversation, by persons on either side, this seems to me to be the plain sense of
the matter, as one may possibly have to declare, or act upon, at least, before
many days. The only Case of danger and distress is where the sanity or insanity of a monarch should not be clearly ascertained or not generally known.
To guard against this, in the instance now before us, I think accounts shd. have
been industriously propagated for some time past: & whatever motives of
delicacy & prudence might have prevailed at first . . . the case seeming now
to be so decided, the actual insanity to be so complete, & the hopes of its
ever ceasing so small, that any attempts further to disguise it will lye open to
very uncreditable suspicions.[1]

Unhappily this point of view was all too prevalent within the Whig
camp. Unpleasant technicalities were brushed aside by confident
assertions of the 'obvious' and 'plain' sense of the matter. The
assumption, too, that the King was in an incurable condition was
fatally attractive, and contributed to the lack of a systematic
formulation of policy. Almost a month had gone by before the
Duke of Portland and the Prince of Wales were formally reconciled, and, despite their happy optimism, the Whigs were even
more hesitant than the Ministry in committing themselves to a
clear and lucid line of conduct. On 2 December a meeting was
held at Carlton House, attended by the Duke of York, the Dukes
of Devonshire and Portland, Grey, Sheridan, Loughborough,
Stormont, and North. But now another factor made its appearance. Fox's exertions during his frantic journey home had
been too much for him. He fell a victim to dysentery and was
too ill to attend the conference. His indisposition was to exercise
no small influence on later developments. At the meeting the

Prince spoke about the conversation he had had with Pitt relating to the adjournment of the two Houses of Parliament.[1] On 4 December he told the Duchess of Devonshire that he had decided to refuse a limited Regency, and after praising Sheridan's conduct he went off to spend the night at Brooks's.[2] The King's removal to Kew on 29 November had relieved the Prince of the necessity of residing at Windsor, a duty which he had found increasingly burdensome. He was soon to throw caution to the winds, and his behaviour, which had originally brought him much credit, became notorious. His enforced residence at Windsor had given the impression of filial devotion, and had prevented him—as Elliot put it to his wife—from 'breaking out into any unseasonable indulgence of his spirits before the public'.[3] Soon parties at Carlton House and gay nights at Brooks's were to be the talk of the town.

As the debate of 10 December approached the Whigs became no more united. On 4 December Fox was ill again. He felt 'weak and low' and his illness reduced his strength and depressed his spirits.[4] Though he was slightly better on the 5th Elliot suspected that the improvement was due to the temporary relief of laudanum.[5] Burke had tried to persuade the party to press for detailed accounts of the King's condition, but he had been overruled. He had also drafted an address to the Prince from the Commons inviting him to assume the Regency, but it had been too extreme for his companions' taste, and in order to keep the peace Elliot wrote a new version, softening the extravagances of Burke's style, but adapting his phraseology wherever possible. This was approved by Burke, Portland, and Fox.[6]

On 5 December another meeting was held, this time at Burlington House, at which the propriety of demanding a Parliamentary discussion on the state of the King was considered. Sheridan and Burke were for it, Fox and Loughborough against. Fox was still ill—so ill that he was convinced that he was dying.[7] Meanwhile Thurlow was flirting with the Opposition. On 7 December the Whigs were sure that he was with them, and on the following day the Duke of Devonshire was told by the Prince that when Sheridan had visited the Chancellor, Thurlow had told him that he was a man of no party—'and to a man of your discernment that is saying enough'.[1] At the same time the feuds between Sheridan and Grey were 'worse than ever', and the party's concord and harmony were disturbed by a quarrel at Brooks's between Fitzpatrick and Grey, which was all the more surprising as initially they had been in agreement as to Sheridan's unreliability. Yet the next day Grey was reconciled to Sheridan, and told him that he would accept any office which three of his friends would advise him to take.[2]

Rumours suggesting negotiation were in the air, nevertheless, and Sir William Young thought that the Opposition would propose a coalition in an attempt to humour public opinion. He did not think that such proposals would be worth listening to. One newspaper went so far as to say that Lord North would play a leading role in supporting a Coalition Government.[3] On 27 November the nearest approach to a formal negotiation took place. Pitt had a conversation with Stormont, friendly in manner and moderate in tone. Stormont agreed that it was impossible to do anything that would hamper the King's full exercise of his powers on his restoration to health, and expressed his opinion that proposals of negotiation, if made, would be on such terms that the Government would find it difficult to decline without making a bad impression on the public. At the same time he conceded the force of Pitt's arguments against negotiation, whilst trying to convince him that the intentions of the Lord Chancellor were as honest as Pitt admitted Stormont's to be.[4] Grenville, writing to his brother on 28 November, told him that 'the general language leans to negotiation', yet three days later the Government were convinced that they were about to meet with 'universal and instant dismission'.[5] The Chancellor had undoubtedly had conversations with the Prince, Sheridan, and Fox, which he had not communicated to his colleagues, and on one occasion his duplicity was betrayed by the innocence of a page when returning his Lordship's hat.[1] But if he had disclosed any of Pitt's proposals for the Regency it is possible that he had done so inadvertently, and with typical caution in uncertain circumstances he carefully refrained from committing himself.[2]

Pitt had become increasingly dissatisfied with the medical opinions tendered by the King's doctors, and he had therefore called in old Dr Addington, who thought that there was a definite possibility of a recovery, and on his recommendation the King was removed to Kew on 29 November.[3] Stories were continually being circulated about the King's behaviour: he had danced with Reynolds, and torn a page terribly in a fit of violence.[4] Nevertheless, Addington maintained that he had cured a patient in his asylum, who had suffered from the same symptoms as the King.[5] On 3 December the physicians were examined before the Privy Council. Three main questions were put to them. Was the King incapable of attending to business? What hopes were entertained of his recovery? How long was his incapacity likely to last? All the doctors—Warren, Pepys, Baker, Reynolds, and Addington—agreed that the King was incapable of attending to business, and, with the exception of Warren, they all said that a recovery was probable. Warren attempted to avoid the question. He was politically committed to the Whigs, and in the past he had attended Portland's wife and children during their illnesses.[6] Now, though he confessed that he lacked the experience necessary to answer the question on the probability of recovery with any authority, it took an hour and a half to extract this concession from him, despite his earlier concession that the majority of those afflicted with all species of the King's illness recovered.[7] The doctors could not give any indication of the length of time which would elapse before the King's recovery. A fourth question was put to them, to elucidate how much experience each had in the treatment of lunacy. The first three had none, Reynolds only a little, Addington, by virtue of his asylum at Reading, by far the greatest.[1] This was a valuable move on the Government's part, for Addington's optimisms now carried greater weight than the pessimistic forecasts of Warren. From the administration's point of view the examination had been more favourable than had been anticipated.[2] The Opposition were correspondingly disappointed and since Fox was too ill to appear at the examination it was said that had he been present Warren's answers would have been much more uncompromising and definite.[3] Hopes and fears of negotiation were now dwindling. By 4 December it was believed that the Prince would not only dismiss the administration, but that he would also dissolve Parliament.[4] Sir William Young had heard from Colonel Stanhope that 'the arrangement of the new administration was firmly settled in everything', with the exception that the Duke of Devonshire had not agreed to go to Ireland.[5] That was something of an exaggeration, for the Whigs were by no means agreed on the constitution of their Cabinet, but opinion was now hardening in favour of a change of administration, and while Opposition newspapers denounced Pitt's policy as one of delay, supporters of the Government criticised the impatience and confidence of the Whigs.[6]

On 4 December the Lord President (Earl Camden) told the Lords that the responsibility for making 'some provision to supply the deficiency' caused by the King's illness devolved upon the two Houses, whilst presenting the report of the examination of the doctors by the Privy Council, and on the same day the first desultory exchanges took place in the Commons. Pitt moved that the report should be considered the following Monday (10 December) and gave notice that he would move the appointment of a committee to search for and examine precedents. On the previous evening he had held a meeting of his supporters at the Cockpit, and had outlined the proposals he intended to put before the House. Fox, in a short speech, took the opportunity to point out that 'if delicacy and their duty should happen to clash, the one ought not to be sacrificed to the other'. Grenville thought that Fox looked ill, and that he spoke poorly in his attempt to feel the pulse of the House.[1]

But a far more significant development than the cautious and hesitant manoeuvres in the two Houses was taking place. The obscure intrigues of November had largely been the result of ambiguous medical prognoses. Now the administration had the encouragement of a confident and optimistic diagnosis on the part of a doctor who had by far the greatest experience in dealing with cases of insanity. On 5 December, Dr Willis, a clergyman from Lincolnshire, saw the King for the first time, and on the morning of the 6th Pitt visited Kew and had an interview with him. Willis was not a formally trained physician, but he kept a madhouse and had built up a considerable reputation in the treatment of mental disorders. He had been called in as the result of a recommendation by General Harcourt's wife, who had given Pitt a testimonial describing how Willis had cured her mother of a nervous complaint, and despite all the charges of fraud and humbug which were hurled at him during the crisis he had the most perceptive and sympathetic approach to the King.[2] He told Pitt that there was no symptom in the King's case which he had not seen to a more pronounced degree in patients who had recovered.[3] He even allowed the King to shave, in his presence, and after a quiet night on 5 December George said that he felt better and that Dr Willis had settled his mind.[4] The King also took the opportunity to question his doctor on his abandonment of the duties of a parson in order to follow his career as a medical practitioner. Though it was agreed that Willis was to have the principal management of the King the other doctors were retained in order to look after the King's physical, as distinct from his mental, welfare.[5] With the advent of Willis the situation was transformed. It was now of real value to the Government to allow a second examination of the physicians, for they had further evidence to confirm their belief that the

King's illness was no more than a temporary derangement. At the same time the Opposition wanted the opportunity to get more resolute rulings out of Warren; thus, for very different reasons, both sides welcomed another chance to question the doctors.

Meanwhile the Prince and the Duke of York were not adding to their reputations for sobriety. On 30 November Sir William Young wrote that the Prince's melancholy 'is not of that deep rooted sort for which no physic of the mind can be found. Drinking and singing were specifics on the day stated to me'.[1] Both the King's oldest sons attended Opposition councils openly, as well as abandoning themselves to the pleasures of Brooks's. At the same time Pitt was receiving assurances of support 'much beyond the expectations we had formed'.[2] Thurlow was veering round to the Ministry once again, for he was now under the influence of Lord Stafford and Lord Weymouth, who from the beginning of the crisis had been 'clear and decided' in their support of the administration.[3]

The ministers also knew of the Prince's disposition 'to go to all the lengths to which that party are pushing him'.[4] It was well known that the Prince had declared his intention of refusing the Regency under any restrictions or in any manner short of full regal power, and that the three royal Dukes had determined to take a similar stand, authorising Fox to say so if necessary in the Commons.[5] But the Government was not daunted by these threats. Once it had been decided to impose restrictions for the protection of the King's rights

no other motive whatever can be a justification for abandoning them, as long as there can be found one individual or set of individuals who will undertake to carry on the government and as long as Parliament continues to think the proposal right and equitable.[6]

On 9 December, however, Grenville was convinced that the Prince's alleged resolve was 'nothing more than a bully intended to influence votes in the House of Commons'. If the Prince did assume such a desperate attitude

I should hope there would be every reason to believe that the Queen would be induced to take the Regency. . . . Nothing has passed with respect to this subject. Pitt has seen her once; but the conversation was nothing more than general, although with the greatest civility, and even kindness, on her part towards him.[1]

Here Grenville was deceiving himself, for the Queen was extremely anxious not to be dragged into British politics. She had devoted herself, since her marriage, to her domestic responsibilities, and the demands of a large and increasing family had taken up all of her time. In any event she had little knowledge of politics, and no inclination to become involved in what must have seemed to her a bewildering succession of incomprehensible disputes. Fortunately for the Ministry the Prince's resolution was short-lived. By 10 December Grenville confessed that the notion that the Prince would refuse the Regency was losing ground, and on the same day *The Times* was sufficiently confident of the outcome of the proceedings in Parliament to publish a full list of appointments in the new administration.[2]

Grenville's spirits were rising, for assurances of support were reaching the Government:

We receive every day new professions of attachment; and I do not hear of any individual of any consequence whom we shall lose, except probably the Duke of Queensbury. The Duke of Grafton has declared himself explicitly. There is no longer any doubt of Thurlow . . . Lord Lonsdale is still uncertain, and the Duke of Northumberland. . . . The general idea is that he is connected . . . with the independents . . . to support Mr Pitt as the Minister, but to oppose the restrictions on the Regent. This is not the less likely to be their conduct, on account of its being absolute nonsense.[3]

There was every reason to believe that 'the country will continue entirely with us', and that addresses would be presented from all parts to the Regent, begging him to continue the administration. Nevertheless, Grenville anticipated that by 10 or 12 January the

Bill would be passed and the Regent installed in office—'we shall then immediately be dismissed'.[1]

On 8 December in the House of Commons Pitt moved a committee to examine the King's physicians, deliberately excluding Burke from the list of members, despite the latter's exhortation to the House to preserve all their capacities, and to 'maintain them with firmness in situations of extreme delicacy and importance'.[2] The King was now improving daily, though Opposition papers diligently strove to convince the public that no improvement had taken place since his removal to Kew.[3] Grenville jubilantly told his brother of Willis's evidence before the committee, which had been 'all but decisive as to the certainty of his recovery in a short time'.[4] There were as yet no signs of convalescence, but there were indications (at least to Ministerialists) that it would not be long delayed.[5] The King's irritation had subsided, and Willis himself was very hopeful.[6] If the King had been a 'common man' he would have had no doubts on the matter, but 'in the King's situation, his own reflections on his situation, when he begins to recover his reason, may retard the cure'.[7] Of ten patients brought to him within three months of their being attacked, nine had recovered; the shortest time involved was six weeks to two months; the longest a year and a half; the average about five months.[8]

All this fortified the hopes which Pitt and his colleagues entertained. The debate of 10 December took place at a time when recent developments had done much to restore the confidence and determination of the Government. Pitt had now left the uncertainties of November behind. He was convinced that restrictions on the Regent's powers were necessary to preserve the rights of the stricken King, and this was all the more imperative if, as Willis maintained, the King's recovery was inevitable. The proposal to search for and examine precedents would gain time, but from his own study of previous Regencies Pitt was satisfied that the course upon which he had embarked was constitutionally correct as well as politically astute. Yet, had he not had the favourable diagnosis of Willis to support him, it is possible that he would have shrunk from engaging in public controversy on the issue of limitations, and only through Fox's blunder on 10 December was he able to prolong the controversy on terms entirely favourable to himself. The intervention of Willis transformed a rearguard action into a battle which it was now possible to win, even if it was still to be fought primarily on the defensive. As a result of his natural caution and austere industry Pitt was equipped with an interpretation of the situation which was both logical and in accordance with previous practice, and if luck was on his side he had earned his good fortune.

The Opposition made a sorry contrast. Even after a month's intrigue, gossip, and discussion, they had reached no decision. For all his reticence Pitt had evolved a policy which was politically and constitutionally defensible; for all their ardour the Whigs were no nearer an agreed approach to the question of Regency than in the early days of November. Their internal feuds and jealousies became more vehement as their advent to power was postponed, and in the midst of their unhappy divisions they took refuge in the complacent expectation of ultimate success. Sir Gilbert Elliot's fears were disastrously confirmed. Fox was ill; Burke was ignored; yet Grey, whose premature ambition made both Portland and Elliot uneasy, was admitted into the party's inner councils, holding private conferences with the Prince of Wales at Brooks's.[1] Thurlow's behaviour continued to baffle and bewilder. On 7 December the Duchess of Devonshire thought that the Chancellor was 'supposed by some to be against us', and on the next day the Duke of Richmond told Carmarthen that he thought it shameful for the Chancellor 'to be making his terms with the Opposition at the same time that he was present at all our Cabinet meetings'.[2] Yet Sheridan was still trying to make Thurlow a party to the negotiation by which the Opposition were to slip into office, silently and conveniently,

without the distressing tumult of controversy.[1] Fox had given
way to Sheridan's demand for discussions with Thurlow, but
with great misgiving and little desire for the scheme to succeed.
On the eve of the most decisive phase of the crisis the Whigs
were divided, hesitant, and about to embark on a serious public
controversy with little forethought and no agreement. Small
wonder that the Duchess of Devonshire could write long
afterwards 'I can trace that beginning of all negligence and want
of ensemble which together with the indulgence of imprudent
language has destroyed the importance of the Opposition'.[2]
Burke had warned Fox of the need for making speedy decisions,
and of the shortness of time, yet little use had been made of the
weeks that had passed since the King's breakdown to think out
the problems of constitutional theory and political conduct.
Chance, not wisdom, dominated the hopes of the Opposition
during the winter of 1788–9, and chance was finally to ruin their
fortunes. Their errors were the consequence of their failure to
apply themselves to the realities of the situation confronting them,
and they contributed to their discomforture by over-confidence
and careless disregard for unpleasant technicalities which seemed
nothing more than tedious pedantries on the part of lawyers and
Ministerialists. They did not realise that the confusions of
November were to haunt them, and finally to frustrate them,
through all the later twists and ironies of fortune.

CHAPTER II

THE PARLIAMENTARY DEBATES
OF DECEMBER 1788

'We shall soon be in a complete ferment', wrote Sir John Eden to his brother William on 11 December 1788, 'Mr Fox yesterday advanced some doctrine which Mr Pitt constructed little short of treason. This brought on acrimony from Fox, a rejoinder from Pitt, and a severe speech from Burke, who termed Pitt a competitor for the Regency.'[1] The exchanges in the Commons caught hold of the popular imagination, and the contest between advocates of 'inherent right' and 'Parliamentary privilege' replaced the King's illness as the topic of the day. Pamphleteers and journalists echoed the arguments which were so hotly disputed across the floor of the House, mingling personal vituperation with constitutional theorising,[2] and, once the passions of the public had been roused, it was impossible for Fox and his friends to prevent the controversy raging with an intensity which was to prove fatal to their cause. By assuming in public a unanimity which they did not possess, and by seeking in the tumult of debate to preserve the semblance of a unity which did not exist, the Whigs made it easier for the Government to press home its initial advantage. Yet, when the Commons met on 10 December, no one anticipated the dramatic events which were to ensue so rapidly, and the significance of Fox's blunder was not immediately apparent.

After the examination of the physicians had been ordered to lie on the table and to be printed, Pitt told the House that he did not wish for any further delay in the appointment of a committee to search for and examine precedents. Though the doctor's report offered reasonable hope that the King would recover his senses, there was no knowing when this would take place, and it was therefore necessary to take action without any further waste of time. Pitt did not think that his proposal would cause any difference of opinion, for it would supply the House with the wisdom of their ancestors, as well as the fullest information on which to act. He therefore moved the appointment of a committee 'to examine into, search for, and report precedents'. It was possible that the committee's report would be presented within a week.[1]

All this was unexceptionable, and free from any undue suggestion of party bias. To appeal to precedent, when confronted with a constitutional problem, was reasonable, and in reply to the criticism that he was merely playing for time Pitt had pointed out how speedily the committee could accomplish its task, if appointed without delay. In spite of all the fuss over the need for speed the King had now been ill for over a month and no catastrophe had resulted. But the Opposition, relying on the Heir Apparent to throw Pitt out and to establish them in office, were straining at the leash. After so many years in the wilderness even another week was too great a postponement. The proximity of power was too much for Fox to bear. With no prior warning to his friends he intervened in the debate with a forthright and uncompromising denial of the relevance of any precedents whatever, and what was even more important he affirmed in the most aggressive terms the Prince's right to the Regency. He conceded that it was essential for the House to lose no time in providing for the exigency, but maintained that this was an argument in favour of dispensing with Pitt's motion:

What were they going to search for? . . . Not Parliamentary precedents, but precedents in the history of England. He would be bold to say . . . that the doing so would prove a loss of time, for there existed no precedent whatever that could bear upon the present case. . . . There was a person in the kingdom different from any other person that any existing precedents could refer to— an heir apparent of full age and capacity to exercise the royal power. It behoved them, therefore, to waste not a moment unnecessarily, but to proceed with all becoming diligence to restore the sovereign power, and the exercise of the royal authority. . . .[2]

Fox failed to recognise that the study of precedents depended, not on the discovery of any identical situation in the past, but on the interpretation of parallel cases, in which the King was incapacitated and a Regent appointed. His blithe dismissal of all precedents appeared all the more irresponsible when he proceeded to defend the right of the Prince of Wales to the Regency. There had been no suggestion that the Prince should be passed over, and the notorious association of the Heir Apparent with the leaders of the Opposition tended to discredit Fox's motives in introducing the matter in debate. The problem was not who was to be appointed Regent, as much as deciding the powers he should exercise and the means by which he was to be invested with the privileges and responsibilities of his office. In his haste to install his patron Fox ignored these issues, taking refuge in his rash and ill-starred assertion:

... the Prince of Wales had as clear, as express a right to assume the reins of government, and exercise the power of sovereignty during the continuance of the illness and incapacity with which it had pleased God to afflict his Majesty, as in the case of his Majesty's having undergone a perfect and natural demise; and, as to this right which he conceived the Prince of Wales had, he was himself to judge when he was entitled to exercise it, but the two Houses of Parliament as the organs of the nation, were alone qualified to pronounce when the Prince ought to take possession of and exercise his right. ... But ought he to wait unnecessarily? ... while precedents were searched for, when it was known that none that bore upon the case which so nearly concerned him existed? ... He should not oppose the motion, but he thought it his duty to say, that it was incumbent upon the House to lose no time in restoring the third estate. ...[1]

Fox was right in stressing the fact that the Prince of Wales was of full age, but this did not in itself determine the argument. To define the Prince's right in terms which relegated the two Houses to the status of mere ratifiers was a more dubious proceeding, and it was dangerously ambiguous at its most vital point—for what was the precise significance of the Prince's alleged right to judge when he was to exercise his right to the

Regency? More important still was the assumption that a temporary incapacity was equivalent to the death of the King. This was to deny the distinction between succession to the Crown on the death of the monarch, and the assumption of the office of Regent. By making this assertion without citing precedents, Fox presented Pitt with another technical issue which had to be discussed if the Regency was to be settled in any way consonant with the constitution. By raising so many difficult issues in language which was both ambiguous and aggressive, Fox had converted a plea for haste into the most provocative incident of the crisis, and by giving Pitt the opportunity of fighting the controversy in defence of Parliamentary privilege against royal prerogative, he enabled the Minister to postpone the entry of the Whigs into office, and finally to defeat the Prince and his friends in a fashion that was as unexpected as it was overwhelming. As Fox was speaking Pitt slapped his thigh in jubilation, vowing that he would unwhig the gentleman for life. He realised the opportunities created by Fox's speech, and he exploited them with the skill of a seasoned and determined campaigner.

Pitt replied to Fox at once, defying him to support his assertion by any constitutional precedent, or to reconcile it with the spirit of the constitution. The doctrine which Fox had advanced was the strongest and most unanswerable reason for the appointment of the committee to examine precedents. Such a claim had to be tried and tested, even if intimated in an informal fashion on the part of the Prince. It was little less than treason to the constitution to assert such a right to the Regency, whether resting in the Prince of Wales or anyone else, without reference to the decision of the two Houses of Parliament. When the personal exercise of the royal authority was interrupted it was the responsibility of the other two branches of the legislature to provide for the temporary exercise of the royal authority. But while he denied the doctrine of inherent right Pitt was careful to admit the force of what he described as the Prince's irresistible claim. Despite the fulminations of Burke, both in private and in public, against the monstrous ambitions of William Pitt, there was never any serious suggestion of ignoring the Prince when choosing a Regent, still less any intention of overthrowing the succession. But a claim was a very different matter from a right:

. . . unless by their decision the Prince of Wales had no more right (speaking of strict right) to assume the government than any other individual subject of the country. What Parliament ought to determine on that subject was a question of discretion. However strong the arguments might be on that ground in favour of the Prince of Wales . . . it did not affect the question of right; because neither the whole, nor any part, of the royal authority could belong to him in the present circumstances, unless conferred by the two Houses of Parliament. As to the right honourable gentleman's repeated enforcement of the Prince of Wales's claim, he admitted that it was a claim entitled to their most serious consideration; and thence . . . it was more necessary to learn how the House had acted in cases of similar exigency, and what had been the opinion of Parliament on such occasions. He would not allow that no precedent analogous to an interruption of the personal exercise of the royal authority could be found, although there might possibly not exist a precedent of an heir apparent in a state of majority during such an occurrence, and in that case . . . it devolved on the remaining branches of the legislature, on the part of the people of England, to exercise their discretion in providing a substitute. . . . The question now was, the question of their own rights. . . .[1]

Pitt had now turned the tables on his adversary. Whilst conceding the most weighty part of Fox's argument, he had represented his opponent's speech as a sustained attack on the privileges of Parliament, and by doing so he made the discussion of a technicality the focal point of political interests, the issue upon which the realisation of the aspirations of both Government and Opposition hinged.

It required all Fox's considerable skill as a debater to reply to Pitt. He attempted to justify, whilst at the same time modifying, what he had said. Like many politicians called upon to explain themselves he claimed that he had been misrepresented. Pitt had used the equivocal word 'Parliament' instead of his own expression 'the two Houses', and in doing so an important difference had been obscured, for Parliament could only be complete when the executive arm was fully operative. He denied that he was advocating 'the antiquated and exploded doctrine of indefeasible hereditary right', but, if the Crown was declared by the law to be hereditary, why should it not be inferred from analogy that the exercise of the sovereign power was also hereditary? On these grounds the claim of the Prince to the right of assuming the Government during his father's illness ought to be admitted. Fox was astonished that anyone should dispute the point. He repeated the distinction he had made between a full Parliament and one weakened by the incapacity of the King. Until the third estate was restored by a recognition of the Prince's right, the two Houses were more truly a convention than a Parliament. He repeated, too, his belief that the situation which confronted the House was essentially the same as a demise of the Crown. The Prince's right was indisputable. The office of Regent belonged to the Prince, and

it so belonged of right, during what he would call the civil death of the King, that it could not be more completely his, by the ordinary and natural demise of the Crown. The Prince, therefore, who maintained that right, and yet forebare to assume it, was entitled to the thanks of his country.... It was the duty of the two Houses to restore the royal authority and that immediately....[1]

But this did not meet Pitt's objections, and the attempt to differentiate between a right and a claim only confused the issue, for if a right required the recognition of the two Houses in what sense was it a right at all? And if it was the Prince's duty to assume the Government during his father's incapacity why was it fitting to congratulate him on his failure to do so? If the Prince had the right to decide when to assume the executive power during the illness of the King, why had he not taken the initiative in seeking the adjudication of the two Houses? By insisting that the King's illness should be treated as equivalent to death, Fox was implying that George III's madness was incurable, but it is doubtful whether he would have made the same assumption had the King been suffering from any disease other than insanity. Fox was hoping that fulfilment was at hand, but he allowed his expectations to cloud his insight into the realities facing him, and this had fatal consequences for his cause. Despite the daily fluctuations in the King's condition Willis was confidently assuring Pitt that his patient was in far from an incurable state.[1] The tragedy of it all, from the Opposition's point of view, was that Fox had not bothered to study the problems raised by the crisis as both Pitt and Burke had studied them. He would have been wise to have followed Sheridan's advice, avoiding the discussion of technicalities in order to get into office without public controversy or debate. He underestimated the importance of the 'abstract' issues, only to raise them in a doubly dangerous form. Ambiguity and aggressiveness made troublesome companions. Fox had thrust his party into a position in which both the advantages of a consistent interpretation of the constitutional predicament, and the benefits of a policy of enlightened self-interest, were lacking. Ironically Fox's self-confidence undid anything which had been achieved by the painstaking negotiations carried on by Payne and Sheridan, whilst failing to make the noble stand for the principle of hereditary succession which was so precious in Burke's eyes. Fox's speech was too polluted and soiled with the sordid realities of day to day politics to be a convincing defence of the sacred principles of the constitution, and by seeking to blur the fundamental differences between Government and Opposition it was not free from a hint of shady self-interest. The controversy which Sheridan feared had been provoked by Fox himself, but it was not the constitutional debate for which Burke yearned.

Pitt had no difficulty in making it perfectly clear what the issue at stake was:

... to make provision for the executive power of the government during the interruption of the personal exercise of the royal authority by sickness ... did rest with the remaining branches of the legislature ... The right honourable

73

gentleman's doctrine was . . . that the two Houses had no such discretion, but that his Royal Highness had a claim to the exercise of the sovereign power which superseded the right of either House to deliberate on the subject. . . .[1]

Fox had only himself to blame if he now found himself called upon to justify himself in the confusion and bitterness of public controversy. He had rushed into the fray, betraying his cause by careless and imprecise language. Even an apologist was to avow that he had used a chance expression, upon which Pitt had swooped in an unjustified fashion.[2] But the distinction between right and claim represented an important change of emphasis, for if Fox was in earnest about the Prince's right, and if he took his analogy with a demise of the Crown seriously, he ought to have adopted the position of Edmund Burke—that the Prince was under an obligation to take the initiative. It was ludicrous to pretend that in strict constitutional practice the Prince had already succeeded to the powers of the Crown, only to commend him to the House on the grounds that he had refrained from taking action.

Burke's own intervention in the debate was unhappy. After saying that the subject before the House called for moderation and good temper, he launched into a furious attack on Pitt, accusing him of using unpardonable violence in charging others with treason because they ventured to mention the rights of the royal family. He continued:

Where was the freedom of debate, where was the privilege of Parliament, if the rights of the Prince of Wales could not be spoken of in that House without their being liable to be charged with treason by one of the Prince's competitors? [Cries of Order! Order! from the Treasury benches.] He had ever understood that our constitution was framed with so much circumspection and forethought that it wisely provided for every possible exigency and that the exercise of the sovereign power could never be vacant. . . .[3]

Pitt's appeal to precedent was both more exact and more flexible. When Burke talked of the constitution, what he had in mind was his own interpretation of the settlement of 1689. The problem

74

of the Regency was that there was no 'obvious' answer in constitutional law or practice. But, unlike all his colleagues (with the
possible exception of Loughborough) Burke took the issues raised
by the King's illness seriously—as worth intensive study and
examination in their own right—and he saw the crisis primarily
in constitutional rather than in political terms. For Fox the
technical issues were mere pawns in the party game, for Sheridan
a series of embarrassing irrelevances. Yet Burke's attempt to
throw the odium of questioning the rights and privileges of
Parliament on to Pitt was a lame stratagem by which he sought
to free Fox from the consequences of his folly. It was Fox, not
Pitt, who wished to prevent the House from debating the
question of right, and who had doubted Parliament's authority
to deal with the situation. All that Fox and Burke said bore out
Pitt's contention that when so wide a difference of opinion was
possible on the question of the Prince's right, it was absolutely
necessary to examine precedents. While Fox attempted to qualify
his original assertion by ambiguities, rather than by genuine
concessions, Pitt was not afraid to maintain his position without
any modifications. He remained convinced that it was little
less than treason to the constitution to assert that the Prince
had

a claim to the exercise of sovereign power, during the interruption of the
personal authority of his Majesty by infirmity and in his lifetime . . . he considered such a claim as superseding the deliberative power and discretion of the
two existing branches of the legislature.[1]

The question was put and carried and the committee named.
Pitt was now well placed. He had been provided with the means
of continuing his delaying action, yet on terms consistent with
his reading of the constitutional position. Not only this, but he
was now the defender of the privileges of Parliament as well as
of the rights of the sick King. With the encouraging diagnosis
of Willis to support him his position was a strong one.

Fox's blunder was promptly talked over, and, although its

decisive nature was not immediately apparent, it became the most popular topic of speculation and discussion. Nor was sharp criticism limited to supporters of the Ministry. As he entered their carriage with Fox and Grey, Sheridan could not refrain from commenting 'I suppose he has some right, has he not?' Fox's statement in the House had taken many of his colleagues unawares. The Duchess of Devonshire confessed that though the Whigs said they were glad of the discussion on the Prince's right, it had had a bad effect. She continued:

Pitt and Charles both blamed for bringing it on. Marsham and the country gentlemen are said to be against us on it. I think Grey and Sheridan, though resolved to go through with Fox, are in their hearts against it. . . . At Richmond House Lord Sydney said that Fox had retracted. . . .[1]

But whatever regrets he expressed in private Fox never publicly retracted his assertion of the Prince's right. His obstinacy prevented him from retreating from the sad predicament into which he had been plunged by his own impetuosity. Confusion in his own mind had resulted in disaster in the House.

Where did Fox learn his doctrine of hereditary right? It is possible that Loughborough was the source of his principle, for at an early stage of the crisis he had prepared a paper for the Prince of Wales (at Payne's request) discussing the technical problems of the Regency. Its arguments are strikingly similar to those adopted by Fox in the Commons:

. . . (T)he principle of the P's conduct is perfectly clear. The administration of government devolves to him of right. He is bound by every duty to assume it. . . . The authority of Parliament . . . would be interposed, not to confer, but to declare the right. The mode of proceeding . . . is, that in a very short time H.R.H. should signify his intention to act by directing a meeting of the Privy Council, where he should declare his intention to take upon himself the care of the state, and should at the same time signify his desire to have the advice of Parliament, and order it by proclamation to meet early for the dispatch of business. That done, he should direct the several Ministers to attend him with the public business of their affairs. . . .[2]

... It is of vast importance at the outset, that he should appear to act entirely of himself, and in the conference he must necessarily have, not to consult, but to listen and direct.[1]

Of course Loughborough, like Burke, wanted the Prince to demonstrate in action what he had a right to demand. This called for initiative and leadership, which the Prince of Wales did not possess, and it was much more dangerous to commit the party by embarking on a series of actions which, however attractive in theory, could be made to look suspiciously like a *coup d'état*. Words could possibly be withdrawn with few complications. Actions were irrevocable.

Loughborough had also prepared a declaration to be made by the Prince on assuming the Regency, and when Fox was told of Loughborough's plans he asked that the 'noble schemer' should not be informed that he had seen them.[2] For Fox was in a very awkward position. He disliked the negotiation with Thurlow, but had reluctantly agreed to it, and he favoured Loughborough's claims to the Lord Chancellorship in any Whig administration. One way of demonstrating his loyalty to Loughborough would be to follow his advice on the technicalities of the Regency, without necessarily committing himself to the course of action, which, in Loughborough's view, was an integral part of the correct procedure. In any case, Sheridan and Payne had not given Fox full details of their discussions with Thurlow. Certainly, before the debate of 10 December, Fox asked Loughborough for his advice:

... I should be happy ... to have half an hour's conversation with your Lordship upon the subject of the measures to be taken by the Houses of Parliament. ... I wish to speak merely for myself, and a few friends, and have no authority from ... any person of higher station. ... I mean to treat this business as wholly unconnected with general politics about which I am afraid our sentiments still continue to be widely different. ...[3]

The ambiguities of the letter are as interesting as the request for advice. Was Fox, by emphasising that he did not want to do more than speak for himself and a few friends, trying to avoid being drawn into Loughborough's plans for the Prince? In what sense could he really hope that the controversy would not involve 'general politics'? Could the conviction—on Loughborough's part—that the Prince should act, without waiting for the decision of the two Houses, be the issue on which he and Fox entertained 'widely different' sentiments? Perhaps Fox was trying to placate Loughborough by adopting his interpretation of the constitutional problem—the doctrine of inherent right—whilst rejecting, as 'general politics', the demand that the Prince should seize the initiative. This would bring Fox into conflict with Sheridan and the Prince on the issue of negotiations with Thurlow, without convincing Loughborough of his good faith. It becomes credible only if one remembers that Fox did not take the constitutional technicalities seriously: the doctrine of inherent right was important as a gesture to one man in the Whig party, a gesture which Fox thought it impossible for anyone but himself to make. And he had no idea that it would alter the situation beyond all recognition. Because he was so confident that nothing could prevent the Prince from becoming Regent in a very short time, and a Whig Ministry entering upon a long tenure of power (providing George III was, after all, incurably mad) Fox saw the constitutional debate as an opportunity for conciliating the discordant elements within the Opposition. In fact his action accentuated the divisions within the Whig party, created a situation in which Pitt had constitutional propriety and political advantage on his side, and ultimately thwarted all the aspirations of his fellow Whigs. At his meeting with Loughborough, when they discussed the constitutional aspects of the crisis in preparation for the debate of 10 December, Fox had little idea of the magnitude of the issues with which he was meddling.[1]

Naturally Ministerialists were jubilant at Fox's miscalculation. Sir William Young expressed his astonishment to the Marquis of Buckingham, saying that it was equalled only by the high

spirits of his colleagues and himself. Fox had provided the
Ministry with the best grounds on which to fight:

> Lord Radnor . . . told me that he understands Fox's doctrine . . . came from
> that constitutional lawyer Lord Loughborough. . . . Looking back to the
> history of this 'Man of the People' and to his present conduct, in despite of
> his talents of logical discrimination, I begin to doubt whether his weakness or
> profligacy is transcendent. Pitt's language was the most masterly and decisive;
> and has been done but little justice to in the papers of the day. . . .[1]

Lord Bulkeley had never been 'so interested in any public
measures' as 'in the support of Mr Pitt and the King at this
moment'.[2] It is significant that he thought of himself as taking
the part of the monarch as well as of the minister, and that he
saw the contradiction between Fox's former conduct and present
opinions, which were all the more extraordinary on that account.[3]
Grenville's delight at the outcome of the debate was unrestrained:

> You will, no doubt, be as much surprised as I was, to find that the notion
> of the Prince of Wales's *right* was brought forward yesterday by Fox in the
> House of Commons. It was a matter of no less astonishment to many of his
> friends, who were by no means prepared for the assertion of such a doctrine.
> One should lose oneself in conjecture by attempting to find out what motive
> could have induced him to take exactly the most unpopular ground on which
> their side of the question can be rested. . . . Only think of Fox's want of judge-
> ment, to bring himself and them into such a scrape as he has done, by main-
> taining a doctrine of higher Tory principle than could have been found any-
> where since Sir Robert Sawyer's speeches. . . .[4]

Nor was astonishment expressed only by Pittites. The Earl of
Charlemont, although firmly of Fox's opinion after further consideration, was 'somewhat startled at the proposition' at 'the
first glance'.[5] Lord Sheffield doubted the expediency of Fox's
argument, whatever its popular support, but consoled himself
with the thought that Pitt had given as much offence as Fox,
and that he was 'playing the game without temper or judgment'.[6]
The Times deplored the violent character of the debate, fearing
that great alarm and dissension would result, while Opposition
newspapers attempted to divert attention to Pitt's ambition, which

his 'temporary fit of honesty' during the debate had revealed for all to see.[1]

Fox's conduct had been a bewildering mixture of optimism and obstinacy, of careless impatience and irresponsible arrogance. Even the Duchess of Devonshire, ever sympathetic to Fox and his fortunes, confessed some years afterwards:

We can trace in these fragments, the virtues and foibles of Mr Fox—the comprehensive mind, undaunted genius, and unabating kindness, which, added to the most unaffected simplicity, constitute his character, but we may also trace what has told, alas, so much against him; a contempt for even necessary expedients, a great imprudence in conversation; and a fear, which in him is superior to anything, of seeming tu yield what he thinks right to the bias of public opinion. . . .[2]

The consequences of Fox's blunder were more readily perceived when the Lords met on 11 December to appoint a committee to examine precedents. The Lord President (Earl Camden) took the opportunity to repeat Pitt's contention that the assertion, which had been made in another place, of the Prince's right to assume the Regency was in itself a strong argument in favour of the proposed scrutiny.[3] Loughborough immediately attacked the other assertion, also made in another place, that the Prince had no more right than any other individual subject. The Prince's right was undeniably founded on law; the dangers of an elective Regency were great and alarming. Were the Lords willing to follow the 'horrible precedent' of the reign of Henry VI, the single precedent (so Loughborough claimed) of a Regent appointed by a House of Parliament? The two Houses could not make a law without the consent of the King, and whilst he was not suggesting that the Prince should rush violently into Government, nevertheless, upon authentic notification of the King's illness, the Prince ought—of right—to be invested with the royal authority.[4] In reply Thurlow confessed that Loughborough's doctrine was something completely new to him, and that in consequence he wished to have the advantage of all the information that could be obtained. But he solemnly reminded their Lordships that it was impossible to separate the natural and political character and capacity of the King.[1]

Many men found this conflict of views perplexing. Lord Stanhope was opposed to any proposal which would saddle the Regent with a permanent council, but he could not sit silent and hear it said that the two Houses had no power to supply any deficiency caused by an interruption in the personal exercise of the royal authority.[2] Stormont thought that an elective Regency would inevitably lead to a republic, and if the two Houses departed from the succession and elected a Regent he feared that the Scottish peers would regard the Act of Union as suspended.[3] But no attempt on the succession had been made (or even contemplated) by Pitt. The danger existed only in Stormont's mind. The search for precedents did not imply any interference with the rights of the House of Brunswick. In this matter there was an air of unreality about many of the criticisms voiced by the Opposition. Their efforts to create an atmosphere of suspicion suffered from palpable insincerity, for it was realised that the sinister picture of the Chancellor of the Exchequer leading an attack on the constitution was a ruse to obscure their own indiscretions in debate.

Lord Sydney, replying to the debate, maintained that no person, however high his rank, however distinguished his birth, had a legal claim to assume the Regency as of right during the temporary incapacity of the King.[4] The personality of the Regent was not in doubt (unless the Prince refused the office); but the right of Parliament to limit his powers was, and although Pitt accepted the Prince's eventual accession as Regent, he was determined that his powers should be restricted by Parliament. Regency was a trust on behalf of King and People. But the Whigs persisted in seeing the crisis in personal terms, with the exception of Burke, who was more than ever a voice crying in the wilderness, ignored, distrusted, and misunderstood by his political associates. The Opposition was as ineffective in the Lords as in the Commons, and a committee was appointed to search for and examine precedents.

Fox soon sought an opportunity to undo the damage his original assertion had inflicted upon his fortunes. When Pitt told the Commons on 12 December that he intended to move that the House should form itself into a committee on the state of the nation on the following Tuesday, to consider the report of the committee appointed to study precedents, Fox attempted to justify himself, and to clear himself from misrepresentation, not only in coffee-houses and newspapers (he had expected that) but 'before a certain august assembly, by a grave person, in high authority, and dignified rank'. He wished to make it clear that on 10 December he had not spoken on the authority of the Prince of Wales. His remarks had been made on his own initiative as an individual member of Parliament. But he was not content with that. He went on to make a distinction between the Prince's right and the possession of that right:

> He conceived the exercise of the royal authority to be the right of the Prince of Wales, but he had spoken of it as a right and not a possession. Before the Prince could exercise that right, he must appeal to the court competent to decide . . . or must wait until that court . . . made such a declaration. That court was composed of the two Houses of Parliament while they were sitting; the Prince had the right, but the adjudication of that right belonged to the two Houses. . . .[1]

Here Fox was trying to answer Pitt's charge that the doctrine of the Prince's right removed all power of deliberation from the two Houses. But it was not easy to appreciate what the precise difference was between a right which required the adjudication of the two Houses, and a claim which merited their consideration. If the Prince had the right to assume the Regency on what grounds was it necessary for him to wait for the two Houses to take the initiative? In what sense was the adjudication of the two Houses valid if they had no alternative but to recognise the Prince's right to the Regency? Astonished as he was at the controversy which had raged, Fox endeavoured to prevent further attention being paid to the abstract issues, which had proved sufficiently embarrassing already. He knew of no difference between an irresistible claim and an inherent right, and, if doubts could be entertained on the Prince's right to assume the royal authority during the King's illness, there could be none as to the propriety of investing him with 'the sole administration of the government, and the unlimited exercise of all regal functions'.[1]

But all this was playing with words. If there was no difference between an irresistible claim and an inherent right why had Fox been so insistent on the difference two days before? And considerable doubts were entertained on the right of Parliament to limit the Prince's powers, on the precise nature of the office of Regent, and on the powers which rightly belonged to him. Government and Opposition were emphatically divided on these issues, for the security of any administration formed by the Prince, and the necessary support for that Ministry in the two Houses, would depend largely on the patronage and influence which the Prince would be able to exercise as Regent. Fox's explanation of the furore as a simple instance of misunderstanding was feeble, and by reiterating his conviction that the Prince should be declared Regent with full regal powers, he made it impossible for the question to be carried with unanimity, despite his avowal that the differences between Pitt and himself were 'extremely minute'. If Pitt's proposals came near to his own he would be able to sacrifice something to unanimity, but if they did not bear a close similarity to his suggestions he would be compelled to divide the committee. It was of no avail to follow this threat with another wistful appeal to sweet reasonableness: 'But what signified differences upon abstract points, where the substance was indisputable?'[2] Unhappily for Fox the substance was highly disputable. He was forgetting that he himself had introduced the 'abstract' point in his speech on

83

10 December, and everyone knew that the question of limitations was far from being an 'abstract' point. If the King's illness was incurable, as Fox and colleagues must have hoped, then they would want to establish their Ministry on the firm basis of a new Parliament. Once in office, and having the full confidence of the Regent, a dissolution would bring them victory at the polls—a victory which they badly needed. But there could be no general election unless the Regent had the right to dissolve Parliament, and without the patronage of the Crown the outcome of the election would be doubtful. It was therefore absolutely necessary to prevent the Regent's powers being limited. Sheridan was in favour of getting into office first and doing away with any restrictions afterwards, but because it reflected political interests so sharply, and would influence political fortunes so radically, the abstract issue could not be shelved so easily. It was debated keenly and relentlessly, for both sides saw the crucial nature of what was at stake.

Pitt had no intention of allowing his opponent to escape un-scathed from a position of vulnerability. During the Regency debates he showed a determination as unyielding as that which he had displayed less happily over the Westminster scrutiny, and by emphasising that however abstract the issues appeared the difference of opinion was fundamental and far-reaching, he rejected Fox's offer of compromise as the worthless gesture it was. The Prince had no right whatever. Fox's latest statements had not altered the situation. The House had to settle the matter one way or the other, before proceeding to other 'great and important considerations'. No right to assume the royal authority independent of the consent and approbation of Parliament resided in the Prince of Wales, and the intimation of such a right presented a question of greater magnitude and importance than the exigency itself. The technical issues were more momentous than the political conflict, and here Pitt and Burke, whatever divergences characterised their respective interpretations of the constitution and their motives for giving priority to the abstract controversy, were in agreement. It was, Pitt continued, the first duty of the House 'to decide whether there was any right in the Prince of Wales to claim the exercise of the royal power . . . independent of the actual demise of the Crown . . .'.[1] He was giving Fox no respite. The suggestion that the King's incapacity was equivalent to death was being put to devastating use. He went on:

> On the ground of expediency it was . . . highly desirable that whatever part of the royal power it was necessary should be exercised at all during this unhappy interval, should be vested in a single person, and that this person should be the Prince of Wales. . . .[T]hat his Royal Highness should exercise that portion of authority, whatever it might be, unfettered by any permanent council and with the free choice of his political servants. . . .[2]

How bitterly Fox must have listened to the concession of the Prince's right to choose his own servants! Unless he was also endowed with the unlimited authority of the King such freedom would be useless. Pitt had not denied that the Prince was the obvious and correct choice as Regent, but by concentrating on the technical issue he had turned to his own advantage the known realities of current politics.

All that Fox could do in reply was to claim that his defence of the rights of the Prince had been inspired by the thought of the liberties of the people:

> The Regency was a trust on behalf of the people, for which the Prince was responsible. . . . Sovereignty was a trust depending on the natural liberties of mankind . . . he had urged the Prince's right to be hereditary, conceiving an hereditary succession the best security to the people for the due discharge and faithful execution of the important trust vested by them in their governors. . . . Restoring the royal power seemed to him clearly the first step that must be taken, and he conceived that the two Houses could not bargain with the Regent beforehand for the diminution of the royal power. . . . The question consequently would be, whether it was expedient to make the Prince of Wales Regent, or a Parliamentary Regent, and thus give a situation and create a power, hitherto unknown to our constitution, by placing a person in the situation of the King without regal powers. . . .[3]

But while Fox's attempted reconciliation failed, Sheridan's intervention now reopened the old controversy in a dramatic fashion. Ironically Sheridan was not interested in the abstract issues, regarding them as an unfortunate embarrassment for the party. His aims were simple to the point of crudity. He wanted to get into office as quickly as possible, and to this objective he was prepared to sacrifice every other consideration. He cared little for the finer points of constitutional controversy, and at the beginning of his speech he questioned the propriety of 'the abstract proposition on the right of the Prince of Wales'. His only motive for speaking was an anxiety to prevent any wrong conclusions being drawn from his remaining silent. He was supporting Fox, whatever doubts he himself felt about the merits or political utility of his friend's case. He was attempting to hide from the public the differences within the Opposition on the issue of hereditary right. He saw himself as a peacemaker, a role which he had had little opportunity of playing during his political career. Any discussion of the abstract question 'was neither likely to tend to the promotion of the good or the peace of the public. It could not conciliate; it might create dissensions and animosities.'[1] But he threw away any advantage he had gained by one rash and aggressive assertion: 'He begged leave to remind the right honourable gentleman of the danger of provoking that claim to be asserted which had not yet been preferred.'[2] It was common knowledge that the Prince and Sheridan were close friends, and Ministerialists assumed that what Sheridan had said was nothing less than a threat from the Prince. Fox's earlier denial that he was in any sense a spokesman for the Prince was forgotten. Sheridan was interrupted by cries of 'Hear! Hear!' from the Opposition benches and vigorous shouts from supporters of the Government.[3] In the face of the tumult he repeated his words. It was an unfortunate end to an otherwise conciliatory speech, and whatever Sheridan's motive for ending on such a truculent note Pitt was once again able to seize upon an error of judgment on the part of an opponent, trusting that the House 'would do their duty in spite of every threat, however high the authority from which it might proceed'.[1] The alliance of Prince and Opposition appeared even more sinister. First Fox, then Sheridan, had threatened the Commons' right of debate, hoping to overawe discussion by dark hints of what might follow should the House come to a conclusion uncongenial to the Prince. At the end of the debate Lord Frederick Campbell was convinced that the question of right would have to be settled before any further discussion could take place: Pitt had consolidated the advantage which he had gained on 10 December.

The Whigs now found themselves involved in a public controversy for which they were ill prepared. They had blundered into debate with little foresight. They were disunited, yet they were following a policy which many of them distrusted and few of them understood, and they could not agree on the division of spoils should they be successful. The constitution of the new Ministry was still uncertain. Although the adherence of Lord Malmesbury strengthened their ranks there were many disagreements and intrigues within them. On 11 December even Sheridan had been depressed and out of spirits. He and Fox were quarrelling, their animosity heightened by possible misrepresentations of Sheridan's conduct during Fox's absence on the Continent. Sheridan and Grey were resolved to go through with the principle of the Prince's right, but in their hearts they disagreed with it and regretted that it had ever been raised. Sheridan saw with misgiving the changed policy followed by the party since Fox's return, especially deploring the latter's lack of enthusiasm for the Lord Chancellor, whom Sheridan was courting so assiduously. The Duke of Norfolk was pressing his claims as Lord Privy Seal, and on 12 December, the day on which Sheridan gave his rash warning of the dangers of provoking the Prince to assert his right, there were 'great disturbances in the arrangements'.[2] The Prince had promised Lord Sandwich the post of First Lord of the

Admiralty, but both Portland and Fox refused to have anything to do with this. Sheridan was given the task of persuading the Prince to change his mind, and was successful. With characteristic indifference to someone else's fortunes the Prince gave up Sandwich 'in the handsomest way in the world',[1] and at the same time Sheridan persuaded Fox to waive Loughborough's claim to the Chancellorship in the interests of a renewed attempt to gain Thurlow for the Whigs. But, on the same day, Sheridan attacked Fox for bringing on the debate on the Prince's right, and when Fox said that it was better to take the bull by the horns Sheridan retorted that it was unnecessary to drive him into the room first.[2]

Sheridan was making great exertions to bring Thurlow over. From 10 o'clock in the evening of 13 December until 3 o'clock the following morning he was engaged in discussions with the Lord Chancellor, carrying with him a written proposal from Fox. Yet Sheridan feared that the negotiations with the Chancellor were already too late, and that he was pledged to the limitations which the Government were preparing. He knew that Thurlow was a great rogue, and said as much, for the Chancellor had tried to sound him on the possibility of undermining Fox, and had also told him that the Ministry intended to put the control of the King's household in the hands of the Queen for six months. All this made Sheridan more than ever convinced that the Prince should accept the Regency, even with restrictions on the creation of peers and of Lords of the Bedchamber for six months. But Fox refused to concede as much, and the natural outcome of these wrangles was further embarrassment in the councils of the Opposition.[3]

Despite his quarrels with Sheridan and his misgivings about the negotiation with Thurlow, Fox remained obstinately, almost blindly, optimistic. Writing to Mrs Armistead from St James's Street on 15 December he cheerfully reviewed the situation:

Though I am fatigued to death, and ought to go to bed it being near three, I cannot let go the opportunity of Carpenter, who sets out in a few hours, to write a few lines to my Liz with more freedom than I can do by Post. We shall have several hard fights in the H of Cs this week, and next, in some of which I fear we shall be beat, but whether we are or not, I think it certain that in about a fortnight we shall come in. If we carry our questions we shall come in in a more creditable and triumphant way, but at any rate the Prince must be Regent and of consequence the Ministry must be changed. The manner in which the Prince has behaved throughout the whole has been the most steady, the most friendly, and the handsomest that can be conceived. You know when he sets his mind to a thing he can do it well, and in this instance he has done so most thoroughly. The Duke of York who is steadiness itself has undoubtedly contributed to keep him to his good Resolutions and seems as warmly our friend as the Prince himself. In short with regard to the Princes every thing is easy and pleasant much beyond what I could form any idea of. In regard to other things I am rather afraid they will get some cry against the Prince for grasping as they call it at too much power, but I am sure I cannot in consequence advise him to give up anything that is really necessary to his Government, or to claim anything else as Regent, but the full power of a King, to which he is certainly entitled. The King himself (notwithstanding the reports which you may possibly hear) is certainly worse and perfectly mad. I believe the chance of his recovery is very small indeed but I do not think there is any probability of his dying. Adieu, my dearest Liz. It is so late that I can only write here what I dare not by Post. The sooner you come the better, but I own I think this next fortnight will be such a scene of hurry that I should have little time to enjoy what I most value in the world my dearest Liz's company. I take for granted you want some money & will if I can send you some by next Post, but I have hardly a minute to myself, either to get the money or to write, adieu my dear Liz, indeed, indeed, you are more than all the world to me.[1]

There is no trace of any self-questioning on Fox's part. He was undaunted by the prospect of several defeats in Parliament, confident that within a week or two the Prince's accession as Regent would settle everything. He ignored the possibility that the King might (despite all that was said and done) recover, and however steadfast the support of the Prince and the Duke of York was, this was of little consequence should the King's health be restored. On the day before he wrote to his mistress, Fox had told his associates at a meeting of the party at Burlington House that he was confident of beating the Government; yet, on 15 December, he complacently accepted defeats in the Commons as an inevitable but not decisive factor in the situation.[1] He did not ask himself whether these defeats would ultimately affect the outcome of the crisis.

He was also involved in the delicate task of reconciling Loughborough to his fate. Fox had given in to Sheridan's demands with great reluctance, and this was clearly reflected in his letter to Loughborough:

> I am so perfectly ashamed of the letter I am writing that I scarce know how to begin. . . . When I first came over, I found a very general anxiety among all our friends, and in the Prince still more than others, to have the Chancellor make a part of our new Administration, and (excepting only the D. of Portland) they all seemed to carry their wishes so far as to think his friendship worth buying, even at the expense of the Great Seal. This idea seemed so strange to me . . . that I took all sorts of means to discourage it, and have actually prevented the Prince . . . from saying anything to Thurlow which might commit him. . . . The difficulties which have arisen within these last few days . . . have had the effect of increasing the anxiety of our friends for Thurlow's support. . . . I feel the part I am acting to be contrary to every principle of conduct I ever laid down for myself and that I can bring myself to act at all I strongly suspect to be more owing to my weakness than my judgment. . . .[2]

The Opposition leaders were anxious to have Thurlow's support before the Lords resumed their deliberations on 15 December, and Loughborough, though bitterly conscious of the persistent sacrifices of his interests on the part of Sheridan and the Prince, wrote to Fox in terms of friendship and respect, while also indulging a taste for pessimistic prophecy:

> I will frankly confess to you that the measure appears to me a strong indication of weakness, and I am deceived if it will not be generally so felt as soon as it is known. This affords additional reason why, even on motives of prudence, I should acquiesce in it, which I do, I assure you, without the smallest interruption of those sentiments of friendship and confidence with respect to you or the Duke of P. which will ever remain in my heart.[3]

Loughborough's forebodings and Fox's secret hope that the Chancellor would prove treacherous were both justified in the debate in the House of Lords on 15 December.

In general the debate echoed what had already taken place in the Commons. Lord Fitzwilliam asked if the House could be given an assurance that it was not the Government's intention to discuss the Prince's right. It was not, in the smallest degree, necessary for such a discussion to take place, and if it did not occur this would give him great satisfaction.[1] The Lord President contented himself with saying that while the committee were still searching for precedents it was 'utterly impossible to advance a single step', but he reminded the House that the ministers had no wish to agitate more questions than were absolutely necessary.[2] This gave nothing away and told the Opposition little of the Government's intentions. Earl Camden concluded by asking Fitzwilliam whether he would declare that the rights of Parliament were admitted in full force, but Fitzwilliam countered this by saying that while he deprecated the discussion of the Prince's rights he could not be expected to admit the rights of others in opposition to them.[3] The Duke of York denied that the Prince had any intention of asserting his right:

His Royal Highness understood too well the sacred principles which had seated the House of Brunswick on the throne to assume or exercise any power, be his claim what it might, not derived from the will of the people expressed through Parliament.[4]

But the only denial which could now serve any purpose was a forthright and uncompromising rejection of the Prince's inherent right, not a mere assurance that he would not exercise it unless invited to do so by Parliament. And to demand this was to ask too much of the Whigs.

The most important incident in the debate was Thurlow's celebrated avowal of loyalty to the King. The Lord Chancellor agreed with the Duke of York that questions of right were generally invidious and often unnecessary—'no question ought to be brought forward which the nature of the subject did not absolutely demand to be discussed'. When the committee

examining precedents made their report it would be possible to
see what should be done 'to restore vigour and efficacy to the
executive government . . . and preserve the rights of the King
entire so that . . . he might not find himself . . . disabled from
the full exercise of all his rightful prerogatives . . .'.[1] Thurlow
then made his gesture of fidelity—'When I forget His Majesty
may God forget me!'—to the accompaniment of the furious
mirth of Burke and Wilkes. The negotiations with the Lord
Chancellor seemed to have been crowned with futility, despite
Sheridan's patience and the cheerful support of the Prince. Fox,
however, was overjoyed that the Chancellor had declared against
the Opposition; but Thurlow's allegiance to his master was much
less definite than his public conduct implied. He continued to
hold tentative negotiations and discussions with the Whigs,
though they were naturally less hopeful of the outcome and more
suspicious of his motives. The Prince was reluctant to give up
hope and persisted in holding long conversations with Thurlow,
despite disappointments and broken pledges, and Sheridan was
still employed as letter-writer and go-between.[2]

But, apart from his public declaration of loyalty to the King,
Thurlow had touched upon a very important aspect of the
constitutional debate when he emphasised that the rights of the
incapacitated King ought to be safeguarded during a Regency.
This was an echo of one of the distinctions made by Pitt in the
lower House, a reminder that the Regent was merely a temporary
substitute for the monarch, not the monarch himself. The
remainder of the debate was undistinguished. Stormont and
Rawdon appealed for moderation, by which they meant the
abandonment of the discussion of the Prince's inherent right.
Stormont thought that nothing could be easier than the reconciliation of the points of view of Ministry and Opposition—an
ingenuous delusion—and that the House should therefore declare
the Prince Regent.[3] Rawdon lamented the introduction of any
topic which would promote disagreement, deprecating the

debate on the Prince's right on these grounds.[1] The Duke of
Gloucester joined the chorus of the innocents, protesting that any
discussion of the Prince's right would have 'most mischievous'
consequences.[2]

Despite their disappointment over the debate in the Lords the
Whigs looked forward to the debate in the Commons on 16
December with some optimism. Many Opposition members
hoped to beat Pitt on the question of the day. Elliot was less
optimistic. He considered a majority 'perfectly doubtful' and
though he still thought that 'the business *must* end well' he
reminded his wife that 'we are in battle and all battles are precarious'.[3] The betting at Brooks's (Thurlow's declaration notwithstanding) was evens against the Minister.[4] Nor had Thurlow
been the only trimmer. Lonsdale was being wooed by the
Prince with some earnestness, at the same time as Pitt was informing him of his proposals for the Regency. Lonsdale was indisposed and this aided his intrigues. He gave the Prince advice
on how to deal with Parliament, and disapproved of the discussion
of the Prince's right. As late as the end of December he was
receiving communications from Pitt giving details of the
Ministry's plans, and in January he was still corresponding with
Payne, who sent him papers outlining the Opposition's case
against the policy of restrictions. Conveniently, his illness saw
him through the crisis unharmed.[5]

More important than Lonsdale was the group which came to
be known as the 'Armed Neutrality'. Rawdon and Northumberland were its principal figures. They claimed that they
wanted Pitt to continue as Minister, but they opposed the
policy of restrictions and the discussion of the Prince's right.
Sir John Eden suspected that their motives were far from
idealistic:

> The arm'd Neutrality met last night at Northumberland House, you have
> probably had their Names and Numbers before: about thirty in the Commons
> & twenty in the Lords, who are ... not pleased in not having their merits

properly rewarded. Among the former [sic] I recollect the Duke of Northum-berland, Ld Rawdon, Ld Kinnaird, Ld Hawke, Ld Breadalbane; among the latter [sic] Sir J. Sinclair, Macbride's [illegible], the two Bastards, Sir J. Moles-worth, Sir J. Swinburne &c; but it is supposed that most of them will upon this occasion vote with the opposition. . . .[1]

Grenville told his brother on 9 December of Lonsdale's un-certain attitude and of the Duke of Northumberland's policy of opposing Pitt's restrictions while claiming to support him as Minister. He could not refrain from commenting that the con-duct of the 'Armed Neutrality' was not the less likely 'on account of its being absolute nonsense'.[2] Thus, when the Com-mons resumed their deliberations on 16 December the Opposition entertained great hopes. A defeat in the House would be a great blow to the Government, in spite of increasing support in the country as a whole for Pitt and the privileges of Parliament. On the other hand only a resounding victory in the House could retrieve for the Whigs the ground lost as a result of Fox's blunder on the 10th and Sheridan's extravagance on 21 December.

After the House had formed itself into a committee on the state of the nation Pitt justified the restrictions which he was bringing before the House. A century, he claimed, had passed since any point of equal importance had demanded the attention of the two Houses. They had to provide for the exercise of the royal authority during the King's incapacity; but they had also to decide a question of 'a greater and still more important nature':

whether any person had the right either to assume or to claim the exercise of the royal authority, during the incapacity and infirmity of the sovereign; or whether it was the right of the Lords and Commons . . . to provide for the deficiency in the legislature resulting from such incapacity?[3]

Pitt was conscious that any decisions reached during the crisis would create constitutional law and determine constitutional practice. However furious the struggle for political survival Pitt did not lose that sense of responsibility which was so often attacked as mere priggery by his contemporaries. The abstract question was fundamental to the predicament confronting the House. Pitt reminded members of Fox's dismissal of precedents, calling upon his rival to cite a single case analogous to the infancy, infirmity, or illness of the sovereign in which the full powers of the sovereign were exercised by any person whatever. Precedent indicated the limitation of the Regent's powers, and the duty of Parliament to appoint a Regent:

The first precedent was taken from the reign of Edward III. . . . The Parliament of those days . . . provided a council about the King's person to act for him; a clear proof that they conceived the power existed with them to provide for the exercise of the royal authority. The next precedent was the reign of Richard II when the counsellors were also appointed to exercise the royal power. The third precedent occurred in the infancy of Henry VI. At that time the Parliament were called together by the young King's second uncle, the first being still living, but out of the kingdom; and that act was ratified by Parliament, they not considering it sufficient that it was done by the authority of the Duke. In that instance again, it was clear that the Regency was carried on by Parliament. . . . Subsequent precedents would prove that no one instance could be found of any persons having exercised the royal authority, during the infancy of a King, but by the grant of the two Houses of Parliament, excepting only where a previous provision had been made. . . .[1]

Pitt admitted that in the majority of cases when the King was absent from the realm, power had been delegated to the Prince of Wales, but he denied that this proved that any inherent right to the Regency resided in the Heir Apparent. The *Custodes Regni* had never been invested with the 'whole rights of the King himself', holding as they did their situation by appointment and not by right. In the case of Henry VI's illness

the Parliament of that day provided for the moment . . . they looked forward to the time when the heir apparent should attain full age, granting him a reversionary patent . . . to take place when he should come of age . . . That instance, though a single one, and where the heir apparent was not of full age, was sufficient to show the sense of Parliament in those days as much as if the heir apparent had been of full age. . . .[2]

If no contrary precedent was advanced the committee should presume to 'admit that no right existed in the heir apparent or the heir presumptive to assume the functions of royalty on the temporary incapacity of the sovereign; nor any rights but those delegated by the two remaining branches of the legislature'.[1] Pitt denounced the suggestion that the discussion of necessary limitations should be avoided, and took care to point out that in his view the thesis that the King's illness was equivalent to death was unfounded: 'Could the committee so consider his Majesty's indisposition, which was not an uncommon case, and generally but temporary; could they conceive that his Majesty had undergone a civil death? He was sure they would not. . . .'[2] He defended the role of the Lords and Commons in providing for the deficiency in the third branch of the legislature, representing as they did the 'whole estate' of the people, as their 'legal organs of speech'. Whenever the third branch of the legislature was 'wholly gone', or whenever it suffered a suspension, the two Houses were justified in acting in their present capacity, as 'organs of the people'. In any event

the political capacity of the King . . . was always considered legally entire, and . . . if any natural incapacity should cause a suspension of the royal authority, it then rested with the remaining branches of the legislature to supply such defect. In every proceeding of Parliament in the reign of Henry VI they had acted upon such a power, and declared in what manner, and by whom, the royal authority was to be exercised, for, and in the name of, the King. In that reign the Duke of Gloucester claimed the Regency, and applied to Parliament for the same as his right; but the answer of Parliament to such claim was, that he neither had by birth, nor the will of his brother, any right whatever to the exercise of the royal authority. They however appointed him Regent, and entrusted him with the care of the young King. Here was an instance of a claim of right having been actually made, and an instance, likewise, that it had been fully decided upon by the then Parliament, who declared that no such right existed, either from the law of the land or from precedent. The rights of Parliament were congenial with the constitution.[3]

Pitt contended that Parliament's right to supply the deficiency in the third branch of the legislature enabled them to appoint a power to give sanction to their proceedings 'in the same manner

as if the King were present', and that the Prince of Wales was
not (as had been claimed) 'one and the same' with the King. He
then moved his resolutions:

... that his Majesty is prevented, by his present indisposition, from coming to
his Parliament, and from attending to public business: and that the personal
exercise of the royal authority by his Majesty is thereby interrupted.

... that it is the right and duty of the Lords ... and Commons ... now
assembled, and lawfully, fully, and freely representing all the estates of the
people of this realm, to provide the means of supplying the defect of the
personal exercise of the royal authority, arising from his Majesty's said
indisposition, in such manner as the exigency of the case may appear to
require.

... that ... for this purpose, and for maintaining entire the constitutional
authority of the King, it is necessary that the ... Lords ... and Commons ...
should determine the means whereby the royal assent may be given in Parliament, respecting the exercise of the powers and authorities of the Crown, in
the name, and on behalf of the King, during the continuance of his Majesty's
present indisposition.[1]

The first resolution was put and agreed to. On the second the
Master of the Rolls (Richard Pepper Arden) affirmed that he had
never heard of any inherent right on the part of the Prince of
Wales until the last ten days, and that he could not accept the
doctrine that the King and the Prince of Wales were one and the
same person. He had no doubt that it was the constitutional
right of the two Houses to provide for the interruption of the
royal authority.[2] Mr Loveden asked whether the resolutions
were meant to preclude the Prince from the Regency, and
whether gentlemen voting against the resolution would have
their votes imputed to 'private interest ... and convenience'.[3]
Pitt denied both of these charges. Mr Bastard—significantly a
member of the 'Armed Neutrality'—questioned the expediency
of pressing the resolution when no claim of right had been made
on behalf of the Prince, taking care at the same time to state that
Pitt stood higher in the esteem of the people than Fox.[4]

The most interesting contribution was made by Lord North.

Now totally blind, he had taken no part in politics for eighteen months, but he had lost none of his debating skill, and the Whigs doubtless hoped that his charm would soothe the irritation which had been caused by the behaviour of Fox, Burke, and Sheridan. That North should become one of the chief spokesmen for the Opposition was in itself an indication of the damage which had already been done by indiscretions in debate. Too proud, or too wilful, to change their reasoning the Whigs clung to the possibility that a new speaker, famous for his moderation, would transform the situation. Apart from his eloquence North had little influence in the House. He had never been a borough-monger, and his supporters in the Commons had dwindled to a handful.[1] Since the ill-famed coalition he had gradually faded from the political scene, seeking, as his eyesight deteriorated, a haven from the storms of public life. The debates on the Regency form a moving epilogue to his career. His speeches were as reasonable, as free from malice, as they had ever been. He maintained that the first step required was the restoration of the legislature. The sooner this was accomplished the less likely were the House's proceedings to be interpreted as inspired by 'personal motives'. The two Houses were a convention, not a Parliament, and since they were a 'maimed and imperfect' legislature they should confine themselves to the necessity of the case. Until the third branch of the legislature was restored they had no legal power, and instead of discussing abstract questions which could only promote dissension they should fill the vacancy without delay. If the House was unanimous about the principle why fall out over 'forms'? On the nomination of the Regent the House would resume its status as part of a full Parliament, and it would then be possible for any necessary legislation to be passed—'either of limitation, restriction, or of any other kind'.[2]

All this was very attractive, for North was not denying the House liberty to impose any restrictions which might be necessary. He had merely questioned the utility of imposing restrictions before appointing a Regent. But here the Prince's political affiliations clouded the issue. Was it practicable for the House to appoint a Regent without first limiting his powers? If Parliament had the right to nominate the Regent why could the two Houses not restrict his powers? North's gesture of conciliation was more apparent than real, but if he could not restore 'unanimity' it was improbable that anyone could. Nor was it true to say that the House was united in principle, but divided over the formal expression of that principle. There was agreement that the Prince ought to be Regent, but the principle upon which he was to be appointed was fundamental to the controversy.

The other speakers followed with little variation the arguments already urged on their side of the question. Mr Powys deprecated any declaration of the rights of the House, but Mr Rolle thought it 'indispensably necessary' that the question of right should be discussed and decided.[1] The Attorney-General (Sir Archibald Macdonald) thought that the resolution was 'a necessary foundation for all their future proceedings', as well as a vindication of the 'rights of the whole community'. He admitted that 'to act and not to determine abstract questions was the duty of the committee; but . . . it was impossible to consider the principles upon which the committee acted to the community at large as an abstract question'.[2] Everybody agreed that the abstract question was unfortunate, but it was possible, and convenient, to define it differently. The patent made when the Duke of York was appointed Regent, in favour of the Prince of Wales when he came of age, demonstrated 'that without a patent the Prince of Wales when he came of age could not claim of right, much less assume, the Regency of this realm. . . . This great question, having been anxiously introduced by a right honourable gentleman, must now be settled for all posterity.'[3]

At this stage Fox felt compelled to break his silence. He found it difficult to believe that the Chancellor of the Exchequer and his friends thought that the committee should take seriously the precedents by which the Government was seeking to justify its policy:

Was the practice of the present times, times so enlightened, and in which the principles of the constitution were so well understood, to be grounded on precedents drawn from so dark and barbarous a period of our history as the age of Henry VI?... From a time ... when the House of Commons was prostrate at the feet of the House of Lords, when the third estate had lost all energy and vigour, and when the power lay wholly in the hands of the barons?[1]

Such precedents were useless. There was no analogy, Fox urged, between the constitution then, and the constitution established at the revolution. He was convinced that a right attached to the Prince of Wales as Heir Apparent to exercise the royal authority, upon the incapacity of the King being declared by the two Houses of Parliament, the Prince's right being considered as subject to the adjudication of the Lords and Commons. To make a law for the appointment of the Regent was to make the monarchy elective, instead of hereditary. The power of making laws rested only in the complete legislature, not in the concurrence of any two branches of it. Fox poured scorn on the government's proposals: 'If the doctrine of the day prevailed ... when the King of England is in good health the monarchy is hereditary; but when he is ill, and incapable of exercising the sovereign authority it is elective.'[2] Such 'legal metaphysics' were unintelligible. Not one of the precedents applied to the case before the House. If they proved anything at all they established the Prince's right:

since, in all of them, the nearest relative to the Crown, if in the kingdom, had been appointed the Regent, and especially the Prince of Wales. In the reign of Edward III, his son, commonly called the Black Prince, was declared Regent at only thirteen years of age, during the invasion of France by his father. . . . The regencies in the reign of Henry VI proved the right of the Prince . . . was recognised, although he was not a year old, in the very patent which appointed the Duke of York protector.[3]

Fox concluded by repeating the well-worn question—what was the use of bringing forward the issue of hereditary right, when the expediency of appointing the Prince of Wales was agreed on all sides?

But his speech was full of contradictions. He had denied the validity of precedents, only to claim that they supported his own point of view. In his haste to condemn discussion of the issue of hereditary right he asserted the doctrine in language which made further debate inevitable. He failed to address himself to the problem of limitations, and contributed nothing to the debate on the procedure by which the Regent was to be appointed. Despite his renewed emphasis on the right of the two Houses to declare the monarch's incapacity, his insistence on their power to adjudicate the right of the Prince to the Regency remained ambiguous and inconclusive.

In reply Pitt concentrated on the practical implications of conceding the Prince's right, the chief of which was the confidence of Fox and his friends that they would succeed the current administration. Pitt put the alliance between the Prince and the Whigs to unexpected use. The Opposition were supporting the Prince in the hope that their influence over him would enable them to nominate any Ministry that would be formed. Pitt did not deny the Prince's right to choose his political servants, but he questioned how free the choice made by the Prince would be. By depicting the Prince as the guileless victim of unscrupulous politicians Pitt exonerated him from the worst excesses of faction, whilst evoking pious memories and old prejudices unfavourable to the imposition of a complete administration on the head of state. Fox and his associates were striking at the conventions of the constitution:

The nation had already had experience of that right honourable gentleman and his principles. Without meaning to use terms of reproach, or to enter into any imputation concerning his motives, it could not be denied that they were openly and professedly active on the ground of procuring an advantage from the strength of party, to nominate the ministers of the Crown. It could not be denied that it was maintained as a fundamental principle that a minister ought at all times to be so nominated.[1]

This made it all the more urgent to decide what powers could legitimately be entrusted to the Regent, since the Prince did not seem aware of the dangers involved, when such 'advisers' sought to create a weight of influence which they could use against the just rights of the Crown. The pathos of the King's condition gave added force to an appeal to recognise the right of the Crown to nominate ministers. Pitt continued:

> The notice which the right honourable gentleman in his triumph had condescended to give the House, furnished the most irresistible reason for them deliberately to consider lest in providing for the means of carrying on the administration during the short and temporary interval, they might sacrifice the permanent interests of the country, in future, by laying the foundation of such measures as might forever afterwards during the continuance of his Majesty's reign obstruct the just and salutary exercise of the constitutional powers of government in the hands of its rightful possessor, the sovereign, whom they all revered and loved.[1]

The rights of both the King and the Parliament demanded that the question of right should be fully discussed, especially when the motives of those who had introduced the subject were politically suspect and demonstrably factious. Fox was being crushed in debate. His errors of judgment (many of them dictated by the growing realisation that he had blundered on 10 December) were being turned against him in relentless fashion, whilst his inability to sustain an argument on abstract terms made it easier for Pitt to trap him in the complexities of constitutional controversy. Fox was the innovator, the advocate of extreme notions of hereditary right, the foe, not only of the privileges of the two Houses, but of the rights of the sick monarch. Only a withdrawal of his original assertion could save his fortunes, but this would mean humiliation, amounting as it did to the concession of victory to Pitt.

The Lord Advocate (Ilay Campbell) rightly pointed out that the question of right could only be waived if the two Houses were prepared to agree, not only that the Prince should be

Regent, but that he should be invested with all the regal powers
without limitation or diminution. To limit the Prince's powers
as Regent implied that the right of supplying the deficiency lay
with the two Houses.[1] After Mr Milnes had contended that the
conduct of Fox and his friends merited the 'utmost reprobation'
the Solicitor-General argued that the King

was still, in the contemplation of law, as perfect as ever, and the positive
right of the Prince ... to the Regency ... was clearly undefined. No precedent, no analogy, could be furnished ... Parliament was called upon to
establish a precedent. ... The Prince ... should be invested with every
authority for managing the public business, but ... the powers of the Regent
ought to be circumscribed.[2]

Precedents existed for the guidance, not the unprotesting submission, of the House. This was an effective answer to the plea that
all precedents were irrelevant. No absolute parallel could be
expected, but to ignore precedent was to ignore the basis on which
the law had to rest. It was of little use for Sir W. Molesworth to
advise the 'prosecution of such measures as would produce
unanimity', for that inestimable virtue had been sadly tarnished
in the dingy atmosphere of debate. Neither side was prepared to
pay the price which would restore unanimity—complete and
total submission that the opposing party was right in its reading
of the situation. Mr Drake's lament, that he dreaded nothing as
much as a change of administration, reminded members of the
struggle for power which was the sinister background to all their
deliberations. When the vote was taken the Ministry triumphed
by 268 votes to 204.[3]

The result was a bitter disappointment for Fox and his friends.
Sheffield was compelled to admit that Fox's declaration had done
more harm than he had imagined, and that Pitt's 'mountebank
speeches ... suited the nonesense of many, however they may
be execrated and disliked by others'.[4] The Prince, though very
much hurt at the outcome of the debate, took it bravely.[5] Elliot
told his wife that the party was 'shockingly beat on Tuesday ...

majority against us 64, which was more than we expected, although I certainly did not expect we should carry our point'.[1] He complained that Pitt was 'the only object which the nation can perceive, and the only thing they think valuable in the world'.[2] Defeat in the Commons made unpopularity all the more difficult to bear. The press commented on Fox's conduct as occasioning much grief to his friends, as well as triumph to his opponents, and the Opposition's overtures to Thurlow were reported with avidity, if not accuracy. It was said that the Prince would refuse a limited Regency, but *The Times* thought that for all the heat and passion of debate Pitt's popularity would see him through. Fox's intemperance had diminished his influence over his colleagues, and Sheridan was named as the principal adviser amongst the Whigs.[3] Writhing under the humiliations which they had endured at Pitt's hands, Fox's colleagues blamed him for introducing the topic of right, a subject which had proved so unhappy for their cause.[4] Sheridan, seeking even after the defeat of 16 December to restore the party's fortunes by negotiation, was manfully striving to gain the 'Armed Neutrality' for the Opposition. On 18 December he met Rawdon and Northumberland, who promised to support the Whigs on the issue of limitations, and on the next day he was confident that all would go well. The Prince would accept a limited Regency, rather than see it pass to the Queen, but if he was to be saddled with Lords Justices he had resolved to refuse 'boldly'. Sheridan was still pressing him to accept the office even with limitations, for the latter could be discarded once the Prince was installed as Regent, and, although Fox and Portland were opposed to this suggestion, North had been persuaded to give it his blessing. There were even further attempts to convert Thurlow, Sheridan holding conversations with the Lord Chancellor and carrying on a correspondence with him. For all their disappointments the Whigs were reluctant to abandon hopes of bringing the Chancellor over; but they soon wearied of the negotiation, and when Fox forced Thurlow to show his hand on 25 December relief and joy were the chief reactions within the party, with the possible exception of the Prince and Sheridan. Certainly Fox's letter to Loughborough, dated 26 December, reflects jubilation rather than regret:

... The negotiation is off with an express desire on his part that no more may be said to him on the subject till the Regency is settled. . . . It was the pleasantest conversation I have had with him for years. . . . In short I think the negotiation is fairly at an end; and if when the Regency is settled the Prince wishes to revive it, it must be considered as a proposition entirely new and treated upon that footing. . . .[1]

Sir Gilbert Elliot told his wife of the 'shabby trimming game' which Thurlow had played, 'keeping himself open to both parties till one should be completely victorious'.[2] Yet there is no definite evidence that Thurlow was betraying Fox to Pitt all the while, any more than there is evidence to prove that he betrayed Pitt to Fox. Both were disgusted with his duplicity and hypocrisy; both distrusted him; and both never forgave him for his conduct during the Regency controversies. Thurlow was possibly less unscrupulous than legend suggests, but his conduct was too subtle, too calculating, and too hesitant, to gain him the confidence of Pitt or Fox. Instead of securing his position in both parties he offended the leaders of the Opposition as well as his colleagues in the Government. Elliot called him 'a treacherous and dangerous character', too dangerous to admit into any Cabinet, despite the value of his support in the Lords and his influence with George III.

Ministerialists could not disguise their joy at the outcome of the debates. Grenville told his brother of the blunders committed by Fox and Sheridan, adding, with some relish, 'You may conceive what an advantage this gives us especially when coupled with the strong hopes entertained of the King's recovery...'.[3] Sir William Young, out for his morning walk on 13 December, noticed 'a long row of handbills, stuck from one end to the other of Devonshire House; in which a few words of "Fox for the Prince's prerogative" and of Pitt, in reply for the privilege of Parliament, and the liberties of the nation, were not badly selected . . .'.[1] In his account of the debate of 16 December, Grenville paid tribute to Fox's ability as a debater, confessing that he thought his speech one of the best he had ever heard him deliver. But Pitt's reply had neglected no opportunity of exposing his opponent's errors, and Grenville thought that he had never heard a finer burst of eloquence. The Ministry were now confident of carrying their restrictions—'probably by a larger majority'—and Grenville could not refrain from adding: 'Fox's declaration of the Prince of Wales's right has been of no small service to us. Is it not wonderful that such great talents should be conducted with so little judgement?'[2] All this was a far cry from the timorous doubts and gloomy fears of the dark days of November. Pitt and his colleagues faced the future with growing optimism and swelling confidence.

The debate arranged for 18 December was postponed until the following day at the request of Fitzpatrick, who told the House of Fox's indisposition. He had not recovered from the dysentery which he had contracted on his journey home from Italy, and he was weak and weary, though not depressed in spirit. Palmerston told his wife that during the debate of 16 December Fox was 'very ill and had much difficulty to go on . . . though he spoke as well as ever I heard him'.[3] Pitt was also feeling the effects of continuous strain and the tribulations of a long drawn out controversy. But while he was suffering from a severe cold and a sore throat, Fox was the victim (so Elliot wrote to his wife) of 'a real illness'. On 19 December Sir John Eden went so far as to say, 'I should not be surprised, according to the surprising luck that has always attended our minister, if during this present contest his enemy Charles Fox should fall a martyr to his exertions, for he is very far from well'.[4] Fox's illness was eagerly discussed in the press. *The Times* informed its readers that he was suffering from 'an obstruction on the neck of the bladder', as well as from dysentery, and that his friends were exceedingly alarmed. These fears were exaggerated, but as time went on Fox found the strain increasingly difficult to bear, and by the end of January he was to seek a cure for his bodily ailments and political disappointments by taking the waters at Bath.

When the debate was resumed on 19 December the discussion covered familiar ground. After Alderman Watson appeared at the bar of the House with the report of the committee on the state of the nation, Sir John Sinclair repeated that he did not think it necessary for the House to make a declaration of its right 'on the slight ground of the expression of a doubt of the right of the Prince of Wales'.[1] The conduct of the Minister was 'highly objectionable'. This well-worn theme was repeated by Opposition speakers and as solemnly refuted by the supporters of the Ministry. Sir Grey Cooper doubted whether the House 'in its present limited and imperfect capacity' could agree to the resolutions which were being debated, and repeated the argument against the precedents drawn from the reign of Henry VI by emphasising the 'wretched state of submission' of both Houses of Parliament at that period. Mr Martin attacked Fox's ambition, and Mr Christian, after regretting that the question of right had been brought forward, thought that the question would have to be decided 'for the benefit of posterity'. The third resolution was extreme, however, for it would be wrong to impose any limitations on the Prince as Regent.[2] Windham had earlier singled out the third resolution as particularly distasteful—'his mind revolted at the idea of a coarse fiction'.[3] All these arguments were thoroughly familiar from previous exchanges in the controversy, and it is difficult to see what it was hoped to gain by repeating them. After Mr Anstruther and Mr Beaufoy had reiterated the platitudes appropriate to their own side of the question, Mr Dempster moved to leave out the word 'right' in the second resolution, together with 'in such manner as the exigency of the case may appear to require', inserting instead the words 'by humbly addressing . . . the Prince of Wales . . . to take care of the administration . . . during the continuance of his Majesty's indisposition and no longer'.[1]

The question was put and carried that the word 'right' stand part of the resolution; but the second amendment was debated, although in an uninspiring fashion. Burke warned the country gentlemen to be more careful of how they voted in future, but, after further discussion, Dempster withdrew his amendment to the second resolution, which was carried as it stood originally, though Dempster then moved that all of the third resolution should be omitted from the word 'determine' and that his amendment calling upon the Prince to take upon himself responsibility for the administration should be inserted in its place. After exchanges between Fox, Pitt, and Marsham, the House adjourned.[2]

But before the resumption of the debate on Monday, 22 December, there were further dissensions within the Opposition. On 19 December Fox was angry with Sheridan for allowing some of their friends to leave town, under the impression that there would be no resumption of the debate, and when he apologised on the following day Sheridan casually told him that for all he cared he could be as cross as he liked.[3] On Sunday, 21 December, Grey suspected that Sheridan had won the support of the 'Armed Neutrality' by 'talking other sentiments than Fox's'.[4] Failure heightened suspicion and distrust, and with such a lack of unity within the party the future seemed all the more depressing. The gay optimism of November was no more, although most Whigs were reluctant to accept the fact that they might not, after all, enter office within the coming week or two, and that even if they did their tenure would not be as secure as they had originally imagined. As defeat in Parliament blighted their hopes they turned more expectantly to the Prince; but if the policy of limitations was successful his support would not be able to save them from the vengeful wrath of George III. To secure their hold on office they needed the patronage of the Crown, for without such assistance they could not hope to build up a majority in the Commons strong enough to withstand the enmity of the King, should he be restored to his senses. And, by the restrictions which he intended to place on the Regent, Pitt was forestalling them at this very point. He had been far-sighted enough to realise that it would be neither constitutionally proper nor politically justifiable to deny the Prince's claim to the Regency. By evolving a clear conception of what the office signified he had found it possible to outwit the Whigs. By their persistent neglect of the constitutional issues, and their careless repetition of the 'irrelevance' and superfluity of the abstract questions, the Whigs had contributed to Pitt's triumph. Sir John Eden could refer to Pitt's surprising luck, but it might be claimed that by earnest application to the problems of the crisis the Chancellor of the Exchequer had earned his good fortune.

Burke opened the debate of 22 December by declaring that it was 'his sole pride and exclusive glory . . . to speak against the wishes of the people whenever they attempted to ruin themselves'.[1] He did not worry whether his principles were labelled Whig or Tory, for he knew as little of the inside of Carlton House as he did of Buckingham House. He was perfectly satisfied with the constitution as he found it, but, while he wanted no alteration, others longed for innovations. The proposed method of giving the royal assent to Bills was a 'glaring falsehood', a 'palpable absurdity'; housebreaking and highway robbery were more excusable than 'law forgery'.

When all the heterogeneous mass of cases, and all the farrago of nonsense under the title of legal distinctions were considered, every man of common understanding and integrity of principle must see the necessity of governing the whole of them by the genuine spirit and fair principles of the constitution.[2]

If the Prince was given unlimited powers as Regent this in itself would prevent cabals, intrigues, and dissensions. Burke singled out for special condemnation the suggestion that the Prince should not have the power to create peers, reminding the House that the 'fountain of honour' had flowed profusely since 1784. In his enthusiasm he betrayed some of the Opposition's secrets: 'Suppose the Prince wished to bestow honours on the House of Cavendish . . . or . . . to revive the title of Rockingham, would it be deemed extravagant or improper?'[1] Here he was pulled to his seat by his colleagues tugging at his coat-tail, but valuable information had been divulged, and strengthened Pitt's determination to prevent the Prince from creating peers of the realm. Small wonder that Burke's speech was severely criticised for its violent tone. Sir William Young thought that he had been wilder than ever, and that he had laid himself and his party open 'more than ever speaker did'. He was 'folly personified, shaking his cap and bells under the laurel of genius', finishing his speech 'in a manner next to madness'.[2]

For the Government the Solicitor-General maintained that in his political capacity the King remained 'whole and entire'. Despite his temporary incapacity, 'in the eye of the law his politic character remained entire . . . there would be no illegality in applying his name to the Bill in question. No regent . . . could be legally appointed but in this way'.[3] Sir John Aubrey differed from those 'with whom he had acted for some time', for, while rejecting the doctrine of a Regency *de jure* in the heir to the throne, he did not agree that the House was competent to exercise its Parliamentary functions. The argument in favour of a restricted Regency savoured more of a prejudice against a particular party in the state than of a concern for the public welfare.[4]

Lord North made another lengthy speech, in which he argued that the House did not have the power to create the third estate, which was to give vigour and effect to their proceedings. If a power created by a necessity was limited by that necessity the wisest course would be to supply the temporary defect in the executive without delay. By addressing the Prince to take upon himself the Regency during his father's illness the House would save themselves and posterity from 'the horrid principle of virtually declaring that an act of legislation may be exercised by the Lords and Commons at a time when the third estate is incomplete . . .'.[1]

Fox supported the amendment in a forceful speech. He claimed that the precedent of Henry VI's reign proved that power had been given in the first instance to the next in succession to the Crown; that the full authority of the sovereign was entrusted to the Regent at the time of nomination; and that the limitations which were imposed on the Duke of Gloucester were made in a full Parliament, when the third estate had been supplied, and when from each of the Bills restraining his authority the Regent might have withheld his consent.[2] No one except the next in succession could hold the Regency, and he was to hold it with the full powers belonging to the Crown. Fox saw no need to depart from this course; if the precedent of Henry VI 'did not make exactly for him' it 'made directly and totally against the right honourable gentleman'. He did not deny the power of the two Houses to supply the deficiency by resolution or address, but they were in no position to legislate. If they did so the judges would laugh at their acts. He conceded the right of the two Houses to nominate the Regent, but, having bowed to their decision, he wished them to go on and appoint the Regent.[3]

But to concede the right of the two Houses to nominate the Regent, without conceding their right to limit his powers, had little significance at the stage reached by the controversy. Fox's treatment of the precedents was wilful and inconsistent, and the vague and imprecise notions which he entertained on them were mercilessly exposed by Pitt. To say that the precedent might not make exactly for him betrayed his lack of clarity and incisiveness on the matter. Pitt could not refrain from commenting on the contradictory fashion in which Fox had dealt with the precedents:

In the first instance they had been pronounced to be wholly irrelevant; and now they had been admitted as authorities, not merely in point against the

mode of proceeding which he had submitted to the House as the most constitutional and most eligible, but as clearly establishing the direct contrary.[1]

The present Parliament was a full Parliament; the throne was not
vacant; an address to the Prince would therefore be constitutionally incorrect. If the Parliament had the right to decide the
issue of Regency it could not be curbed in the exercise of that
right. Fox and Sheridan protested. Sheridan tried to save something from the wreck by affirming that the first act of the Prince's
Regency would be to assent to limitations. But the House was
not convinced, and in the division the Ministry triumphed by
251 votes to 178. 'Never', wrote Sir William Young to Buckingham, 'did any debate of nice discussion go off better . . . than that
of last night; never was I more agreeably surprised than by the
result—having gained nine on our former majority.'[2] The
resolutions were ordered to be communicated to the Lords at a
conference, and this was done on 23 December.

On 26 December, and again on the 29th, the Lords debated the
resolutions. Much of the argument was couched in familiar
language, so familiar as to be almost stale. Rawdon moved an
amendment to the second resolution, calling on the Prince to
take upon himself the Regency. Stormont denied the relevance
of the precedents cited by the Ministry; Porchester accused the
resolutions of inconsistency; Carlisle reminded the House that
there was no reason to pass the resolutions simply because the
Commons had done so. Loughborough maintained that the
Prince had a right to the Regency which was 'beyond all com-
parison'. The Government was seeking to make the Regency an
elective office. All precedents were invalidated since the two
Houses were not a Parliament as long as the executive power was
vacant. The difference between an hereditary right and an irresistible claim was slight, and, since everyone agreed that the
Prince was the only person fit to be declared Regent, no more time
should be wasted in putting that intention into effect.[3]

For the Ministry Richmond defended the resolutions on the ground of necessity, while Lansdowne emerged from his enigmatic silence to support the resolutions. The throne was not vacant; Parliament was regularly assembled; the precedents named by the Ministry were relevant and convincing. It was necessary to decide the question of right, though he did not mean by this that the Prince should not be nominated Regent. But he had never given his vote with more conviction than he felt in voting for the resolutions, which he hoped would set the question of Regency at rest for ever. What could strengthen a Government more than

to have it declared on the full authority of both Houses of Parliament, that the right of nominating the Regent rested in the people, and that the Prince of Wales was chosen Regent, not from any right on his part . . . but with the unanimous voice of a nation of freemen.[1]

Thurlow objected to the amendment moved by Rawdon. What did the term Regent mean? He had heard of *Custodes Regni*, of Lieutenants for the King, of Guardians and Protectors, of Lords Justices; but he did not know where to look for an explanation of the office and function of Regent. In the eyes of the law the political character of the King of Great Britain was always 'whole and entire'. The King's natural character could not be separated from his political character:

A king, even when a minor, was always and in all circumstances, considered as competent to exercise the royal authority, though from the frailty of human nature he might not be adequate to perform the duty of executive government, whence it became necessary to provide for the supplying for that defect.[2]

The interests of the Prince of Wales would be best served by acceding to the resolutions and grounding a Bill upon them, in which the degree of authority and nature of the functions to be vested in the person who was to stand between the Crown and the two Houses should be precisely marked and ascertained, as well as the extent of any necessary limitations.[3] After Rawdon had defended his amendment on the grounds of propriety and appositeness the original resolution was carried by 99 votes to 66.

The third resolution was debated on 29 December, but the Opposition gained no advantage, and the Whig peers had to content themselves with entering a protest against the resolutions in the Lords' Journals. They maintained that the third resolution violated the Act of 13 Charles II by which no Act of Parliament could be made without the consent of the King. The proposal to put the Great Seal into commission was stigmatised as 'a simulate appearance of the royal assent'.[1]

The first stage in the Parliamentary struggle was now over. After a month's debate the question of right had been settled overwhelmingly in favour of Pitt and the Ministry, an outcome which could not have been foreseen at the beginning of the month. If the Whigs had defeated the Ministry in the Commons—as, relying on their future use of the royal patronage, they hoped to do—Pitt would not have been able to prolong discussion until the recovery of the King, as he was eventually able to do. The indifference of the Opposition leaders to the technical issues of the Regency resulted in blunders which allowed Pitt to retain the support of moderate men who did not understand the technicalities of the crisis, but who were frightened by Fox's doctrine of hereditary right, and distrustful of what seemed ominously like an attack on the privileges of Parliament. If Fox had succeeded in getting into office, without first of all provoking a full-scale debate, many of these members would, as was their wont, have veered round to the support of the Government of the day, regardless of its political complexion, providing that it was not especially unpopular. The debate on the question of right destroyed such a possibility, and the primary responsibility for this rested on Fox. He had ignored the constitutional issues, yet, in his eagerness to install the Prince as Regent, and because of his desire to make some gesture of confidence towards Loughborough during the negotiations with Thurlow, he had provoked a debate on precisely those questions for which he and his colleagues were least prepared, and on terms which placed them in a position of extreme vulnerability. Significantly the only two members of the Opposition to grapple with the technicalities of the crisis seriously—Burke and Loughborough—were those whose claims to Cabinet office were deemed subordinate to party interests. Yet Fox never realised the astonishing dimensions of his mistake, and he persisted in his belief that Pitt had simply been more fortunate, more unscrupulous, more subtle in his craft and cunning. That the Whigs were not united on the issue of hereditary right, that they had not discussed it in any detail at their conferences, and that Fox's initial assertion came as a surprise to his friends, made the blunder all the more catastrophic. They were thrust into a technical controversy when they were preoccupied, not with 'abstractions', but with the no less intractable problems connected with the allocation of posts in the new Ministry, which, they fondly imagined, would be formed within a week, a fortnight, a month—but (in any case) soon. They never realised how great was the contribution they made to their own undoing.

Nor was Pitt's success in Parliament his only source of encouragement during December. First of all, the King was making progress under the care of Willis and his son, despite the antagonism which Warren and Willis felt for each other. On 18 December Pitt was assured that notwithstanding the pain which the King had to endure from the blisters on his legs no doubt was entertained of his complete recovery. On 25 December Willis told Pitt that although the King had a fever, a white tongue, and a hoarse voice, these symptoms were constant attendants on illnesses of the type from which His Majesty was suffering, and there was no need to change the opinion which he had previously formed on the prospects of the King's recovery.[1] Pitt was also popular in the city. During the week before Christmas there was talk of the merchants and bankers of the city voting him a pension, and *The Times* noted these suggestions with approval. There could be no more fitting means of disposing of the surplus revenue of the capital than by granting part of it to the Minister 'who had restored this country to its most flourishing period in the administration of Lord Chatham, and who deserves so well the thanks and reward of the nation at large'.[1] However sentimental the reference to Chatham's Ministry may have been the emotion of gratitude to the younger Pitt was commonly and sincerely felt amongst supporters of the Government.

In the last days of December the first steps were also taken in the struggle in the country over addresses of support for the Government. On Saturday, 27 December, the *Morning Chronicle* carried an advertisement announcing the resolution of the corporation of Cambridge to thank Pitt for his conduct. The previous day twenty merchants and bankers of the city of London had unanimously agreed to call a meeting of bankers, merchants, and traders, to vote an address of thanks to Pitt and the majority which had supported him in the Commons. The meeting was to be held on 7 January.[2]

In the last week of the old year Fitzwilliam was receiving news from his agents in Yorkshire of how the Whig interest stood there. It had been hoped to revive the fortunes of the party in York by persuading Lord John Cavendish to stand as candidate, and if he agreed the Whigs thought it possible 'to carry the entire representation of this place and thus revive the interest'.[3] But the situation was no easy one. Robert Sinclair admitted that the enemy had 'reaped much benefit from having got the start of us some days', and, although Fitzwilliam was eager for an address in support of Fox to be obtained from York, Sinclair warned him that such an attempt would have 'an injurious effect upon the general interest'. It would, he thought, cause much confusion, as well as disgusting the moderates, who disliked political disputes, and who would otherwise lean to the Opposition. It would also call forth intensive exertions on the part of the Pittites, perhaps rekindling 'that spirit among the mob, which was so injurious to us upon the last election, and which it has been our constant inclination and endeavour to extinguish altogether'. If the other party called a meeting they would naturally be opposed with the utmost vigour, but it would be wise to wait for them to take the lead in provoking public discussion. Sinclair thought that the corporation of York favoured the Whigs, so that if the Ministerialists wanted an address of support from the city they would have to rely on the general public and call an open meeting. If that should transpire the Whigs would rely on the corporation to get their own measures adopted.[1]

On 24 December, John Dixon told Fitzwilliam of his own distaste for the measures which Pitt had taken, but he lamented that in Yorkshire 'the neighbourhood hereabouts seem so horridly infatuated in their opinions of the rectitude of Mr Pitt's conduct, that I by no means think any forward step at present advisable, and indeed some friends to our cause . . . coincide with me in the same opinion'. It would be by no means unsatisfactory if the supporters of the Ministry refrained from seeking addresses of approval for Pitt's conduct, but any attempts which they made would be resisted. Unhappily the prevailing opinion was 'decidedly with Mr Pitt'.[2] Mr Wentworth, writing on Christmas Day, related how Sir William Milner had told him that the popular cry 'was very much against us . . . and no wonder, as I don't know any gentlemen of any consequence, that will give themselves the least trouble.'[3] On 28 December, Sinclair, writing from York, emphasised that the suggested donation of coals to the poor would have no good effect, for the Pittites had made their donation only a few days before and it would therefore be wise to wait a little longer, until the winter weather should give the transaction the appearance of humanity, not policy. If any public meeting should be called by the Sheriff for the purpose of an address complimentary to Pitt, Sinclair and his friends would try by every available means to procure as strong a weight of interest as possible to defeat the proposal. How short-sighted the public were in their failure to see the imprudence, indecency, and dangerous tendency of Pitt's ambition! Yet his plausibility and hypocrisy had gained him a high degree of popularity, which, though astonishing to men of 'discernment', it was not easy to suppress or diminish. At the same time Sinclair trusted that by getting enough rope Pitt would 'at last hang himself'.[1]

The weakness of the Opposition interest in Yorkshire is reflected in the way the members for the county voted on the question of right on 16 December. Seventeen supported the Government; nine the Opposition.[2] However much the Whigs might fume they had been outmanoeuvred on every front, and during January Pitt was to receive a large number of congratulatory addresses. Sympathy for the mad King strengthened support for Pitt and the claims he had made for precedent. Perhaps because they relied too exclusively on Carlton House politics the Whigs found themselves outgeneralled in the battle over addresses from corporations and boroughs; and in the stress of conflict the party failed to resolve the dissensions within its own ranks. Grey and Sheridan found themselves compelled to advocate in public a policy which they deplored in private, yet they could not commit the folly of making their breach with Fox open and avowed. Burke had brooded over the crisis in his own intense and searching way, and the conclusions which he drew from his researches divided him alike from friend and foe. Portland had failed to show any sense of leadership. Still nursing old wrongs, still distrustful of Sheridan's influence at Carlton House, the Duke was at the mercy of events, not their master. Christmas was a depressing season for the Whigs. Fox and Windham had planned to visit Burke at Beaconsfield over the festive season, but their respite from politics was brief.[3] Fox had had his decisive interview with Thurlow on 25 December, yet four days later Sheridan and the Prince had a lengthy conference with the Lord Chancellor at Carlton House.[4] The old year went out in a flurry of negotiations, dominated by the sour remembrance of defeat, and on 30 December Pitt informed the Prince of the restrictions which he intended to impose on the powers of the Regent.[1] He must have seen the new year in with some relief and pardonable optimism. The King was recovering; the Opposition had been vanquished in debate; opinion in Parliament, in the press, and in the country, was veering to his side. All of this must have seemed something of a miracle when compared with the situation at the beginning of November, despite the fact that the care which he had taken to prepare himself for the technicalities of the case had enabled him to exploit the errors of his opponents to the full. For the Whigs, defeat in the two Houses was but the prelude to further squabbles. The crisis disrupted their fragile unity, heightened their personal animosities, and (what neither Government nor Opposition anticipated) frustrated their most precious hopes. George Cavendish, writing to Mrs Ponsonby on Christmas Day, sought to explain his disappointment:

. . . (T)he Minister has carried his questions by a greater majority than it was thought, or perhaps he thought it should. On our side was some misfortune & perhaps some mismanagement. We despise Parliamentary craft too much, & are sadly deficient in it.[2]

The Whigs had foolishly underestimated that most unpredictable of gentlemen, the independent member of Parliament, who, whatever his views on hereditary right, was acutely sensitive to any attack on his rights and privileges as a member of the House of Commons. To 'despise Parliamentary craft' was to indulge in the worst form of escapism, and for this extravagance Fox and his friends paid an exorbitant, but not unjustly extorted, price.

CHAPTER III

THE POLICY OF RESTRICTION AND THE DISILLUSIONMENT OF THE WHIGS

December had seen Pitt's victory in the struggle over the Prince's inherent right to the Regency; January was to confirm his supremacy in the two Houses, both Lords and Commons voting his restrictions by comfortable majorities, and to give him the added encouragement of popular support. In the early weeks of January, 1789, addresses of thanks to Pitt and the members who had sustained him in the debate of 16 December were approved in boroughs and townships throughout the country, whilst the Whigs could do little to stem the mounting flood. For the Opposition reverses in Parliament were ominously complemented by a series of local defeats, and, although the 'Armed Neutrality' finally threw in their lot with the Whigs, trusting their future to the same uncertain fortune, Fox retired to Bath at the end of the month, a sick man, worn out by strife, and wilting under the bitter burden of defeat. The allocation of Cabinet places was virtually settled by the end of January, yet, in the last week of the month, Edmund Burke expressed his disappointment with the way in which his friends had handled the crisis, and roused himself to fight the battle more furiously than ever in February, despite the fact that he, too, had sought refuge from the unhappy combination of ill-health and political disappointment at his Beaconsfield home.

The new year began badly for the Whigs. On the morning of 2 January, Cornwall, the Speaker of the House of Commons, and brother-in-law of Lord Hawkesbury, died, and before they could proceed to the business of the Regency the Commons had to elect a successor without delay. On 5 January, William Wyndham Grenville, the Paymaster of the Forces, and a reluctant ministerial candidate for the office, was elected, receiving 215 votes as against the 144 cast for his rival, Sir Gilbert Elliot. The Opposition had mismanaged the affair. Palmerston told his wife of his surprise on hearing of Elliot's candidature on the morning of the election:

I did not imagine that there was any intention of contesting the Speakership, but this morning I was surprised with the information that it is intended to propose Sir Gilbert Elliot. I am sorry I cannot go there to vote for him but I have totally incapacitated myself for that, having made use of a little James's powder and some physic. Perhaps they may not divide upon it, as I suppose there can be no chance of carrying it. Sir Gilbert would make an excellent Speaker . . . a better one . . . than the other, who has one very strong objection against him, being very short-sighted, and . . . subject to violent headaches. Sir Gilbert has likewise been talked of to be Chancellor of the Exchequer, as has also Tom Pelham. Our side are much at a loss for a proper person to hold that situation, as it seems a measure decided that the Duke of Portland is to be First Lord of the Treasury, and Lord John Cavendish who was not very equal to the Chancellorship five years ago, and has been out of Parliament ever since, wishes not to take it again. . . . I was in hopes that Fox meant now to stand out boldly as First Lord of the Treasury, and that the Duke of P. . . . would have been the ministerial leader in the House of Lords. . . . I do not think we have any person but Fox at all suited to the situation.[1]

Involved as it was in the complicated wrangles accompanying the formation of the new Cabinet, the Speakership was the subject of contention and confusion amongst the Whigs. It took three days for the decision to contest the election to be made, and though Portland and the Prince were in favour of Elliot's candidature, Fox had only committed himself on the afternoon of Sunday, 4 January, the day before the House was to vote. Even then he had allowed Burke and Charles Pelham to take the lead in deciding the issue. Grey and Sheridan, on the other hand, were opposed to the candidature, possibly because it would only intensify and embitter party feeling. The Whigs were looking ahead to the new Parliament, which they fondly hoped would be the most gratifying result of the Prince's accession to the Regency, and it was felt that by opposing Grenville's election it would be

easier for them to put their own man into the post when circumstances were more favourable. Charles Pelham told F. F. Foljambe
that he did not think Elliot stood a chance against Grenville, but
that it was necessary to fight the issue 'to lay claim in a new
Parliament'. Elliot himself was severely critical of Fox's inertia
and apparent inability to make up his mind, and Robert Liston
thought that the Opposition would have done better if they had
decided to oppose Grenville sooner. No cards had been sent out
and no visits made on Elliot's behalf until the morning of the
election, yet the Government had been canvassing for Grenville
as soon as the office had fallen vacant.[1] As soon as Grenville was
installed as Speaker Pitt announced that he would submit his
restrictions to the consideration of the House on the following
day.[2]

But when the Commons resumed their deliberations on 6
January, Mr Loveden claimed that before any further discussion
could take place on the steps necessary for supplying the Regency
it was essential to know 'precisely what the present state of His
Majesty's health' was, and 'whether the probability of his
recovery was increased or lessened'.[3] This was unexpected, and
at first Pitt was unsympathetic. He agreed that prudence was
necessary, but, unless any good reason could be suggested why
the House should change the opinion it had formed on the
evidence of the last examination of the physicians, he would
contend that the order of the day be read in opposition to Loveden's proposal.[4] The Whig leaders took a curiously ambiguous
attitude towards another examination of the King's doctors, for
while they disliked the additional delay which would inevitably
follow another inquiry, they could not resist the temptation of
calling in question the hopeful diagnosis which had proved so unfortunate for their plans. Yet they were hesitant, evasive, awkward in their call for another examination of the doctors. It was
almost as if their errors had made them over-cautious, timorous
lest they should commit some new indiscretion which would

blight their hopes. They wanted the advantages of another inquiry into the King's health without the responsibility of initiating the proceeding. Fox reminded the House of the importance of precise information on the health of the King. Though the doctors were agreed that the King would probably recover, there had been no unanimity on the length of time such a recovery would take. Many contradictory reports were in circulation. Rumours were dangerous, for the people might be deluded with false hopes. Perhaps the wise course would be to act on the report of the committee which had examined the doctors. If no new sign of convalescence had appeared then another examination of the medical situation was necessary.[1] Here Fox was trying to emphasise the lack of evidence indicating an imminent recovery on the part of the King. If Pitt denied the need for another examination, then it could be claimed that this was little less than a tacit admission that there had been no improvement in the King's health. The confidence which was felt towards Willis's prognosis would be undermined, and yet the impression would be given that the Opposition were simply seeking further information on the condition of the King, not wantonly stirring up old disputes about the relative merits of his doctors. Fox had been bitterly disappointed in Warren's evidence before the committee which had examined the doctors a month before; perhaps he was hoping that, given a second chance, the 'Buff and Blue' doctor would redeem himself.

Support for the new inquiry came from Mr Edwards, and—much more forcefully—from Burke. The House had been assured that the King's incapacity was only temporary, yet here they were, fully a month later, in exactly the same state of expectancy. Burke claimed that the evidence of the doctors before the Lords' committee suggested that the King's recovery was less, not more, probable; and when, in reply to a query from Vansittart, he gave Warren as his authority for the statement, he was greeted with ironic cries of 'Hear! Hear!' from the Treasury benches.[1] Lord North called upon someone to rise and justify the shouts and when his challenge was not taken up he commented that they must have been inspired by nothing more than a sudden burst of zeal for his Majesty's recovery: Warren's skill and integrity were unquestioned.[2] Pitt denied that he had called in doubt either Warren's personal character or his professional competence, but he repeated his objections to any unnecessary delay. The positions in debate were now reversed. Pitt, the subtle master of the art of postponement, was being hustled into further delays by the advocates of an immediate and precipitate solution of the problems of the Regency. Pitt thought that the original examination of the King's doctors gave ample grounds for the House's future proceedings.[3]

But Burke was not silenced so easily. If there was a difference of opinion amongst the King's physicians why was Dr Munro not called in? The keeper of one mad-house ought to be set against the keeper of another.[4] All this made Mr Pulteney regret that so much warmth had been shown in debate.[5] Fox then reminded members that they had been assured that the King's recovery was probable, though no one could say when it would take place; surely it was necessary for them to have some idea of when the King might be expected to recover before they could proceed? In the face of these demands Pitt gave way, moving the appointment of a committee for the examination of the royal physicians. Sheridan moved an amendment questioning the probability of the King's recovery, but this was negatived, Pitt's motion being carried by 221 votes to 141.[6]

It is difficult to see why the Whigs favoured another examination of the King's doctors, unless they hoped that by some miracle sufficient evidence would be produced to discredit Willis, and thus to buttress their secret hope that the King would never recover. Yet here they were deceiving themselves. Despite Warren's gloom there had been no deterioration in the King's condition, and the bitterness between Warren and Willis owed as much to professional jealousy as to political loyalty. For Warren, the fashionable physician, disliked the prospect of being proved wrong by an amateur in Holy Orders, who had learnt how to deal with lunatics by the instructive experience of keeping an asylum. Even if there had been some possibility of a dramatic reversal of medical opinion further delay in Parliament could only help Pitt. The Chancellor of the Exchequer must have been pleasantly surprised to find that his opponents were obliging him still further, and it is paradoxical that whilst he wanted to push on with his restrictions his adversaries (who had accused him of deliberately wasting time) should provide him with another opportunity to play for time. Yet it was only with reluctance that Pitt accepted the suggestion that the doctors should be re-examined, for he did not want to give the Whigs the chance of claiming that because the King had not yet recovered, the optimistic diagnosis, on which so much of his policy was based, was an illusion.

There were possibly other motives behind this change of front on the part of the Opposition, by which impatience gave way to a scrupulous insistence on full and reliable information on the King's condition, prior to any further steps to meet the exigency. The Whigs had not yet decided on the composition of their Cabinet, and time was still needed to reconcile conflicting ambitions. The proximity of office had intensified, not diminished, the clamour for posts of responsibility and profit, and there was keen rivalry for almost every appointment. The failure of the party leaders to agree in good time over Elliot's candidature for the Speakership had been the consequence of the multifarious demands of self-interest. The choice of a Chancellor of the Exchequer presented special problems. Lord John Cavendish was the favourite for the post, but he was unwilling to involve himself again in public affairs, complaining to Mrs Ponsonby that London was not very entertaining 'as Politicks and the snow have spoilt all society'.[1] He could not bear the thought of taking up any office, but had gone so far as to agree to come into Parliament again—'they want me to do more but I think they will not persuade me'.[1] Yet if Cavendish refused the Chancellorship it was difficult to find any mutually acceptable substitute for him. Sheridan and Grey were both known to be casting ambitious eyes on the Exchequer; and at the same time Grey, Elliot, and Windham were in the running, possibly for the Chancellorship, and, failing that, for one of the Secretaryships, Fox being the obvious choice for foreign affairs. Burke was regarded as unacceptable in Cabinet office, and Sheridan, sensing the opposition to his own hopes, cut his losses and contented himself with the office of Treasurer of the Navy, wishing, so the story went, to prove his abilities in some less dignified office. But it was never fully believed that he had abandoned all hope of the Chancellorship or at least of a post in the Cabinet.[2]

What was to be done for Burke was an even more baffling problem. Portland, inspired by his regard for Burke's character and abilities, wanted to do something worthy of his great gifts, but which would, at the same time, be 'exempt from the many difficulties which seem to be in the way'.[3] On 9 January, Portland, Pelham, and Elliot settled the matter over dinner. Burke's brother Richard was to become Secretary to the Treasury, worth £3000 a year, until an office for life in the customs, worth £1000 a year, should fall vacant. Burke was to have his old post at the Pay Office at £4000 a year; but since this was precarious, and made no provision for his family, it would only be of 'real substantial value' if 'some more permanent provision' was added to it:

In this view the Duke is to grant him on the Irish establishment a pension of £2,000 a year clear for his own life, and the other half to Mrs Burke for her life. This will make Burke completely happy, by leaving his wife and son safe from want after his death, if they should survive him. The Duke's affectionate anxiety to accomplish this object, and his determination to set all clamour at defiance on this point of justice, was truly affecting, and increases my affection for the Duke. . . .[4]

Burke knew nothing of these discussions and arrangements. In fact his family were apprehensive that he was to be overlooked in the general scramble for jobs and pensions.[1]

In the meantime Fox was ill again. He was too weak to attend a party conference on 10 January, and on the following day the Duchess of Devonshire recorded that there was nothing but treachery going forward—'Sheridan hears Grey has abused him, Grey is abused by others'.[2] Two days later it was the same story:

Great private treachery—Sheridan . . . says Lord John Townshend and Stanhope have made Tickell think that Grey and Lambton had abused him— this was the old attack of Sheridan courting the Prince and encouraging the Praise of him in the world and papers where Fox is abused.[3]

In the midst of intrigue, disappointment, and further defeats in the Commons, the news from the country was discouraging. The battle over addresses had begun, and was to prove, in the long run, as depressing for the Whigs as the conflict at Westminster. In Yorkshire the initiative had been seized by the Pittites, who had not refrained, as their opponents had hoped, from calling public meetings to secure addresses of support for Pitt and the members who had voted with him on 16 December. At Halifax a meeting of gentlemen, clergy, merchants, and principal inhabitants was called by public advertisement, and held on the last day of 1788. The Reverend Henry Wood was in the chair, and an address of support for Pitt was unanimously approved. All that the Whigs could do in reply was to insert advertisements in the local press to the effect that the meeting had been attended by a mere forty people. On 7 January, Sir George Armytage, writing to Fitzwilliam, told him that he and his friends had decided to call a meeting at Halifax of their own supporters—'in order for to reprobate so gross a falsehood'.[4] At Leeds John Beckett was attempting to invigorate the Opposition interest—a formidable task—and he was driven to confess that any dissolution of Parliament on the Prince's accession to the Regency would be unwise, for Leeds and its neighbourhood were decidedly unfavourable to the Whigs. The question of right had raised a storm—'and sorry, very sorry I am to say that it takes much the same direction now as it did in '84, and as to this town is likely to burst in a few days in an Address which though staved off a little while we are no longer able to prevent'.[1] On 15 January he consoled Fitzwilliam with the news that things were not quite as bad as he had expected. Instead of the anticipated address 'containing a deal of obnoxious matter' they had escaped with 'a simple vote of thanks', and there were even indications that 'things were mending again'.[2] At Rotherham an address of support for Pitt and his followers was unanimously voted and signed by 265 persons at a meeting held on Saturday, 10 January,[3] and addresses in favour of the administration had also been voted at Perth, Aberdeen, Stirling, Glasgow, Gateshead, Cambridge, Southampton, Maidstone, and Leicester.[4]

The meeting at the London Tavern on 7 January proved less agreeable to the Ministry. Both sides claimed that the meeting favoured their own point of view. At the commencement Samuel Beachcroft was in the chair, but when the address of support for Pitt was proposed by Edward Payne and William Waddington a tumultuous debate ensued. Beachcroft announced that a majority for the address had been indicated by a show of hands, but this was challenged and a division was demanded. The voting ended in uproar, with the Pittite chairman and his friends escaping down the backstairs, whilst Alderman Pickett, duly installed as Whig chairman, presided over a comfortable majority against the address. But, although they claimed that the voting had been five to one in their favour, the Whigs did not give any figures in the jubilant accounts which they advertised in the press; and the Pittites, putting as brave a face on the situation as possible, persisted in contending that the meeting had voted the address before it broke up in uproar and confusion. A series of advertisements which appeared in the newspapers on 19 January announced the presentation of the vote of thanks from 'the

Merchants, Bankers, and Traders of the City of London' to Pitt for his very able defence of the privileges of Parliament, as well as publishing Pitt's letter of thanks to Samuel Beachcroft. Whatever happened at the meeting Beachcroft had succeeded in procuring over four hundred signatures in support of his address, and these were printed in the advertisements. Although they had succeeded in throwing the London Tavern meeting into disorder the Whigs had not deterred Beachcroft from presenting his vote of thanks to the Minister.[1]

The conflict was now being fought out at the local level with little quarter asked or given, and in the majority of cases the Pittites were successful, their seizure of the initiative standing them in good stead, whilst the popular cry of Parliamentary privilege as against the Prince's prerogative gave them a valuable slogan. On 12 January a meeting at Reading voted an address of thanks to Pitt, and to all members who had voted with the administration, in particular the two members for Reading, Francis Annestey and R. A. Neville.[2] On 16 January an address of thanks to Pitt and his supporters passed at Birmingham with only three dissentient voices,[3] and by 19 January the list had swollen to no less than forty-five addresses of support from towns and boroughs.[4] On 17 January a meeting of the clergy, gentlemen, and freeholders of Devon, held at Exeter, resolved that Sir John Chichester, the High Sheriff of the county, Lord Fortescue, the Lord Lieutenant, and Mr Rolle and Mr Bastard, the members of Parliament for the county, should be desired to wait upon the Regent immediately after his appointment, to request that Pitt and his colleagues, enjoying as they did 'the marked approbation of their Sovereign, the confidence of both Houses of Parliament, and the general good opinion of the country', should continue in office.[5]

Both Government and Opposition attacked the validity of those proceedings which had gone against them, and sought to discredit the motives or the status of those who had distinguished themselves by their enthusiasm for the opposing cause. On

Tuesday, 20 January, the *Morning Herald* poured scorn on the address which the Chancellor of the Exchequer had received from Gateshead—'a borough which probably most of our readers have not heard of before'. In the first place, the writer continued, 'it is *not*, nor *ever* was, a borough; in the next, it is the wretched avenue from the South to the town of Newcastle upon Tyne, where shopkeepers of the *lowest* order, *keelmen*, and *pitmen* reside'.[1] The place was so shabby, the *Morning Herald* claimed, that it was necessary for Mr Rowland Burdon, a Newcastle banker and the son-in-law of Mr Brandling, the Pittite member for Newcastle (the other member was a Whig) to cross the river Tyne with 'a squad of Bankers' Clerks' and assume the chair to 'give a little respectability to the meeting'.[2] *The Times* replied in kind about the meeting at the London Tavern. Whatever the partisans of the Opposition might say, the property of those who had signed Beachcroft's address amounted to forty millions sterling—or so it was arrogantly asserted. Could the Opposition 'carry up such an Address, even to the Regent, with such a list of names, and such a mass of riches'? Ridicule was cast upon the regret which would be inspired by any limitation of the Regent's power to distribute pensions and offices: 'No certain stipend for Mrs Armistead, Mrs Benwell, Mrs Windsor, and the other virtuous matrons belonging to the immaculate party.' And further contempt was heaped on the anti-ministerial faction in the city of London:

We hear no more of the respectable majority who voted Alderman Pick-axe to the chair at the London Tavern. What were the names must ever remain a secret—they are ashamed and afraid to commit them to the public scrutiny. Indeed . . . the publication of names and residence might afford some very disagreeable visits to garrets and cellars from Messrs. Jealous and Carpmeal. This is a fact well known to *the Party*, who are composed of a heterogeneous mixture of the lowest and highest of his Majesty's subjects—an assemblage of Dukes, Earls, Blackguards, Sharpers, Captains of the Road, and Parsons of the Fields—all seeking for power, places, and pensions, by any means, fair or unfair, by which they can be attained.[3]

An advertisement in the *Morning Herald* for 21 January, and in *The World* the following day, reported a meeting at Halifax protesting against the address of thanks to Pitt, and on 19 January the *Morning Herald* had printed a bitter attack on the dinner which Pitt's supporters at Manchester had held in the Bull's Head Tavern. At Doncaster the Whig members of the corporation had prevented the Mayor and the Pittite Aldermen from sending up an address of thanks, by absenting themselves from the meetings of the corporation and thereby making it impossible for a quorum to be present.[1] Yet, despite all this, the majority of meetings went against the Whigs. This is not to say that the Pittites did not meet with important reverses, such as that which they experienced at the Morpeth meeting on 21 January. However enterprising and successful Pitt's supporters had been in Newcastle they were less fortunate in Northumberland, where they had to compete with the formidable Grey interest and with the veiled hostility of the Duke, whose opposition to the policy of restriction did damage to the Government's cause, for all his supposed desire for the continuation of the Ministry. Rowland Burdon, the indefatigable organiser of the Gateshead address, and William Ord of Fenham, proposed an address of thanks to Pitt at a meeting at Morpeth on 21 January; but the motion was defeated, and a resolution passed thanking Sir William Middleton and Charles Grey for their conduct in Parliament, and Sir Francis Blades and Grey for 'explaining the *true* principles of the constitution and declaring the real rights of the people'.[2] Meetings in Montgomeryshire and Denbighshire voted addresses of thanks to their M.P.'s for their steady support of the Prince of Wales, but when compared with the magnitude of the ministerial triumphs in the provinces this was small consolation for the Whigs. For Pitt's supporters never lost the initiative which they had seized in the struggle over addresses, and Fox could not claim that despite his defeats in Lords and Commons the mass of opinion in the country was behind him. The succession of favourable addresses enabled Pitt to press home even more relentlessly the thesis that Fox depended solely on the goodwill and patronage of the Prince of Wales—dubious advantages in the party contest. The warnings which Sinclair had dutifully sent to Fitzwilliam about the necessity of avoiding a 'popular' controversy were more than borne out, though Burke was later to claim that not enough had been done in the way of public agitation, of meetings, addresses, and petitions.

Increasing frustration met the Whigs at every turn. Their internal rivalries remained unabated, their bitter memories unforgotten and unforgiven. The composition of their Cabinet was still uncertain; and, as the controversy dragged on, and Portland's deficiencies as a leader became ever more apparent, the party became more and more divided. Constant accusations of treachery and intrigue, of betrayal and of slander, instances of bad temper and impatient petulance, soured personal relationships within the party, creating an atmosphere of suspicion and distrust, and though they still clung to the hope that their entry into office was imminent, the Whigs were less united and more harassed by ambition and self-interest than in the dismal days after the defeat of the coalition in 1784. The proximity of the promised land only made everyone more vociferous in demanding that his own claims should not be overlooked. In addition to these cares Fox's ill-health was a continual worry; his political judgment was weakened by the lethargy and indecision caused by his physical debility, the enervating effects of his attack of dysentery. As the month progressed his condition deteriorated. But, whilst contemporaries exaggerated the seriousness of his plight, they were also mistaken in their emphasis on the 'political' nature of his illness. At the end of January he was so ill that he sought a respite at Bath from the stress of continual debate and the strain of successive defeats. Without a fit Fox the party foundered, and in losing control of themselves the Whigs lost control of their destiny. They became the victims of the same circumstances which had originally filled them with hope. For their salvation they looked to the accession of the Prince of Wales, either as Regent or King. Their blunders in debate; their ineffectiveness in the struggle over addresses; their personal piques and hatreds— all these had broken the back of the party, shattered its morale, and destroyed the slender loyalties on which unity so precariously rested.

Even the Prince had to give way. For all his brave words and bellicose gestures he had replied to Pitt on 2 January. His language was dignified, but he could not disguise his distaste for the policy of restrictions, despite his assurances that if the restrictions were approved by Parliament he would accept the Regency upon terms which he himself thought ill-advised and mistaken. Burke, Loughborough, and Sheridan had all helped to draft the Prince's reply, and the acceptance of the Regency was couched in stately terms.[1] For a moment there was a revival of rumours suggesting a compromise, and although most of the Cabinet were convinced that 'absolute dismission' would be the immediate consequence of the Prince's accession as Regent, Buckingham, writing from Dublin on 15 January, earnestly hoped that all suggestions of an accommodation were false, that

> Pitt will not think of sacrificing his fair name by so paltry an attachment to office. . . . He cannot surely after what has passed with the Prince hesitate on his resignation; but I must point out to you most explicitly my determination not to remain here from the moment of the appointment of a Regent unless I clearly understand myself to be a permanent Governor, and not a 'locum tenens' to the Duke of Norfolk.[2]

There was in fact little danger of a reconciliation between the opposing parties. The controversy over the Prince's inherent right had raged too bitterly and too publicly for that. Nor did the new examination of the King's doctors achieve anything, other than the publication of the extreme distaste which Warren and Willis entertained for each other.[3] When Pitt presented the report of the committee to the House on 13 January, Burke questioned the way in which the committee had done its duty, but his motion to have the report recommitted was negatived.[1] That the Opposition should react in this way was the measure of their disappointment. Another week had been wasted, and no tangible advantage had been gained from the inquiry. The doctors had merely repeated their previous opinions, which were accepted or rejected according to one's party loyalty. The Archbishop of Canterbury told William Eden of the report on 16 January:

The report of the committee, after their very long sitting, was made to the Commons on Wednesday. Dr Willis insists that the symptoms of the Malady are become much more favourable than at his former Examination—that the time when a recovery may be expected no mortal can say, but that the Patient *will completely recover* he has, in consequence of his Experience & Observations, the strongest grounds of hope—that he reads with attention & intelligence & converses with more of both than he could a few weeks ago. Warren and Baker controvert some of these Positions & deny in general that there is amendment. The Others, Pepys, Reynolds, & Gisborne, agree in improved symptoms, and in their opinion of probable recovery. Warren and Willis have greatly disagreed from almost their first meeting. The most dispassionate think Willis's long experience gives him great advantage of Judgment in this particular disorder, but that he is rather too sanguine in his hopes, which he states as scarcely checked by any shade of doubt. On the other hand they think Warren unqualified by any Experience he has had to pronounce so decidedly as he does unfavourable prognosticks as to Recovery. It is a strange subject for Party to exist upon, & disgraceful to the country that it should be so: but so it is, & many pronounce Warren a party man in his accounts of a dark Dye—while Willis is supposed to delude himself by his ambition to recover the Patient. Fox's illness seldom leaves him without severe attacks a week together, and, under the circumstances of that Party, their difficulties and their Quarrels, they are not likely to diminish. . . .[2]

Mr Storer's impressions of the inquiry were less favourable:

. . . From their examination it clearly appears that his Majesty is as far from being in a convalescent State as ever he has been, & that perhaps there has been some endeavours made use of to keep his situation a secret from the public. . . . Mr Pitt is so powerful he may do as he pleases. . . . If he has been guilty of

any Error . . . it has been in not having foreseen his strength in Parliament. . . .
The delay in appointing a Regent has proved serviceable at least to Mr Grenville, who will, however short the duration of this Parliament may be, receive
a handsome sum from his office. . . . The examination of the Physicians, as it
has brought to Light many things which people were not aware of, may
produce some alteration in Parliament, but of this the wisest cannot prophesy,
more than they can concerning any particular period for his Majesty's recovery.
I am so tired with perpetual conversations about Insanity, that I wish for any
new Event for think of, or talk of. There is no circle into which one goes,
where one person does not tell you that the King is now so near the re-
establishment of his bodily and mental health, that he will meet his Parliament
in a fortnight, & some other contradicts him flatly by asserting that both his
mind and body are in a most desperate situation. One cannot say that Doctors
disagree—they are all on the same side but Willis, of whom you will not long
be at a loss which opinion to entertain. The examination is conclusive with
regard to him. . . .[1]

Storer's dislike for Willis blinded him to the realities of the
situation. It was not true that all the other doctors shared Warren's standpoint; and in any case Warren himself hesitated to
affirm the absolute impossibility of a royal recovery. There had
been some slight improvement in the King's condition at the
beginning of the new year. On the evening of 1 January the
King had played fifteen games of backgammon with Willis, and
four games at picket with Hawkins, and had been in a collected
state of mind throughout. Two days later he was rather 'flut-
tered', for though he had had a good night his bowels were in a
lax state; but on the morning of 5 January he was very calm,
and on the next day Willis thought him 'as well, or rather better
this morning than the Doctor has ever seen him in a morning'.[2]
It was still difficult, however, to be over-confident about the
King. He seemed to need Willis or his son about him to maintain
the improvement in his mind, and usually he was unruly in the
morning before becoming quiet and submissive in the evening.
Yet on 17 January he was calm before noon 'and . . . remarkably
composed during the rest of the day'.[3] One of William Eden's
friends confessed that 'upon the whole I think no doubts can be

entertained of his being better, and in a train more decidedly mending'.[1]

Accusations of fraud against Willis were common on the part of the Whigs who could not bear the thought that the reverend gentleman's diagnosis should prove more accurate than the more acceptable assurances of the polished and sophisticated Warren. *The Times* defended the Lincolnshire clergyman against the slanders of the Opposition, denouncing the 'political conspiracy' against him, inspired as it was simply by the hopes he gave of the King's recovery. He had done his duty, daring 'in opposition to a most desperate and dangerous faction to declare that his Majesty's disorder has taken a *favourable turn*'.[2] But one member of the Opposition was determined to find out for himself what the symptoms and patterns of behaviour and recovery were in cases of insanity. Burke was weary of Warren's shadowy hints and hesitant predictions, and at the end of the second week in January he visited a mad-house belonging to a Mrs Harrison at Hoxton in order to ascertain 'such facts as he thought might the better inform him in the discussion of his Majesty's unhappy disorder'.[3] Mrs Harrison had about three hundred people under her care, and Burke was particularly interested in the proportion of patients of the age of fifty and upwards who recovered their understanding. Perhaps Burke suspected that Warren's opinions, on which Fox relied so implicitly, were discredited and useless. In any event Burke was too independent to take his opinions— even on insanity—at second hand. Just as he studied the constitutional precedents more carefully and closely than any other Whig statesman so he tried to procure the fullest and most reliable information on the subject of mental instability. To his contemporaries his diligence appeared ludicrous and tiresome, and when he lectured the Commons on instances of insanity amongst the royal families of Europe from the fifteenth century, together with various symptoms in particular cases, his medical reports and psychological commentaries sorely tried the patience of most members, who could not understand what he was talking about. Yet Burke was making a praiseworthy attempt to form his own judgment of the case, on evidence, not hearsay. Fox was bitterly disappointed with Warren, but he failed to see that he was asking more of the doctor (whose bedside manner and high fees were famous in society) than he could reasonably be expected to give. It was impossible for Warren to save the Whigs from the consequences of their own errors of judgment, and in the public mind his Whig sympathies were more of a liability than an asset. At least Warren did his best to hamper Willis. The two doctors were constantly at loggerheads, each regarding the other with suspicion and repugnance. On 12 January they had another dispute. The King's pulse was at 100, and he was sweating profusely, but Willis, who had promised him an airing in his carriage, ordered him to be taken for a ride. Warren countermanded the order, insisting that the King should be kept indoors. Sheffield thought that 'the whole history of what has been going on, is not fit to be trusted to paper'.[1]

Thus disappointment with the physicians' report added to the depression which the Whigs naturally felt over the unwelcome outcome of the struggle over addresses of thanks to Pitt—how was Pittite influence in the constituencies to be overcome without the patronage of the Crown? Other factors contributed to the mounting distrust with which many members of the Opposition regarded each other's actions. Sheridan and his wife had been evicted from their own home by the bailiffs and were now living with Mrs Fitzherbert. The suspicion that his influence over the Prince was correspondingly increased, inflamed and intensified the jealousy which many of his colleagues already harboured towards the brilliant but unreliable Irishman. His longing for a Cabinet place inspired only distrust, and his sincerity was universally questioned.[2] Portland was determined that Sheridan should hold no Cabinet post, and had gone so far as to say that they could not both be in the same Cabinet. It was rumoured that Fitzwilliam would possibly replace the Duke as the head of the new administration, for, despite fair words and gestures of forgiveness, the latter had not made up his old quarrel with the Prince in sufficiently fulsome a manner. There was no serious intention of replacing Portland as First Lord of the Treasury in any new Whig Government, but the Archbishop of Canterbury confided to Eden that the seeds of discord threatened to break up the Opposition—'they are sown so thick'. The 'cry in favour of the falling minister' was 'beyond example', but 'with the knowledge one has of mankind' once the Prince became Regent, and if the King's recovery was delayed for any length of time, the fickleness of public opinion would rally to the Prince.[1]

On 16 January a long debate took place in the Commons on the restrictions which Pitt placed before the House. He referred to the difference of opinion amongst the doctors, reminding the House that whilst Warren and Baker were the least confident of a cure, the other doctors were much more optimistic, Willis, 'who attended his Majesty more than any of the others', being more sanguine than them all. It was agreed that the King would eventually recover, and that no unfavourable symptoms had made their appearance. Pitt affirmed his confidence in Willis, and then moved his resolutions:

(1) That it is expedient that his Royal Highness the Prince of Wales . . . shall be empowered to exercise and administer the royal authority . . . subject to such limitations . . . as shall be provided.

(2) That the power so be to given . . . shall not extend to the granting of any rank or dignity of the peerage of the realm . . . except to His Majesty's royal issue . . . of twenty one years.

(3) That the said powers should not extend to the granting of any office, salary, or pension whatever in reversion . . . or for any other term than during his Majesty's pleasure, except such offices as are by law required to be granted for life or during good behaviour.

(4) That [the powers] . . . should not extend to the granting of any part of his Majesty's real or personal estate, except so far as relates to the renewal of leases.

(5) That the care of his Majesty's royal person, during . . . his illness . . . shall be committed to the Queen . . . and that her Majesty should have the power to remove . . . and nominate and appoint such persons as she shall think proper to the several offices in his Majesty's household.[1]

Mr Powys denounced the whole system as a 'monstrous fabric, tending to mutilate and dismember the constitutional authority of the Crown', and moved an amendment:

To leave out from the word illness in order to insert 'And preserving the constitution of Great Britain undisturbed and the dignity and lustre of the Crown unimpaired, his Royal Highness the Prince of Wales be appointed during the present indisposition of his Majesty, and no longer, in the name of the King . . . to exercise . . . the regal power and government under the style and title of Regent of the kingdom. . . .[2]

Lord North warned the committee of the dangers of separating the public duties and prerogatives of the Crown—'suspend some and parcel out others, and there existed that fatal interregnum which the constitution had forbidden'. There was no precedent for the restriction of the Regent's right to create peers, nor had there been a time when that power had lain dormant. To restrict the granting of offices and pensions was to prohibit the proper reward of merit. Pitt had proposed to make the Prince Regent, but while he was expecting him to accept the responsibilities and perform the duties of the King he was withholding from him the full exercise of the royal authority. The Prince's irresistible claim was a claim to something which had existed before, not to something new; nor was it a right to sustain a burden, to submit to all the duties without enjoying the prerogatives of a King. No restrictions ought to be imposed on the Regent.[3]

This was rather different from the moderate tone of the Prince's reply to Pitt. Though critical of the proposed restrictions, and of the conduct of the Ministry, the Prince had signified his assent to the Regency, even if limited. Why, then, were the Whigs fighting the restrictions in the House? What did they hope to gain by it? They had suffered defeat after defeat in

Lords and Commons. Not only had the controversy over inherent right proved disastrous to their interests, but the division over the Speakership had demonstrated the strength of the Ministry. They could not hope to prevent the restrictions being imposed, for those who had supported Pitt over hereditary right were unlikely to desert him when he gave practical expression to his defence of Parliamentary privilege. In a House which had already expressed its mind on the issues raised by the King's incapacity no benefit could accrue to the Opposition from a lengthy debate on the restrictions. Though the limitations would hinder the consolidation of a new Ministry, once the Prince became Regent it was conceivable—as Sheridan claimed—that it would prove possible to dispense with Pitt's safeguards, providing the Prince gained the confidence of the two Houses by the way in which he carried out the duties of his office. The longer the King's recovery was delayed the more probable it was that opinion would rally to the Whigs. Perhaps North felt that however hopeless the struggle it was necessary to fight it out to the bitter end, in order to make the conduct of the Whigs in the controversy appear a serious and disinterested contribution to the constitutional debate. Belgrave, in reply, asserted that to vest the full royal prerogative in the Regent would be entrusting too much power to one person during the lifetime of the monarch. The rights of the Crown ought to be secured, not exposed to the hazard of events.[1]

Sheridan made a witty speech in which he cast scorn and derision upon the medical experts and their prognostications. He boldly affirmed that Willis's answers before the committee were 'prevaricating and evasive':

When he heard Dr Willis attribute his Majesty's illness to seven and twenty years of extreme study, abstinence, and labour, and declare that his Majesty was recovering, assigning as a reason, that the physic which he had that day given him, had produced the desired effect, what must he think of Dr Willis? When he heard him assert that his physic could in one day overcome the effects of seven and twenty years hard exercise, seven and twenty years study, seven and twenty years abstinence, it was impossible for him to maintain that gravity which the subject demanded. Such assertions reminded him of those nostrums which were to cure this and that malady, and also disappointments in love and long sea voyages.[1]

The real inspiration of Pitt's policy (Sheridan continued) was the knowledge that the Prince would choose other ministers. Had the Prince intended to keep the present Cabinet the limitations would never have been heard of. The whole of Pitt's conduct was governed by party considerations and by the impulse of his own ambition. The Chancellor had more than once attacked his opponents as a 'political party'. Sheridan thought it the honour and glory of his life to belong to that party:

Was it a disgrace to have been formed under the Marquis of Rockingham, and under his banners to have combatted on behalf of the people with success? Was it a disgrace to be connected with the Duke of Portland, a nobleman, who, swayed by no mean motives of interest, nor influenced by any ambitious designs to grasp at power, nor with a view to any other purpose than the welfare of the country, dedicated his mornings unremittingly to the promotion of the public good?[2]

Sheridan referred in glowing terms to his friendship with Fox:

... it was the characteristic distinction of his heart to compel the most submissive devotion of mind and affection from all those who came under the observation of it, and force them by the most powerful and amiable of all influence to become the inseparable associates of his fortune.[3]

After attacking Pitt's restriction on the creation of peers, and reminding the House that Pitt himself had created no less than forty-eight peers during five years in office, Sheridan repeated his accusation that the only motive for the policy of restrictions was the knowledge that the Prince was going to take into his service a different set of men from those in office. The public must surely 'despise and detest the cunning and the craft from which so wretched a proceeding had originated'.[4] Unhappily for the Whigs the public refused to do so.

A good deal of Sheridan's speech was directed to his own side of the House. Rumours in the press had suggested a division between Fox and himself, and, although these reports were exaggerated, the appeal to Rockingham's memory and the noble affirmation of loyalty to Fox, presented an image of the party to the outside world, as well as reminding its members (many of whom suspected Sheridan of the basest designs) of the old affections upon which the party had been built. Certainly Sheridan's speech was quoted in the press as proof of the unity of the Opposition, but it needed more than a few generous phrases and heart-warming protestations of undying fidelity to restore unanimity. Debate was an unsatisfactory means of moulding party policy, of supplying the lack of a coherent and intelligible solution to the problems which the Whig leaders, because of their indecision and disagreement, had failed to solve.[1]

Grenville, taking advantage of the fact that the House had formed itself into a committee on the state of the nation, made a lengthy defence of Government policy. He had none of Sheridan's wit and sparkle, and after his opponent's exposure of the motives underlying Pitt's conduct, the new Speaker's contribution to the debate made dull listening. But he addressed himself to the task in hand. If the restrictions were to be supported they must be shown to be consistent with constitutional practice, and this Grenville sought to establish. He denied the relevance of the Statute of 13 Charles II, and the analogy between the address to William of Orange at the time of the 'Glorious Revolution', and the correct procedure to supply the deficiency created by the King's illness. The duty which lay upon the House was not that of putting a King into the possession of an authority which had devolved upon him by inheritance, and the limits of which were clearly indicated by existing laws, but rather of 'creating a new and delegated trust to be exercised for a temporary purpose, and to be vested in an office unknown to the constitution of the country'. Nor were they supplying a vacancy in the throne by an election of a sovereign. They were to consider by what person, in what form, and with what degree of authority, it was proper for the government of the country to be administered during the indisposition of the King; and how this was to be restored to him without delay or difficulty immediately upon 'the happy event of his recovery'. The choice before the House was either a Regent controlled in the exercise or limited in the extent of his authority. He himself had little doubt that the latter course was 'infinitely more agreeable to the spirit of the British constitution'.[1]

This put the Government's case in a nutshell, and however the Whigs might bluster they could not escape from the logic of the situation. Sheridan's speech, however brilliant, disclosed the essential poverty of the Opposition's position. Again and again they brought the discussion back to questions of personal distaste and antipathy, ambition, covetous designs on power and influence. Only Burke was to make a sustained and consistent apology for their conduct, but the terms on which he did so hardly reflected the feelings of his associates. After Grenville's contribution the quality of the debate deteriorated. Welbore Ellis denied that two branches of the legislature could make a law without the concurrence of the third—a stale argument. Mr Drake contented himself with a eulogy of Pitt, and Colonel Fullerton pleaded, in somewhat bewildered tones, for the royal authority to be exercised in its entirety. But all this was unavailing. Powys's amendment was defeated by 227 votes to 154, and the original motion was then carried without a division. The resolution limiting the Regent's power to create peers was carried by 216 votes to 159—a slight swing to the Opposition on that issue. All the other resolutions, except that dealing with the King's household, were then put and carried.[2]

Though the debate on 19 January centred on the resolution relating to the King's household, discussion ranged more widely over the whole field of governmental policy. Old arguments against the restrictions in principle and in general were solemnly repeated. Pitt, in a long speech, justified the resolution as consistent with his policy throughout the crisis, but he also denied the supposition that members of his Cabinet would engage in an organised opposition to the subsequent administration. He and his colleagues would never indulge in a factious opposition. The resolution dealing with the King's household was justified by the necessity of not destroying the system which the King had adopted for the management of his household.[1] Lord Maitland, Mr Sturt, Mr Taylor, and Sir John Swinburne all denounced the resolution as improper, and as tending to introduce a weak and divided government. Mr Pulteney and Sir James Johnstone defended the proposals, but Mr Bouverie moved to leave out the words relative to continuing or removing officers of the household. Lord North claimed that the resolution consisted of three distinct propositions, and that these ought to be discussed separately: the care of the King's person; the power to remove or continue the household establishment; the measure of appointing a permanent council. Fox supported North's contention, for if Pitt refused to separate the questions involved in the resolution the committee would be much embarrassed in their proceedings.[2]

Pitt replied that he was decidedly of the opinion that the Queen should have sole care of the King's person, and that it would be wrong to give her that responsibility without the necessary powers. Anyone who thought that part of the resolution objectionable should move to have it left out.[3] Mr Bouverie immediately acted on this suggestion, moving that the second part of the resolution should be omitted.[4] Grey condemned limitations as nugatory. They would obstruct the Regent in the just and useful exercise of his powers and in the choice of his political servants.[5] Dundas reminded the House that the limitations followed logically from the assertion that the responsibility for supplying the deficiency in the executive branch of the legislature lay with the Lords and Commons. The King's political capacity was whole and entire, but it was necessary to provide for him in his personal capacity, and in doing this the substitute should be given such powers—and such powers only— as were absolutely necessary for the purpose for which he was appointed, and for the duration of the emergency and no longer. If the King did not recover as soon as was expected, or if it later appeared that no recovery could be expected, only then would it be time to think of adding to the powers of the Regent, or of voting powers without restriction.[1]

This was moderate and reasonable. But the Opposition did not move from the ground they had taken up. North attacked the resolution as establishing a bad precedent. He knew of no regal duty which the Regent was not expected to perform. Why, therefore, were regal powers withheld from him? The power of creating peers, and the patronage of the household, were necessary to the Crown as the fountain of honour, and they were equally necessary to the Regent.[2] Sir Gregory Page Turner thought that the resolution would create two governments, and for that reason he intended to vote against it.[3] The Solicitor-General defended the resolutions as temporary expedients providing for a temporary exigency.[4]

Fox, in his longest and most forthright speech for some weeks, attacked the measure whole-heartedly. He had never heard a measure supported with so little argument, and he denied that the King could be considered as unaffected in his political capacity. As for Pitt's avowal that he would not indulge in factious opposition, Fox confessed that he himself had been accustomed to opposition for so long as almost to have a kindness for it. Nor was he unwilling to have a strong, watchful, sympathetic Opposition. The wisdom of our ancestors, he continued, had vested all the prerogatives necessary for good government in the hands of the King, yet now a government was to be established without the powers essential to its well-being and efficiency. It was a serious innovation to change the nature of the royal office:

It might be for a short time; it might be for a long time; it was certainly for an indefinite time that they were to change the constitution of the country, and all this was to be done on the report of the physicians. Physicians had acknowledged that the science of physic was the most uncertain of all arts; and that of all branches of physics, this particular malady was the most uncertain. So then they were, for an unlimited time, to change the nature of the third estate, to impoverish and weaken the executive arm, to create a new estate in the country; and all this, on the report of the most uncertain case which can come within the view of the most uncertain of all sciences.[1]

Wilberforce defended the resolutions, for as long as the King was alive the House had to take special care not to place the Prince on the throne. Mr Drake urged the House not to take the Queen out of her domestic sphere by forcing her to become a politician.[2]

Pitt, replying to the debate, admitted that if the King's recovery was protracted then the restrictions could be removed altogether —should great difficulty and inconvenience result from a delayed recovery on the part of the King. When the committee divided on the motion that the words in the middle of the question should stand, the Ministry was victorious by 229 votes to 165, and when North proposed that the words 'for a limited time' be added his suggestion was rejected by 220 votes to 164.[3]

The end of the debate was enlivened by an incident which could have proved extremely embarrassing for the Whigs, and from which they were saved only by Pitt's restraint. Mr Rolle told the committee that he had voted for the appointment of the Prince as Regent under a conviction, derived from an assurance which had been given by Fox, that his Royal Highness was unmarried. But his constituents had directed him to solicit fresh information on the subject and he therefore begged leave to appeal once more to the right honourable gentleman.[4]

The squalid story of the Fitzherbert marriage was always

threatening the Whigs with disaster, and Rolle was just the man to introduce the subject into the discussions on the Regency. Fox's original denial of the marriage in April 1787 had only served to diminish his influence with the Heir Apparent, and to increase Sheridan's standing with Mrs Fitzherbert. The obvious and painful contradiction between what he had said, and what Sheridan later affirmed, with all that it implied, had discredited him in the estimation of the public. Either he was lying or he had been deceived by the Prince of Wales—a sure sign that the latter had lost confidence in him. If the truth came out Fox and his colleagues were doomed. The Prince had violated both the Act of Settlement and the Royal Marriages Act. And, especially in the tense and suspicious atmosphere of the Regency debates, searching inquiries about the Prince's private affairs would expose the divisions within the Opposition, the reciprocal distrust, the thinly veiled hatreds. It would be difficult for Fox to avoid offending the Prince or betraying dark and intimate secrets, should Rolle press the issue; and, in either case, decisive damage would be inflicted on the Whig cause. But it suited everyone, with the exception of a few hardy troublemakers, to turn a blind eye to the realities of the situation at Carlton House. If he had cared to press the issue Pitt could have added acute embarrassment to the discredit which was already heaped upon the Opposition; but, fortunately for Fox, he was content with the victories he had gained. He had no wish to provoke another sordid controversy over the unsavoury details of the Prince's private life, and since it had been agreed that whatever restrictions might be imposed on his powers the Prince was to be nominated Regent, Pitt did not want the dignity of the office, and by inference the dignity of the Crown, to be defaced by public discussion of the Heir Apparent's personal relationships. To know that rumour followed rumour in the Press; to be aware of the suspicions which Horne Tooke and Withers roused and encouraged—this was a different matter from debating the affair in the Commons. Rolle's inquiry was not received sympathetically. Sir Francis Bassett condemned his conduct in introducing the subject as indecent; and when Rolle appealed to the chair Lord North saved the situation by parrying the question. But the ominous issue had been raised. Would it blaze up at a later stage, a more ignominious controversy than hereditary right, and even more fatal to the Whig cause?[1]

The several resolutions were then reported to the House, agreed upon and ordered to be communicated to the Lords at a conference. They were debated in the Upper House on 22 and 23 January, the debates echoing those in the Commons. On 22 January the Earl of Sandwich moved the addition of the words 'for a limited time' to the resolution, but his amendment was defeated by 93 votes to 67, the original resolution then being carried by 92 votes to 64. On the following day the resolution on the granting of pensions and places and that securing the King's personal property were passed without a division, but when the resolution on the custody of the King's person and the management of the household was read Lord Rawdon sought to separate the care of the King from the control of his household. His amendment was defeated by 94 votes to 68. The resolutions were then reported to the House and ordered to be communicated to the Commons at a conference.[2]

The administration had triumphed; they had pressed home the advantage which they had gained in December. Gloom and depression were now replacing the too-careless optimism which had been so characteristic of the Whigs during the first two months of the crisis. Their arrangements for a new Cabinet were still uncertain, and Fox, suffering from persistent bouts of sickness, was corresponding with Portland about the allocation of places. There was also a move afoot to hold a great public meeting at Westminster to offset public support for the ministry. On 21 January Fox wrote a long letter to Portland, discussing the situation in detail:

I send you inclosed a sketch of the arrangement which, imperfect as it is, may be of some use to you. I believe there are some places, and probably still more claimants, wholly omitted in it, but I have found myself so apt to forget when I have seen you some points that I had meant to mention to you that I thought it best to set down something on paper. . . . I have seen Adam and entirely approve of stirring without doors as soon as possible, and avoiding if we can any more divisions. My health must so far be attended to, as not to appoint for the Westminster meeting a day likely to follow a long night in the House of Commons.

I hear the Duke of Northumberland certainly refuses Ireland; if the Ordnance can be kept for Conway, pray do it, and surely if Lord Rawdon is at the cabinet *they* ought to be satisfied. I suppose a Commoner cannot be President otherwise it might be stated to them that either that office or the Ordnance must be kept for Conway. You will think I harp very much upon this part of the arrangement, but I really do feel considerable uneasiness about it. I suppose it will be impossible for you to call here after the House of Lords tomorrow, but I hope we shall meet the day after, and settle finally a greater part at least of this troublesome business. . . .[1]

In the list of appointments which he enclosed Fox had Portland as First Lord of the Treasury, himself and Stormont as Secretaries of State, Fitzwilliam as First Lord of the Admiralty, Loughborough as Lord Chancellor (the long courtship with Thurlow was now over), Fitzpatrick Secretary of State at War, Carlisle President of the Council, Rawdon Privy Seal, Northumberland Master General of the Ordnance, whilst Cavendish, who had not yet formally accepted the post, was down as Chancellor of the Exchequer. The Cabinet list is interesting in that it proves that Northumberland and the 'Armed Neutrality' were now wholly with the Whigs, forgetting their initial support of Pitt as Minister whilst opposing the policy of restriction. Their conversion had not been difficult, and it is probable that from the start their denial of any attack on Pitt's Ministry was no more than a veil by which they hoped to hide their change of allegiance. Grenville had denounced their original position as absolute nonsense, and so it was, for if Pitt was defeated on the issue of restrictions he would have little hope of continuing in office. Now it would seem that

Northumberland and Rawdon agreed with him. Yet, while the support of the 'Armed Neutrality' was welcome to the Whigs, the price which had to be paid—the inclusion of the Duke and some of his friends in the Cabinet—caused infinite worry and Fox was later to lament the unco-operative nature of his new allies, referring in his letter of 6 February to the great difficulty which he felt in giving any advice on how to deal with 'these most unreasonable people'.[1] The alliance brought no material advantage to the Whigs, for Northumberland and his associates were not numerous enough to sway the fortunes of debate in either House, and the anticipated victory was as far away as ever. Nor were Northumberland and his friends the only causes of friction. Fox was hoping to retain Dorset as ambassador at Paris, and although Dorset was uncertain about his future he was coming to the conclusion that there was no reason why he should not stay on if the Whigs wanted him to do so. Writing to Hawkesbury on 5 February he went so far as to say:

... A few days now must decide our fates. I own I am impatient to know mine, their anxiety about me here is very flattering, but I don't think they will persuade me that a change of ministry ought to affect me provided the Regent's ministers wish me to continue in my station. . . .[2]

But how fickle the ambassador's sentiments were can be seen from his letter to Hawkesbury on 24 February, when he had not yet heard of the King's convalescence, but when prospects for the sovereign's recovery were more favourable than at any earlier stage of the crisis:

... I am provoked that insinuations have been spread about me, they were I can with great truth assure you totally void of foundation. Lord Stafford knows fully my sentiments upon the subject, and that I was determined to follow the same line of conduct with him, the Chancellor, and I hoped your Lordship. It had been hinted to me by some of the Prince's friends that I *might remain* in my station if I pleased. I answer'd constantly to these hints that whenever that offer was made to me in a proper manner I should return a proper answer, but I never gave anybody *the least reason* to think I should desert His Majesty's ministers supposing a total change of administration to take place. If the King really quite recovers I own I should like to take a trip to England for a fortnight. . . .[1]

No doubt he had a lot of explaining to do, however urgently he protested his loyalty to Pitt. The difficulties which confronted both Fox and Pitt in trying to form their plans and their ministries are amply illustrated by the ambiguous and unstable outlook of Dorset, who while a naïve and willing victim of flattery in both Paris and London must surely have realised that if a Regent was installed nothing less than a total change of administration was contemplated.

Fox's reference in his letter of 21 January to the proposed Westminster meeting shows the concern felt by the Opposition leaders about the advantages the ministry had gained by its extra-Parliamentary activity. In fact when the meeting took place it was much less than the monster rally which they had originally had in mind, and Burke was to express his dissatisfaction with the way the affair had been handled, and the lack of thrust and initiative shown by Fox and Portland. Had Fox been in good health the outcome might have been different, but Portland was ill-fitted to take the lead in organising public opinion. Fox finally came to the conclusion that the decision to drop the Westminster meeting was justified, but he was also 'afraid of the same timid disposition which was the occasion of our doing perhaps right in this instance, causing much mischief in future'.[2] And even the decision not to hold the meeting was later contradicted by what took place at the Crown and Anchor on 14 February.

Thus, whilst the ministry were gaining their victories in the two Houses on the restrictions which they were determined to impose on the Regent, the Whigs were striving to satisfy their allies, and to gain public support. The air of unreality which Holland Rose noted as characteristic of the Regency debates was the fruit of the frustration which was rotting the Whig party. The debates only revealed their ineptitude, and their weakness in Parliament threw into greater relief the multitude of local set-backs which they had sustained in the struggle over addresses. The patronage of the Prince had proved a dubious, if not a disastrous, factor out of office, and Pitt remained master in the controversy.

In 1788 only the friendship of the Prince promised any break in the series of defeats which the Whig Opposition had sustained since 1784. The least doubt, however, that the Prince would not exercise full powers as Regent, or that the King's illness was not incurable, was enough to make the timorous keep silence—to wait and see appeared the wisest course to take before committing oneself to a party from which it was not clear what one could expect. The best policy for the Opposition to adopt was that of fighting the controversy as a constitutional issue, creating a focal point of conflict between Ministry and Opposition which seemed to transcend the intrigues of faction and the petty clashes of interest. But the Whigs misunderstood the abstract questions raised by the crisis, and because they did not understand them they persistently underestimated their influence on public opinion. If the party was to survive, if the Rockingham tradition was to mean anything in the changed circumstances of 1788, the Whig party had to identify its fortunes with a particular interpretation of the constitution, to make a stand for principle at the expense of expediency, in the hope that this would provide the party with that unity which it had lacked since the death of Rockingham, if not from the end of the American War. This was what Burke hoped to accomplish, but Fox's assertion of the Prince's right failed to do this because it was not based on a logical exposition of constitutional principle or practice. Fox's speech of 10 December (despite its echoes of Loughborough's interpretation of the demands of the constitution) had all too clearly been political interest masquerading as constitutional rectitude. For Burke the key to the crisis lay in putting the question the other way round. Although he overestimated the potentiality of the issues raised by the crisis, Burke at least saw the poverty of politics by negotiation. Pitt's administration was popular and successful; even more significantly, he enjoyed the support of the King and of the two Houses, and in this sense he was the perfect eighteenth-century Minister. There was little hope here for a policy of intrigue, of promised rewards, and of remitted punishments. Both Fox and Burke were disillusioned at the end of January. But whilst Fox went to Bath on the 28th,[1] where the waters were to restore his health and his morale, leaving behind him a situation full of foreboding for the Whigs, Burke braced himself for the final struggle. On 24 January he unburdened his heart to Windham, outlining in his letter his main differences with his colleagues, and his dissatisfaction with the way in which the crisis had been handled, and expressing his fears for the future. It is time, therefore, to turn to Burke's interpretation of the crisis, and to discern the insight and perception which lay behind the violence of his speeches and the extravagance of his conduct.

CHAPTER IV

EDMUND BURKE AND
THE CRISIS OF 1788

The part played by Edmund Burke in the crisis of 1788–9 has frequently been criticised for its violence and extremism, and at the time his conduct confirmed the suspicions which many of his contemporaries entertained regarding his mental stability. Addington, telling his father of the debate of 5 February 1789, thought that Burke 'discredited himself. Indeed he was violent almost to madness; and I believe his party may thank him for a diminution of their numbers. . . .'[1] Madame Huber, writing to Mrs Eden on 21 February, was convinced that he was almost mad, 'and will be quite so, no doubt, if the King recovers'.[2] George Selwyn, lamenting the fact that the King was insane, pointed his moral by remarking, 'Burke walking at large and him in a strait waistcoat!',[3] and an anonymous writer of the period asserted that Burke was 'so vehemently affected at the delay of the ministers in offering their resignation, that he appeared to have lost his own reason in describing the malady which preyed upon that of the King'.[4] The more sober pages of the *Parliamentary History* tell a similar tale. During the debate of 7 February Burke was continually interrupted by laughter from the ministerial benches,[5] and on at least four occasions during the Parliamentary debates he was called to order for the extravagance of his rhetoric.[6] Small wonder, therefore, that Lecky thought it 'impossible to dismiss the debates on the Regency without noting what a painful and humiliating spectacle his speeches on this question present . . . if full of genius they were also full of the most extraordinary exhibitions of passion, indiscretion, exaggeration, and ill taste'.[7] The chorus of condemnation is virtually unanimous. Lapses of taste and proximity to madness constitute a formidable indictment.

But Burke himself was not unaware of the need for restraint in dealing with the problems raised by the King's madness. In his notes on the Regency Question he comments:

> If anything in the world can *call* us, I had almost said *command* us, to temper and moderation, it is this solemn and awful hour; when the most humiliating of all *human* calamities has fallen upon the *highest* of all human situations and when the stroke is not on the frail and perishable portion—but on the proud, the distinguishing part of our nature. . . .[1]

This was paralleled in his speech in the Commons on 10 December, when he reminded the House that 'if ever there was a question which peculiarly called for temper and moderation it was that to which the present argument referred. . . .'[2] It would seem, therefore, that Burke was guilty of self-contradiction, as well as fanaticism. He was conscious of the need for caution, and yet he wilfully ignored his own precepts. This is surely Irishry with a vengeance. It is partly explained by his growing isolation within the Whig party since the death of Rockingham, but it was primarily inspired by his approach to the constitutional problems precipitated by the King's illness, and his interpretation of the policies of the Government. Although in one aspect his speeches were the frantic denunciations of a desperate man, in another sense they were the only coherent interpretation of the predicament on the part of an Opposition spokesman in the Commons. Even when he was ill, lonely, and subjected to cruel misrepresentation, he persisted in fighting the administration with all the determination of which he was capable. What goaded him into such a course? What prompted him to follow a line of conduct which was denounced from the Government benches and severely criticised (and little understood) within his own party? He had little to hope for from a Whig administration. He knew that it was extremely unlikely that he would be given a Cabinet post.

His speech in the Commons on 6 February 1789 gives a clue to his behaviour:

> With regard to the charge of passion . . . he confessed that he had expressed himself with warmth, originating from a deep consideration of the great importance of the subject, and not from any censurable imbecility of temper. So far from it, it would have been censurable in him, or in any man possessed of common feeling, to have refrained from that indication of warmth which he had betrayed, when speaking of a Bill, from the provisions of which the whole House of Brunswick were expressly excluded. . . .[1]

His warmth and his violence—so he claimed—were inspired by the gravity of the issues involved, and provoked by the conduct of the Government. Pitt's denial of the Prince's right, and his proposals to limit the powers of the Regent, undermined the principle of hereditary succession, and threatened to alter the role which the monarch played in the affairs of state. As long ago as 1765 Burke had criticised the Regency Bill of that year for 'inattention to the honour of the Crown', and had even suspected the ministers of harbouring 'a design against it'.[2] And, just as his violence in 1788 foreshadowed that which he was to display over the French Revolution, so his defence in 1791 echoed the terminology of 1788. After his break with Fox he wrote to Fitzwilliam:

> The difference between me and the party turns upon no trivial objects. . . . I was persuaded that the succession was the moment, and probably the only moment, favourable to the power of your party; at the same time, that the moment favourable to your power would of all others be the most critical to you and to the whole state. I was convinced to a certainty that whatever tended to unsettle the succession, and to disturb the recognised ranks and order and the fixed properties in the nation, would be of all men the most fatal to your friends. . . .[3]

Thus, the succession, which Burke thought vested for all time in the House of Brunswick by the Act of Settlement, was his point of departure from the administration in 1788, and from his companions in 1791. The proposed limitations on the powers of the Regent, stemming as they did from the Government's refusal to admit the right of the Prince of Wales, constituted as real a threat to the succession as *The Rights of Man*, and were as startling an innovation. Despite Fox's statements in the Commons on 10 December, Burke's principal criticism of his associates was that they were too lukewarm in their devotion to the doctrine of hereditary right, too prone to subordinate it to the whims of party fortune. To attack the constitution in one place was to weaken its whole structure, and when faced with Pitt's proposals Burke warned his contemporaries of the dangers of abandoning the hereditary succession. But whilst his primary aim was to maintain the constitution intact this brought him into conflict with those of his colleagues who did not share his crusading zeal. Sheridan thought that the first object of policy ought to be the party's speedy entry into office, and Fox, for all his fervour in debate, found the abstract issues an increasingly wearisome embarrassment, offensive alike to ambition and common sense. For Burke, however, they were the core of the crisis, the essential issue, and he therefore strove to bring the constitutional technicalities to the fore, whatever the dictates of political advantage might suggest. (That he also believed the interests of the Whigs to be inseparably linked with the welfare of the constitution does not invalidate his primary concern for the latter's preservation.) His preoccupation with the constitution was associated in his own mind with independence and took precedence over all claims of party: '[I have] sat here three and twenty years and have steadily opposed all innovations in our constitution. No advantages, but sincerity—Freedom, Truth, without *fears*, without favour—unconcerted . . . and unbiassed I believe by any human influence. . . .'[1] Whilst Fox and Sheridan were chiefly concerned with the Minister's hold on office, Burke was worried, not so much by Pitt's prolonged tenure, as by the means he was using to perpetuate it.

The central issue was the position of the King as the executive power in the state. To attack the monarch was to attack the constitution, and if one part of the constitution was nullified the whole would be ineffective. At the same time Burke was conscious of the need to supply the want of an efficient head of the executive, and the delay which formed so great a part of the Cabinet's policy infuriated him even more. A crucial constitutional issue was being settled in the hurly-burly of political strife, but for Burke the national welfare was the most important consideration:

> The first object of *policy* is the good of the state. The first justice is *justice* to the people. On that principle what do justice and the public good require? ... The trusts to be exercised by the Crown are not light and trivial things. With such things at stake we ought to be sure that a real incapacity exists to suspend them. But when that one great fundamental fact is thoroughly ascertained then our whole deliberation ought to be that there should not exist for a moment a want of efficient and capable Government in the country. . . .[1]

It was therefore urgent to discover the true basis on which all action must rest: 'You must try acts of state by the principles of the constitution and not decide the constitution by acts of state.'[2] Burke criticised Pitt for making expediency a substitute for constitutional practice, and denied that the policy of examining precedents was appropriate:

> I must observe once for all concerning *precedents*, that we ought in matters so various and contradictory as *acts*, of *State conveniency* and State necessity, to be very cautious how we take every *event* in constitutional history as a *precedent of Law*. If you do, I will be bold to say, that there is not one kind of arrangement of your Throne, nor any one opinion concerning the right to it, that is not somewhere or other to be found in the records of this Kingdom. . . .[3]

Burke was objecting to precedents, not as Fox did, as irrelevant abstractions or excursions into the horrors of a more barbarous age, but as inevitably inconclusive and contradictory. For Burke there could be only one constitutional interpretation relevant to the needs of 1788. In his speech in the Commons on 10 December, he made his position clear: 'He had ever understood that our constitution was framed with so much circumspection and fore-thought that it wisely provided for every possible exigency and that the exercise of the sovereign executive power could never be vacant. . . .'[1] In other words, whilst Pitt was attempting to discover, by an examination of the precedents, what the correct procedure was, for Burke this problem did not exist. One necessity could not make a precedent for another necessity, he wrote in his notes,[2] and he did not think it irreverent to the constitution to suppose that it was 'wise enough to furnish principles for its own exigencies'.[3] Precedents had nothing to do with the case, for they were 'precedents of civil violence and the specious pretences of usurpers whilst their power was green and immature, ready to let others into a share of it'.[4] For all his talk of precedents Pitt's policy was aimed at the succession, and for Burke this was no mere war-cry covering, on his own part, a lust for place and power. His denunciations of Pitt's ambition, furious and violent as they were, were inspired by his regard for the succession. Popular feeling was as irrelevant as were precedents: 'The disposition of the Sovereign power is not in the will of the People.'[5] Pitt's ambition was precisely the sort of threat which the hereditary succession had been established to prevent: 'Why is Government made an Inheritance? For this single and sole reason, because it limits and qualifies ambition. . . . That having a fixed and invariable rule of known law it can never become the object of private pursuit.'[6] This was not simply royalist sentiment, nor mere concern for the rights of the Heir Apparent, important though his rights were. The rights threatened by Pitt were those of the nation and the interests at stake were national interests: '. . . the settled, known, hereditary succession of the Crown is an invaluable part of our Constitution. That is as much our inheritance as the inheritance of the Royal Family.'[7]

Burke's conduct during the crisis was dictated by an interpretation of the constitution which, although principally inspired by the Revolution Settlement, was constantly expanding into a consistent scheme. Inevitably he was driven to state what that Settlement implied and why it was pre-eminently the guide for all future constitutional developments. The administration, too, claimed that they looked to the Revolution as the justification of their policy, but Burke denied the validity of any interpretation which differed from his own. He saw the politicians of 1788, not as creators of law for the future, but as morally bound to apply the exact requirements of the constitution in one particular situation. He defended one revolutionary settlement, but ruled out the possibility of an equally valid one occurring at any time in the present or future. It would seem that his argument was a circular one, moving round a given premise, which many of his contemporaries (and even some of his colleagues) did not share. While endowing one historical event with final authority Burke poured scorn on mere 'events' as precedents and guides for future conduct:

> Now *necessity* neither does nor can make a precedent; because it is above precedent and above Law. Nay in cases of necessity, no two of which were ever alike, to talk of precedent would be to renounce common sense and govern yourself by the momentary exigencies ... of other times and not by the demands and exigencies of your own ... affairs.[1]

He defined certain historical events as cases of mere necessity:

> Thus the things done at the restoration of Charles II are not precedents. In fact you had ... [neither] King [nor] Parliament nor any constitution at all in the footing of the foregoing or the subsequent.... How was he restored? Why as irregularly as he had been expelled. [R]estored under the shadow and power of a part of the Army which then governed the Nation....[2]

Even when considering the Revolution of 1688 he was compelled to retain the same distinction, though, as one would expect, the Revolution was described in glowing terms:

> Then comes the Revolution—a memorable period in the History of this Kingdom—full of light—full of instruction—never to be blotted out of the memory of mankind—nor is a man worthy to be enrolled in the high class of

Englishmen who does not hold it in eternal honour, first in his memory and closest to his heart. . . .[1]

But he continued:

The Revolution as a precedent is for a Revolution, and if this is the object if you please you may use it—but you must first establish your case—and then proceed to repeal the acts of Settlement—for at present the rights of the Crown stand on the firm bases of those acts of Parliament and not on the revolution, which political event was a *cause producing it*, but not itself by any means the *Title to the Crown*.[2]

He was here resting his case, not upon any 'historical event', but on legislation—that legislation which had vested the hereditary right to the Crown in the House of Brunswick. This gave him the opportunity to question the validity of the legislation by which the Government intended to enforce its restrictions on the Regent. Since the King was mad, and the hereditary principle abandoned, there was no executive power by which the proceedings in the two Houses could be given the force of law. Burke rejected the proposed expedient of putting the Great Seal in commission in order to give the royal assent to the Regency Bill, denouncing it as a dangerous innovation, motivated by Pitt's desire to remain in office. In his speech in the Commons on 22 December he did not hesitate to speak out on this issue. He considered it 'his sole pride and exclusive glory . . . to speak against the wishes of the people whenever they attempted to ruin themselves'. And, though he was content with the constitution as he found it, there were others who wished to alter it.[3] The language of the resolution 'excited his astonishment', whilst the proposed method of giving the royal assent was 'a glaring falsehood, and a palpable absurdity . . . housebreaking, highway robbery . . . were each of them . . . more excusable than law forgery. . . .'[4] He went on:

When all the heterogeneous mass of cases, and all the farrago of nonsense under the title of legal distinctions were considered, every man of common understanding must see the necessity of governing the whole of them by the genuine spirit and fair principles of the constitution.[1]

The two Houses were arrogating to themselves rights which belonged only to the Crown. Not only was Pitt selecting the person who was to be Regent, but, by imposing his limitations, he was changing the character of the executive branch of the constitution. A passage from Burke's notes on the Regency supplements his comments in the House:

The two Houses are then to choose not only who shall execute the Kingly office—but what the Kingly office may be . . . The Kingly office may therefore originate from the two Houses and they are to set up if they please not one who has any interest whatsoever in preserving it, but the direct contrary has an interest in sacrificing it.[2]

Burke saw Pitt as the real ruler of the country during any limited Regency, and in his concern to defend the succession he attacked Pitt's proposals as the culmination of a long campaign against the constitution. The Minister's ambition threatened the achievement of 1688: 'The King is absolute in the choice of ministers and the King chuses Mr Pitt and Mr Pitt makes a Parliament and that Parliament chuse a King and the regal power is encountroulable in the choice [of ministers]. . . '.[3] And again:

It is curious to observe how the power of Mr Pitt . . . revolves unto itself and forms a compleat . . . unity. He first establishes in the Crown the sole power to nominate its minister. The chance of events then enables him through Parliament to name a King. It is established as a principle that the Crown is incontroulable in the appointment of its ministers; and it devolves upon the ministers to appoint those who have the power of appointing ministers without controul.[4]

It was, therefore, a preoccupation with the constitutional aspects of the crisis which led Burke to make his violent attacks on Pitt. It was almost as if he saw in Pitt's conduct during the Regency debates the clue to the meaning of his previous career. Only the most ambitious and arrogant of men could make such an un-scrupulous attack on the foundation of the nation's liberties and welfare. The denunciations of Pitt became progressively more violent: 'I know that there are those amongst us who consider themselves as born for the supreme government of this country— that it belongs to them at the age of 21 as much as the estates they derive under their family settlements . . . that to take their place is usurpation. . . .'[1] Pitt was neither Whig nor Tory. His career had been inspired by one motive only:

. . . to get power as soon as he could; and to hold it as long as he could by every means, by . . . despotism, by the wildest popularity—by destroying Parliaments, by exalting them, by electing, by deposing, to him was a thing totally indifferent. . . .[2]

During the debate of 10 December Burke described Pitt as one of the Prince's competitors and had been called to order for doing so.[3] But he was convinced that the Government's policy was nothing short of usurpation, and in one jotting, in which the shade of Rockingham was significantly invoked, he wrote of the crisis in precisely those terms:

Marquis of R. defended the H. of C. against reformers. The people against the H. of C. The H. of C. against the corruptions of the Crown and now the Crown against the usurpation, against the heads of faction in the H. of C.— whose Terms were in all times the good of the people.[4]

At first the relevance of Rockingham is not apparent. But Burke was aware that the Opposition could look back to the campaigns fought under the Marquis's not excessively dynamic leadership with pardonable nostalgia, and in any event his name would revive memories of a past which was less humiliating than the present. If the criticism was made that Burke's thesis was excessively monarchical, Rockingham's ghost would confound the accusation.

On 24 January 1789 Burke wrote to Windham from Beaconsfield. He was weary of politics and in poor health, but there was an additional reason for his retreat to the country:

I have already, I think, received some small benefit to my health by coming into the country; but this view to health, though far from unnecessary to me, was not the chief cause of my present retreat. I began to find that I had grown too anxious; and had begun to discover to myself and others a solicitude relative to the present state of affairs, which though their strange condition might warrant it in others, is certainly less suitable to my time of life, in which all emotions are less allowed. . . .[1]

He had been letting the whole business get on top of him, deeply worried as he was about its outcome. In this mood it is not surprising to find that wistful longing for retirement, noticeable in earlier stages of his career, making its reappearance:

I sincerely wish to withdraw myself from this scene for good and all; but, unluckily, the India business binds me in a point of honour; and whilst I am waiting for that, comes across another of a kind totally different from any that has hitherto been seen in this country, and which has been attended with consequences very different from those which ought to have been expected in this country, or in any other country from such an event. . . .[2]

Not that he had been entirely surprised at the turn events had taken; he had been taught by 'some late proceedings' and by the 'character of the person principally concerned' to expect something 'extraordinary'. Perhaps here he was referring to the Prince's marriage with Mrs Fitzherbert or to the question of the Prince's debts. Or by the person 'principally concerned' he might have been thinking of Pitt. He went on to tell Windham of his objection to the way in which the party's affairs had been handled:

. . . the Prince ought to have *done* what has been *said* it was his right to do; and which might have been as safely done as was unsafely said. He ought himself to have gone down to the House of Lords, and to *them*, by himself, and to the House of Commons by *message*, to have communicated the King's condition, and to have desired the advice and assistance of the two Houses. His friends would then have been the *proposers*, and his enemies the *opposers*, which would have been a great advantage . . . we admitted the official ministers as the King's *confidential* servants, when he had no confidence to give. The plans originated from them. We satisfied ourselves with the place of objectors and opposers—a weak post always. . . .[3]

This was consistent with the advice he had given Fox shortly after the latter had arrived in London from the Continent; and it was also parallel to the advice given by Loughborough in the early days of November.[1] Burke had tried at a later date to impress upon his colleague the importance of taking the initiative but his advice had been spurned:

Though I went to town strongly impressed with this idea,[2] which I stated to Fox, when I saw him in his bed, and to others, it met with so ill a reception from all to whom I mentioned it, and it seemed then a matter of course that the men who remained in place . . . without character or efficiency in law were under an exclusive obligation to take the lead. . . .[3]

Some of his colleagues thought that the Government should be encouraged to produce their plans, and this so distressed Burke that he ceased to press his own viewpoint, overborne as he was by this 'almost universal conceit'. He had written to his brother, telling him that he had found it necessary to give up his attempt to persuade the party to take the initiative. He was little consulted in Opposition councils, and there is no reason to doubt the sincerity of his statement in the House of Commons that he knew no more of the inside of Carlton House than of Buckingham House.[4] It was probably as a result of this public avowal that the Prince wrote Burke a hurried note on 8 February inviting him to a meeting of the Opposition leaders at Lord Loughborough's, and emphasising that 'there is no man whose advice is so necessary to us, at all times, and particularly in this singular and dangerous crisis, as you'.[5]

But Burke was not merely complaining that his own opinions had been rejected. He was denouncing what he considered a fundamental error underlying the Opposition's conduct, the cause of all the frustrations which had fallen upon them. At the same time things had turned out 'so contrary to all my rational speculation'[6] that he hesitated to make confident prophecies for the future. Instead he was throwing out ideas to Windham in the hope that 'you may urge them in time and place with a force, which, for many reasons . . . I can no more hope for. . . .'[7] He proceeded with his criticism of the Opposition's reaction to the demands which the crisis had laid upon them and as he wrote he warmed to his subject. The intensity with which he held his convictions gave his writing a fervent note, rarely struck in much of the artificial debating which was so characteristic of the controversy. He denounced the lack of sufficient consultation within the Opposition: 'though there have been very few consultations upon particular measures, there have been none at all *de summa rerum*.'¹ Here Burke is borne out by the testimony of the Duchess of Devonshire, who lamented in her diary that 'many of the subjects were brought before the House without previous consultation'.² Burke was distressed by the failure of the party's leaders to face the problems raised by the King's lunacy:

> It has never been discussed, whether all things taken together, in our present situation, it would not be the best or the least evil course, for the public and the Prince, and possibly in the end for the party, that the Prince should surrender himself to his enemies and ours. . . .³

If victory was out of the question defeat could be partly redeemed by artifice:

> It has always hitherto been thought wise rather to foresee such an extremity, and to act in foresight, than to submit to it when it happens; to make peace whilst there is some faint appearance of choice left upon the subject, has hitherto been the policy. If that surrender be thought necessary . . . this, I think, would be best done in the way of a strong, well reasoned memorial on the subject, advising the Prince, for the sake of the public tranquillity, and to prevent further outrages upon the constitution, to yield to the present exigence. . . . This, in my poor judgment, ought to be signed by all the Lords and Commoners amongst us, and possibly by other notables in the country; and then, without a formal secession, to absent ourselves from Parliament until favourable circumstances should call us to it. . . .⁴

Though Burke was counselling retreat the terms on which he did so are interesting. His principal reason for retiring from the fray was to prevent 'further outrages upon the constitution', whilst restoring public tranquillity. His suggestion of secession was an attempt to emphasise in action the Opposition's complete disapproval and total rejection of the Ministry's policy. Perhaps

the 'favourable circumstances' which would recall the Whigs to
Parliament were a dissolution and election as soon as the Regent
was installed, but in any case, although circumstances had con-
spired to give the Government victory in the struggle for office,
there was no reason to concede, even by implication, anything
more than a political defeat. It would be improper for the
Whigs to appear to accept the Government's interpretation of the
constitutional questions raised by the crisis. Burke was en-
deavouring to preserve his party's self-respect and to maintain
unalloyed the purity of their doctrine, despite the humiliations
attendant upon defeat.

But, if surrender was not accepted as inevitable, then adjust-
ments were necessary in the tactics which were to be used in the
struggle:

. . . if we choose the other way . . . to fight it out against a majority in the two
Houses and a very great, bold, and active party without doors, making, for
aught I know, the majority of the nation, then I am sure we ought to prepare
ourselves for such a combat in a different manner, and to act in it with a very
different spirit from anything which has ever yet appeared amongst us. In the
first place we ought to change that tone of calm reasoning which certainly
does not belong to great and affecting interests and which has no effect, but to
chill those upon whose active exertions we must depend much more than on
their cold judgment.[1]

If the fight was to be continued no concern for the normal conventions of polite debate was necessary; indeed, one of the
criticisms which Burke made of the Opposition's tactics in the
Commons was that the style of argument had been 'so very
much different from that by which Lord North was run down'.[2]
The party had erred on the side of moderation:

I suppose a more excellent speech than Fox's last has never been delivered
in any House of Parliament; full of weighty argument, eloquently enforced,
and richly, though soberly, decorated. But we must all be sensible that it was
a speech which might be spoken upon an important difference between the
best friends, and where the parties had the very best opinion of each other's
general intentions for the public good.[3]

That Pitt had commended Fox's speech for its moderation was not, in Burke's opinion, a further argument in favour of the approach which had been so mistakenly adopted in an attempt to undo the effects of Fox's blunder on 10 December. As Burke wrote his earlier pessimism and tone of melancholy resignation were transformed into zealous assurance. The choice was clear— either to concede the Government's triumph, but not their case, or to fight to the finish, regardless of the consequences. All thought of surrender vanished from Burke's mind as his enthusiasm grew. Scorning his associates for their lack of zeal, he was now indifferent to the fate of a mere party. He could even suspect that there was a faint glimmer of truth in the rumour that a coalition between Pitt and Fox was not impossible:

If a foreseen coalition with Mr Pitt should make this style of debate[1] advisable for Mr Fox, the word ought to be given to others, who may bring much mischief upon themselves when such a coalition shall be made, for having spoken of Pitt's conduct as highly corrupt, factious, and criminal; and, in the meantime, they may be considered as hot and intemperate zealots of a party, with the main springs of whose politics they are not acquainted, so far as the general style of debate.[2]

It is difficult not to see Burke defending himself here against prevalent criticism. His sense of isolation within the Opposition, the consciousness that he was not at the centre of events, the conviction that crucial decisions were being made by others, all break through his condemnation of the policy of appeasement, heightening the scorn and contempt which he felt for all who sought a happy compromise. Yet he was careful to make it clear to Windham that no charge of 'illegality' ought at any time to be provoked by the Opposition—for what could be more illegal than the conduct of the administration?

... [I]t is universally admitted that the acts of the two Houses are not legal, but to be legalised hereafter, and that our proceedings are not founded upon anything but necessity. The submission of the smaller number to the greater is a mere voluntary act and not an acquiescence in a legal decision. . . . Our conduct cannot be more irregular than theirs. If it is objected that this principle might lead us a great deal further, I confess it; but then their principles would lead them further too; and they have, in fact, gone to ten times worse and more serious lengths against the substance and solid maxims of our government, than we can be suspected of going, who, should we take the steps I suggest, would only trespass against the form and decorum. . . .[1]

Here Burke was reverting to the constitutional implications of the crisis. He went on to discuss the statement which Sheridan had made to the effect that the Prince of Wales considered himself bound to comply with the requirements of the House of Commons. Burke felt that this could only mean submission. If the statement was an accurate reflection of the Prince's views, then all resistance to the Government was useless. The dangers implied by such an attitude outweighed any political advantages:

I should contend as much as anyone . . . for the constitutional propriety of the King's submitting, in every part of his executive government, to the advice of Parliament. But this, like every other principle, can bear a practical super-structure of only a certain weight. If the two Houses, without any sort of reason, merely from faction, or caprice, should attempt to arrogate to them-selves, under the name of advice, the whole power and authority of the Crown, the monarchy would be a useless encumbrance upon the country, if it were not able to make a stand against such attempts. . . .[2]

This had been a constant theme in his notes. All his proposals were derived from his conception of the essentially constitutional nature of the crisis, and his conviction that the administration's policy threatened the constitution. In his eagerness to defend the constitution from Pitt's onslaught he was prepared to condone extra-Parliamentary action:

If . . . such a stand is to be made . . . the way ought to be prepared for it, by a previous strong remonstrance to the House of Commons from West-minster, against their whole proceedings. I am told we may depend upon Westminster . . . I am not very fond of these things; but on occasions they may be used. . . .[3]

But, whilst every effort was to be made out of Parliament as well as in it, the greatest security for success was the Prince himself:

All his actions, and all his declarations, ought to be regular, and the consequences of a plan. . . . All his written proceedings must be so many manifestoes . . . in this precarious show of government a party must be made and it must be made as parties are formed in other cases. . . .[1]

It is significant that Burke saw himself—saw the Prince of Wales—as undertaking the creation of a party dedicated to an interpretation of the constitution and deriving its validity from that interpretation. And this was the conviction which made Burke so unhappy at the way the Leaders of the Opposition— Fox, Portland, and, especially during the early weeks of November, Sheridan—had handled the party's affairs. They were preoccupied with what was to Burke a subordinate aspect of the crisis, the attainment of office with the support of the Prince of Wales, and they failed to give sufficient attention to the technicalities of the crisis. Over confident of success—a confidence which Burke, for all his initial trust in Portland and Fox, never fully shared—they had relied too complacently on the expected flow of events. At no stage had they appreciated the complexity and decisive nature of the 'abstract issues', and the controversy over inherent right was no substitute for that consistent stand for principle which Burke thought necessary in the circumstances of 1788. Fox had stumbled onto the doctrine of hereditary right, taking his ideas from Loughborough and casually omitting to consult his friends beforehand as to the best course to take in the House. No sooner had the doctrine been raised than the Whigs, fearful of its consequences and concerned primarily with political success, sought to undo the damage by qualifying the doctrine, minimising the differences between themselves and the Ministry. For Burke this was sheer folly, and his violence was the inevitable outcome of his horror at Pitt's proposals and dismay at the ignoble behaviour of his colleagues, who put power and place before principle and right. His increasing loneliness in the party—a

loneliness which was to culminate in the estrangement of 1791—
was the result of ideals, as much as of aristocratic exclusiveness;
and it is a measure of how little the Whigs had learned from their
erstwhile tutor that his behaviour should seem so bewildering
and so perverse to so many of them. They were irritated,
puzzled, and annoyed by his lapses of taste and exhibitions of
passion in debate. Three years after the Regency Crisis, when he
had broken with his colleagues over the French Revolution,
Burke told William Weddell how little he had been understood,
and maintained that his conduct in 1791 was consistent with his
ideas in 1788. Behind his behaviour on both occasions lay a
concern for the hereditary principle, yet few people realised
this—least of all the Prince of Wales or Charles James Fox:

. . . As to the Prince I had thought him deeply concerned that the ideas of an
elective crown should not prevail. He had experienced . . . the peril of these
doctrines on the question of the Regency. You know that I endeavoured, as
well as I could, to supply the absence of Mr Fox during that great controversy.
You cannot forget that I supported the Prince's title to the *Regency* upon the
principle of his hereditary right to the Crown; and I endeavoured to explode
the false notions, drawn from what had been stated as the revolution maxims,
by much the same arguments which I afterwards used in my printed reflections. I endeavoured to show, that the hereditary succession could not be supported, whilst a person who had the chief interest in it was, during a vital
interregnum, excluded from the government. . . . For this I am in disgrace
at Carlton House. The Prince, I am told, has expressed his displeasure that I
have not mentioned in that book his right to the Regency; I never was so
astonished as when I heard this. In the first place, the persons against whom I
maintained that controversy had said nothing at all upon the subject of the
Regency. They went much deeper. I was weak enough to think that the succession to the *Crown* was a matter of other importance to his Royal Highness
than his right to the *Regency*. . . .[1]

Misunderstood by friend and foe, Burke did not spare himself in
the cause. Those on whose behalf he laboured showed little
comprehension of the principles for which he fought, and little
gratitude for the selfless determination with which he defended

their rights. The opportunism of Sheridan, and Fox's careless appeal to inherent right, were alike anathema to Burke. In their preoccupation with his violence and extremism, qualities which they regarded with slight sympathy and less understanding, his contemporaries neglected the inner logic of his thought and the essential consistency of his conduct.

CHAPTER V

THE FINAL DEBATES AND
THE RECOVERY OF THE KING

The events of February 1789, form an epilogue to the principal controversies of the crisis. In Parliament Pitt's Bill was debated in language which echoed the struggle over hereditary right and the policy of restriction, and William Wilberforce complained of the staleness of discussion in the Commons after Fox's departure for Bath.[1] Only Burke brought fire and enthusiasm to the consideration of clauses which were merely giving effect to principles which the House had already approved, and even in his case it is possible to discern a feeling of hopelessness, which was all the more intense because it bore no trace of resignation to the inevitable.

The final flickers of controversy were overshadowed by the news from Kew. In the early days of February London was full of rumours that the King was recovering, much as in November there had been persistent whispers that he was dying. But now the official bulletins were encouraging. On 4 February the King had had a good night, and on the morning of the 5th he was quiet and composed; four days later the doctors felt that his condition gave grounds for cautious optimism.[2] On 10 February *The Times* assured its readers that his Majesty 'has been for the last week past in a state of more general composure and tranquillity and for a longer length of time than since his illness', and on the same day *The World* announced that 'the avowed amendment of His Majesty's health has diffused joy over every countenance in Great Britain. We say *every countenance*, because we will not be inhuman enough to suppose, that there are any who suffer their *Politics* to supersede their humanity.'[3] The favourable reports continued. The King was composed on the 9, 10, and 11

February, and on the 10th Willis assured Pitt that the King was continuing to mend 'in the most rapid manner', though he begged the Chancellor of the Exchequer not to divulge 'these sanguine thoughts'. On the 14th Willis found it impossible to speak too strongly of an amendment, and two days before *The Times* had been jubilant:

It will be a happy circumstance, and may be expected from the flattering accounts daily received of the King's state of health for a week past—that before the Regency Bill is ready for signature His Majesty may be enabled to resume the reins of government, and save all the trouble which will arise to the Opposition Gentlemen, of taking their seats at the different boards, which they have for some time past been preparing themselves for; such a fortunate event, will, we doubt not, meet the earnest prayers of nine tenths of his Majesty's subjects.[1]

Eager anticipation became more frequent as the prospects for the King improved and the spirits of all but the Whigs rose. The Archbishop of Canterbury wrote to William Eden to tell him of the good news:

The last ten days have past without a single interruption of good accounts from Kew. They have been clearly better & better; & this day's is the best of all— & signed by the Physicians whose hopes have hitherto been the least sanguine. Private accounts more than confirm the Public Ones. . . . In short, the minds of *all* men, of *all* descriptions, are strongly impressed with the Idea of *perfect* recovery; & those of most men with that of its being near at hand. And yet (strange to say!) even amidst these circumstances, no man has a doubt, but that there will be a change of Government the moment the Regency takes place. . . . Further it is possible, to be sure, that as the Regency can scarcely be complete yet these ten days, there may be such an improvement in the King, as to furnish still stronger arguments . . . for letting things remain undisturbed. And surely the Present Arguments are strong eno' without any addition. . . . Fox is not yet returned from Bath, & yet I am assured by his particular friends that he is very well. The general Idea of Mr Pitt's firmness, principles, & ability is much raised by the wonderful manner in which he has supported his business through the H. of Commons on ground much of it so new; & proof that it is so raised & continually rising, appears every day by addresses unsought for, & by the particular earnestness of all the Great Towns, with very few exceptions, in the Kingdom.[2]

The next day Mr Fraser wrote to Eden in much the same strain:

I do not know a moment . . . so promising an Appearance of the Recovery of the King as the present. . . . The necessary Caution has prevented the Physicians from being Sanguine, but I am sure I may say that there are very little doubts of his Majesty's perfect Recovery. It now under these Circumstances seems to be very doubtful whether there will be a change in Administration, particularly as those who wish to come in are not of a Mind on the particular Posts they are to hold, and the very respectable Conduct of Mr Pitt, throughout the whole of the Proceedings in Parliament on the Regency Bill, added to the whole of his disinterested and beneficial Administration have deservedly raised him in the opinion of the nation . . . if his Majesty continues to mend . . . as he has done for the last Seven Days. I shall trust that we shall remain as we are. Certain it is that Mr Fox . . . remains at Bath, & I do not find that he is much indisposed. . . .[1]

Even the pessimistic and cautious William Wyndham Grenville allowed the bulletins from Kew to raise his hopes. Though he was of the opinion that the Bill would pass by 18 February, at the earliest, and that letters of dismissal were already prepared to be sent out as soon as the Prince took over, he confessed that he and his colleagues derived a 'strong hope' from the improvement in the King's condition.[2] On 7 February his feelings were more gloomy. He thought that the Regent would be in possession of his authority on or about the 19 or 20 February, and, though the reports on the King's health remained favourable, he had not heard exactly what deductions Willis had made from the period of tranquillity enjoyed by the royal patient. But a week later he was much more cheerful and confident. He had been with Pitt to Kew, and the account given by Willis had been 'such as to confirm and strengthen all our hopes . . . every circumstance . . . affords us room to entertain the most sanguine hopes'.[3] The prevailing opinion was that the Prince would not, after all, turn the Ministry out, and that Portland had told him that, in the circumstances, it would be impossible for him to take any share in the new administration. It was also suggested that they had quarrelled again over the Prince's debts. Just as in November the feelings and expectations of both Government and Opposition had risen and fallen with the King's fits of madness and spells of lucidity, so now the improvement in his condition was the greatest factor in determining public opinion and in establishing or shaking the confidence of the politicians.

So common was the inclination to take a hopeful view of the situation, and so irresistible the evidence that the King was recovering his senses, that Sir Gilbert Elliot admitted the magnitude of the change which had come over the situation:

> The King has been really considerably better the last two days. Sir G. Baker saw him the day before yesterday, and says that he conversed rationally and coherently, with a good deal of recollection, for twenty five minutes. . . . Baker . . . does not consider this amendment an actual convalescence . . . but it is certainly an amendment. . . . Warren also . . . found him considerably better, but he does not seem to think the hope of a perfect recovery even now a probable one. . . .[1]

Even when confronted with undeniable evidence Warren was reluctant to admit that he had been mistaken in his original diagnosis, for it was humiliating to confess that the 'mountebank' Willis had been proved wiser than the society physicians. It was a bitter moment for the 'Buff and Blue' doctor, and with an obstinacy that was as rigid as it was ineffective to influence the course of events he persisted in holding out hopes to his Whig friends which were never realised and which only intensified their disappointment. There was a reprehensible ambiguity about much of Warren's conduct. On 7 February he told Thurlow that the King's amendment was so material that he thought it his duty immediately on coming to town to give the Prince an account of the situation. Yet, four days later, he told Portland that he would be foolish not to accept the Government should the Prince press it upon him, as it was impossible for the King to resume his duties in less than a year despite the improvement in his health. Behaviour of this sort did little to help his friends and his reputation suffered in consequence.[2]

Fox's absence at Bath did not mean that he took no further interest in the development of the controversy and the formation of the Whig Cabinet. Whilst taking the waters he wrote regularly to London, discussing the negotiations with Northumberland and the 'Armed Neutrality' and the proposed meeting of the Westminster electors. Nor was rumour silent about Fox's stay at Bath, the reasons which had sent him there, the progress of his cure, and the motives which kept him out of London for most of February. It was said that his illness was brought on by political disappointment; that he was afraid of Rolle and the eternally recurring and increasingly embarrassing Fitzherbert question; that jealousy of Sheridan had played a great part in his decision to remove himself from the scene. His physical tribulations were followed with as much interest as those of the King. Some reports claimed that he was dying, that the waters had caused a deterioration in his condition. Others asserted that they had invigorated his enervated frame; that his respite from politics had restored his health, and that he was feigning illness for political reasons. So eager were the journalists to give the public the latest news of Fox, that they assured their readers on several occasions that he had returned from Bath, when the object of their curiosity was amusing himself by attending lectures by a Mr Lloyd on a machine of his own invention, called the Eidouranion.[1]

The business of the Regency was never far from Fox's mind, but he benefited from his stay at Bath; yet, ironically, as his health returned, his fortunes declined. Pitt's victory over the restrictions had made it absolutely certain that any Whig Ministry would be less powerful than Fox had anticipated, and should the King recover a brief tenure of office by the Whigs would be nothing more than a sour reminder of the extent of their failure to realise the high hopes and complacent expectations of December. During most of his time at Bath Fox was preoccupied with the arrangements for a new Ministry, and although he remained incurably optimistic to the end, he became all the more aware of the difficulties of satisfying Northumberland and his associates. The Whigs found it no easy task to agree with their new allies, who were determined not to be swallowed up by Fox and Portland. Northumberland knew how greatly his new friends valued the support of the 'Armed Neutrality' in the two Houses and he was determined to exact a good price for it. Fox was resigned (so he wrote to Portland on 6 February) to having 'many dissatisfied people', but he was unhappy about the suggestion that Rawdon should become President of the Council. His own preference was for Carlisle, but Carlisle had no wish to accept the post even if it was offered to him. Perhaps Loughborough would succeed if he made another attempt to bring him round. Fox urged Carlisle's claims to the Presidency again on 11 February, but, at the same time, in order to placate the Duke of Norfolk, Rawdon would have to be given a Cabinet post. Fortunately the news of Lord John Cavendish was more encouraging—'it is a great comfort to have that point, which I think the most important of all, finally settled'.[1] Yet, while Cavendish had at last given way to his friends' entreaties, he had done so with great reluctance and some misgivings. Perhaps he secretly hoped that he would never have to implement his decision. As late as 9 February he wrote to Mrs Ponsonby:

> I do not know what to tell you about the King, the report is, that he is better, but I believe him to be the same in point of his mind; but they have made him rather more governable. I cannot tell you much about myself, they plague me to death to be a great man again, but I have a vast aversion to it. I do not know how it will end. . . .[2]

He gave way out of weariness, rather than any intense political conviction.

Busy as he was with the arrangements for the new ministry Fox was obstinate in his refusal to believe in the King's recovery. He knew that whenever George III came to his senses the Opposition's last hope would be dashed. Consequently in his haven at Bath he clung desperately to Warren's predictions, pouring scorn on the reports from Kew as mere pieces of Government propaganda. To be so near to the consummation of his dearest wish was too severe a disappointment to be borne with stoic fortitude. For Fox was nearing middle age. His political career had been a series of brilliant, but effervescent, displays in Opposition. Only in office could he find fulfilment, only then could he give the lie to accusations of extravagant and unscrupulous ambition. And now the news from Kew, flaunted by his opponents and trumpeted by *The Times*, *The World*, and the *Morning Chronicle*, seemed ominously frustrating. Fox took the simplest way out. He refused to believe that the accounts were true. On 12 February, whilst congratulating Portland on the success of the Whig interest in the Irish Parliament,[1] he confessed that he had not been quite so well, attributing his relapse to the extreme cold, and that he had 'no belief in the K's recovery, but I dare say some of our friends are a good deal alarmed'.[2] Secure in his delusions he remained oblivious to reality. On 16 February he was telling Portland that the bulletins, whether they were good or bad, ought not to make the 'slightest difference in the conduct of the Prince or of us'. He was anxious that no alteration in the party's conduct should imply the tacit abandonment of 'every principle on which we have relied'.[3] As late as 17 February he wrote to Fitzpatrick in optimistic vein. Encouraged by the majority in the Irish House of Lords for the Address to the Prince, he could not refrain from hoping that

all ideas of the Prince or any of us taking any measure in consequence of the good reports of the King are at an end; if they are not, pray do all you can to crush them; and if it were possible to do anything to cure that habitual spirit of despondency and fear that characterises the whig party, it would be a good thing, but I suppose that is impossible. I rather think, as you do, that Warren has been frightened, I am sure, if what I hear is true, that he has not behaved well. . . .[4]

This was little more than a blind refusal to face facts. However suspicious Fox was about the reliability of the doctors' reports he allowed his desires to cloud his judgment. For four months the Ministry and their supporters had seized upon every instance justifying hopeful speculations about the King's health, but that was no reason for Fox to assume that any favourable report must therefore be hearsay. He could not contemplate the possibility of another defeat, issuing this time out of a situation which had promised so much; but, if there had been a change for the better at Kew, it did not mend his fortunes simply to ignore it. The deficiencies of Fox's leadership are nowhere more clearly exposed than during the final stages of the long-drawn-out conflict. However weary he was, however exhausted by the state of tension in which he had been living for four months, he had little justification for retreating from politics, from the realities of the situation, and none for insisting that his colleagues should base their conduct upon his illusions, grappling as they were with the day-to-day problems of negotiation and debate. Yet, whatever they decided to do, they were caught in a sequence of events which they could not control. The frequent changes of plan over the Westminster meeting illustrate the fatal lack of consistency which rendered the tactics of the Whig opposition so futile during the Regency controversies. Fox and Burke had originally welcomed the suggestion of a great meeting of the Westminster electors at which an address of support for the Prince would be approved. In this way the successes gained by the supporters of the Government in the struggle for 'popular' approbation could be offset. Yet, on 2 February, Fox assured Adam that he thought it was right to drop the Westminster meeting. But that was not the end of the story. On 14 February a meeting was held at the Crown and Anchor in the Strand, at which an address of support for the Prince, condemning the Regency Bill and complimenting those who had opposed it, was passed unanimously. A petition against the Bill was distributed amongst the various public houses, as well as being left for signature at Debrett's in Piccadilly.[1] But this was hardly the mighty upsurge of agitation which Burke had hoped to rouse, and it was now a month too late to make any impact upon public opinion. No objective was realised because no objective had been defined. Negotiation went on by fits and starts; constitutional debate depended upon political expediency; and even the standards governing expediency changed from day to day. Fox found it convenient to congratulate the electors of Westminster for embarking upon a course of action which less than a fortnight earlier he had thought it wise to discard. Small wonder that Burke felt that no stand had been made for the principles threatened by Pitt's proposals for dealing with the emergency—proposals which were the consequence of an erroneous interpretation of the constitution.

It was no accident, therefore, that Burke played such a lonely part in the debates of February 1789. He was doing what he held his party ought to have done, and what his colleagues had manifestly failed to do. The policy which he outlined in his notes on the Regency was (so far as was possible) put into operation without the support of his companions. Someone had to speak up for the legitimate rights of the House of Brunswick. Had he not told the Commons that he considered it his 'sole pride and exclusive glory . . . to speak against the wishes of the people whenever they attempted to ruin themselves'?[1] Thus, when on 2 February the Commons debated the resolution respecting letters patent for opening Parliament and for a commission to be appointed under the Great Seal for giving royal assent to legislation, Burke denounced the proposal in a vigorous speech, declaring that the House had no right

'to authorise the Lord Chancellor to put the Great Seal to forgery, fraud, and violence, and that giving them the form of the royal authority, instead of the substance, was to give them the sweepings of the cobwebs in Westminster Hall, and the smoke of the dish . . .'.[2]

In contrast, Sheridan, full of sweet reasonableness and moderation on this occasion, reminded the House that no assertion had ever been made of the Prince's right to assume the royal authority without the consent of the two Houses. The question of right had been unnecessarily agitated. There was little in common between this and Burke's denunciation of the Ministry's proposals as nothing less than fraud. The expedient for giving the royal assent to the Bill was the most questionable part of the Government's case; but it was not indefensible. The Solicitor-General defended it on the grounds that the consent of the Crown was necessary for legislation, and that though the King was incapable in his private capacity the throne was not vacant. Therefore

the only mode of obtaining the King's consent was by putting the Great Seal to the commission for passing it, and making it a public act. If it was so authorised, that rendered it a public act; and if, upon the face of it, it expressed that it passed by the consent of the King, Lords, and Commons, the judges of the land could not dispute it. The Great Seal, once put to it, gave all the authority of law, and no inquiry could be instituted as to the mode of its having been passed. . . .[1]

The Opposition claimed—with some justification—that such a proceeding removed the right of assent from the King, since he had no means of expressing either approval or disapproval. But once it had been agreed (or conceded) that it was more correct to proceed by a Bill establishing the Regency than by an Address to the Prince calling upon him to accept the office, the 'legal fiction' was necessary. As Holdsworth has pointed out, both the rule and the presumption which lay behind the Government's policy were well established; the rule that in law no distinction could be drawn between the natural and political capacities of the King; the presumption that a document bearing the Great Seal was binding. Furthermore, the Government freely acknowledged that their expedient was limited by the necessity which it was intended to meet.[2]

On 5 February Pitt introduced his Regency Bill, which had an uneventful first reading; but on the following day Burke launched a vigorous attack upon the policy of the administration and the provisions of the Bill. The proposed piece of legislation would 'totally ... separate and parcel out the royal authority', and was designed to forward Pitt's ambition. Not only would it degrade the Prince of Wales, but it was also an insult to the House of Brunswick, 'who were to be outlawed, excommunicated, and attainted, as having forfeited all claim to the confidence of the country'.[1] The violence of his language provoked some mirth on the Government side of the House but Burke was undismayed. Gentlemen on the other side of the House might smile, but the conduct of the Ministry verged on treason 'for which the justice of the country would, he trust, one day overtake them and bring them to trial'. Here there were lusty shouts of 'Order! Order!' and Pitt interrupted to support the House's disapproval of Burke's language and sentiment. But Burke was not perturbed. He confessed that he had expressed himself with warmth, but this had not been inspired by 'any censurable imbecility of temper'. His vigour had sprung from 'a deep consideration of the great importance of the subject' and he would have been in error 'to have refrained from that indication of warmth which he had betrayed, when speaking of a Bill from the provisions of which the whole House of Brunswick were expressly excluded'. Nor was his charge of ambition irrelevant—'in examining a Bill that tended to cause a total revolution in the splendour of the Crown, to separate it from executive government, and to give it to other and unknown persons, he had a right to look to the private views of those who had brought in such a Bill'. He went on to criticise the provisions for the care of the King's person, from which the Prince was 'expressly excluded'. Perhaps that was proper, but why were the Dukes of York, of Cumberland, and of Gloucester, and the rest of the royal family excluded? The House had declared the King incapable of exercising his royal authority after a full examination of the physicians, but he was to be deemed capable of resuming the exercise of the royal authority without an examination of the doctors: 'This was putting the whole power of changing the government into the hands of Dr Willis and his keepers. . . . The whole was a scheme under the pretence of pronouncing his Majesty recovered to bring back an insane King.'[1]

When on 7 February the House discussed the Bill in committee, Burke returned to the attack. He stigmatised the clause enjoining the Regent to bind himself on oath to take care of the King's personal safety, and to govern according to the stipulations and restrictions of the Bill, not only as a mockery of the Prince of Wales, but as

an insult to common sense; for he found that the Prince, who was not to be entrusted with the custody of the royal person, was to swear that he would protect it; whilst those who were in fact to have the care of his Majesty were not to be called upon to give any pledge whatever for the faithful discharge of the trust committed to them. . . .[2]

There was some sinister intention underlying the Bill, otherwise it would not have been 'marked by such a departure from the established rules and customs'.

But on this occasion the most colourful contribution came, not from Burke, but from the indefatigable Rolle, who took advantage of the clause insisting that the Prince should forfeit his authority as Regent should he marry a Catholic, by moving an amendment adding the words 'or shall at any time be proved to be married in fact or in law to a Papist' to the Bill. He was merely giving a coherent shape to the inquiry he had made on 19 January about the Prince and Mrs Fitzherbert, and though in his speech he avowed that Fox's denial two years before had satisfied him he maintained that the doubts and rumours which were commonly entertained 'without doors' compelled him to raise the matter once again. If these could be effectually silenced the question might be set at rest for ever.[3] After a lively debate the amendment was defeated, Pitt acting throughout with great restraint and forbearance. North, Grey, and Sheridan all condemned Rolle's motion. They claimed that no such marriage could be legally contracted; the agitation of the question could answer no wholesale purpose whatever; such suspicions were not only derogatory to the honour of the Prince of Wales, but dangerous to the public welfare.[1] But the Whigs did not need to be reminded of the dangers of the Fitzherbert affair, for it was constantly clouding their prospects and dimming their hopes. That Rolle had returned to the attack after Pitt had disdained to countenance his original introduction of the subject into the debates on the Regency was ominous. That the Chancellor of the Exchequer had no need to exploit the issue was a sorry reminder of their situation.

The debates in committee continued, and on 9 February Burke singled out for special condemnation the clause restricting the Prince's right to create peers:

> His Majesty might continue ill for twenty years, and then what sort of anarchy, disunion, and difficulty the divided government they were setting up would create! By depriving the Regent of the power of making peers they had shut the door of the House of Lords against the people. They had put it out of their own power ever to correct their error, and made the House of Lords the great, independent and omnipotent branch of the legislature.[2]

Two days earlier he had been so vehement in his criticism of the motives of the Government that he had provoked laughter amongst the Treasury benches, imputing the restriction to 'the blackness of their hearts, and the rooted degree of their malignity'. Now he was called to order for the language in which he described the King's situation: 'They were talking of a sick King, of a monarch smitten by the hand of Omnipotence, ... the Almighty had hurled him from his throne, and plunged him into a condition which drew upon him the pity of the meanest peasant in his kingdom. ...'[3] He also referred to Pitt's leaving office, but the Ministry had now gained confidence to such a degree that Pitt took the opportunity to refute the insinuation:

> The right honourable gentleman had charged him with having told the House he was going out of office; the fact was he had never told them any

such thing, nor did he know he was to go out. But whether he stayed in or went out, he should endeavour to be serviceable to his country.[1]

All this was a far cry from the dark forebodings of November.

On 11 February the House debated the provisions for notifying the King's recovery by an instrument under the Queen's hand. Sheridan agreed that no one disputed the right of the King to resume his government on his recovery, but

the real question was, the fact of his Majesty being restored and capable of resuming his government, and the manner in which it should be ascertained, and the resumption of his powers made. . . . No person had doubted the propriety of their going into an examination, to prove the incapacity; it was their duty to do so, and it was equally their duty to take care to provide against any act of his Majesty until his capability was known.[2]

Mr Powys thought that the real issue was whether the King ought to resume his government on the authority of Parliament, or of nine members of the Privy Council, but a more impatient, self-righteous note was struck when Burke lectured the House on lunacy in general and royal lunatics in particular:

he had taken pains to make himself master of the subject; he had turned over every book upon it, and had visited those dreadful mansions where these unfortunate beings are confined. . . . Mr Burke read an extract from the volume to which he alluded, which stated that some of these unfortunate individuals after a supposed recovery, had committed suicides, others had butchered their sons, others had done violence to themselves by hanging, shooting, drowning, throwing themselves out of windows, and by a variety of other ways. . . .[3]

Here Burke was interrupted by cries of horror and amazement; yet he concluded his speech by painting a lurid picture of a supposed recovery—which would be 'most happy, if really cured' but 'horrible in the extreme, in its consequences, if a sudden relapse took place'.[4] Sheridan urged once more the necessity of Parliamentary investigation into an alleged recovery, and moved that the Regent not the Queen should be obliged to notify the two Houses of the King's restoration, but this proposal was defeated by 181 votes to 113.[5]

The Bill received its third reading on 12 February. Burke took no part in the debate on that occasion. He had now done all that he could in the way of fighting for the principles of the constitution, as he understood them, against what he considered nothing less than a conscious betrayal of them. Pitt was now so confident that he could afford to accept a suggestion made by Pulteney, and pressed home by Sheridan, that a time limit should be imposed on the restrictions on the Regent's power of creating peers. Pulteney proposed a three-year limit; Sheridan wanted this reduced to one year. After a debate the three-year period was decided upon, Pitt saying that he had no objection, either in theory or practice, to the new clause. Three years were, in any case, 'the extremest time to which, in any possible consideration, anything like a restriction could be supposed proper to extend'.[1] Yet, even in the debate's final stage, Grey could not refrain from remarking that no right to exercise the royal authority independently of Parliament had either been raised or urged. Fox had merely stated his private opinion without any authority whatever.[2] Even after two months heated party strife the Whigs were reluctant to admit their responsibility for the error of 10 December; yet, despite their hesitations, they had been defeated primarily as a result of that 'opinion' and of the manner in which it had been expressed. The Bill was passed and ordered to be carried up to the Lords.

Their Lordships debated the Bill on 16 February after it had been formally read for the first time and ordered to be printed on the 13th. On the 18th they were in committee but they were not to be troubled with the Regency business much longer. On 19 February Thurlow informed them that the King was in a state of convalescence.[3] The struggle was now over, and instead of celebrating their greatest victory since the fall of North, the Whigs had to accept their most humiliating reverse since the coalition.

The Lord Chancellor's announcement was the natural

consequence of the medical situation. On 17 February the bulletin had announced that the King was in a state of convalescence, and bore the signatures of Warren, Pepys, and Willis. *The Times* published the report the following day. On the 20th Thurlow visited Kew and saw the King and on 23 February the Prince of Wales and the Duke of York had an interview with their father. Later that day George III resumed his correspondence with William Pitt:

> It is with infinite satisfaction I renew my correspondence with Mr Pitt by acquainting him of my having seen the Prince of Wales and my second son. Care was taken that the conversation should be general and cordial: they seemed perfectly satisfied. I chose the meeting should be in the Queen's apartment, that all parties might have that caution which at the present hour could but be judicious.

> I desire Mr Pitt will confer with the Lord Chancellor, that any steps which may be necessary for raising the annual supplies or any measures that the interests of the nation may require, should not be unnecessarily delayed; for I feel the warmest gratitude for the support and anxiety shown by the nation at large during my tedious illness, which I should ill requite if I did not wish to prevent any further delay in those public measures which it may be necessary to bring forward this year, though I must decline entering into pressure of business and indeed for the rest of my life shall expect others to fulfil the duties of their employments, and only keep that superintending eye which can be effected without labour or fatigue.

> I am anxious to see Mr Pitt any hour that may suit him tomorrow morning, as his constant attachment to my interest and that of the public, which are inseparable, must ever place him in the most advantageous light.[1]

Significantly, no sooner was the King restored to health than he was doing his duty, issuing orders as usual, and attempting to expedite public business promptly. Pitt visited Kew, as requested, on 24 February, and on the 27th the King's recovery was deemed so complete that public bulletins on his health were discontinued.

Relief amongst supporters of the Ministry was profound and immense. The crisis had ended as suddenly as it had begun.

Lord Sydney, writing to Cornwallis on 21 February, commented on the bitterness which had been aroused:

We have seen no times when it had been so necessary to separate parties in private company. The acrimony is beyond anything you can conceive. The ladies are as usual at the head of all animosity and are distinguished by caps, ribands, and other such ensigns of party. They have old Queensbury out of England by calling him a Rat. . . . Lothian is a conspicuous figure among the deserters. Sir James Harris was created Lord Malmesbury. . . . He went to Pitt and declared his approbation of the intended measures and . . . restrictions. . . . He then went to the Prince and turned right about. The Duke of Northumberland . . . has been with Lord Rawdon at the head of the Armed Neutrality. These two have joined with the Prince, are the most inveterate and hostile of anybody covered as they are with the poor King's favours. Gratitude was not . . . to be expected from Stormont and Loughborough, and they boast that . . . their attachment is to the Constitution. . . . North . . . is led down to the House to act under Sheridan to joke upon the King's misfortunes. Thank God, the country in all parts, and both Houses of Parliament, have nobly stood by the King. . . . Mr Pitt has conducted himself with the greatest judgment and ability—Fox has been dangerously ill. . . . He has been absent some weeks from the House at Bath. I hear he is a good deal recovered.[1]

Naturally disappointment, tinged with bitterness, overshadowed all other feelings within the Opposition. Rawdon, one of those who had changed his tune to suit changed circumstances, told Cornwallis his side of the story:

. . . Before this reaches you, you will have had the news of the King's recovery; probably also of his resumption of the functions of government. . . . As to the extent of that recovery, there is great scepticism; and to speak truly I am very doubtful of it. That his mind is at present tranquil, and clear upon ordinary subjects, is without dispute; but the suspicion is that there are certain strings which will whenever they are touched, produce false music again. The care which is taken that neither the Prince nor the Duke of York shall see the King alone for a moment, whilst the Chancellor and Mr Pitt have severally conferences without a witness, marks an awkward apprehension. . . . (T)he view of what has passed within these last three months enables one to judge so far upon the probable conduct of Pitt, that I look forward with rather an uneasy eye to the coming time. Pitt will without scruple hazard the public tranquillity, if not designedly embroil it, rather than be removed from power; and the popular cry which has been excited and kept up in his favour by extraordinary management will enable him to cope (under the King's name) with all the influence of the Prince . . . that any moderation should be shown in such a struggle is more than can be hoped.

I, as you would probably expect, have taken part decidedly with the Prince upon this question, thinking the combination against him the most mischievous . . . that could possibly be conceived. By this means I have slidden into a kind of alliance with the Duke of Portland. Had a new administration been formed I should have had a seat in it: this . . . having . . . been stipulated by me . . . that I should never be considered as absorbed into the Duke's party, but should remain with my particular friends a distinct body. . . .[1]

Mr Storer described the situation created by the recovery of the King, when writing to Eden on 24 February:

The vessel has righted again; ministry is perfectly afloat . . . & probably this very day will put an end to the progress of the Regency Bill. The King has seen the Chancellor, the Prince of Wales, & the Duke of York. Many tears were shed, much paternal as well as filial tenderness expressed. More I cannot tell you. If the persons attached to Ministry do not bear their honours, & their success with more moderation & philosophy than they did their tendency towards disgrace and dismissal they will be insufferable. . . . How Burke and Sheridan must be disappointed. Charles Fox has been at Bath taking care of his health. At the moment [the] King recovers his understanding. Whether this is merely a lucid interval, or not, is more than I, or the Physicians, can say, but the King is so, & sanguine. Politicians will tell you that the King's understanding now is better, than it ever was. . . .[2]

For a time the Whigs clung to the hope of a relapse, but even this consolation proved illusory, and when Parliament was opened on 11 March, the town celebrated in style. Lady Kenyon wrote to her sister-in-law at Chester, telling her of the illuminations:

. . . how fine we look in this square, all lighted up as brilliant as possible. Mr Lee has ten candles in each window, four more than anybody else, to make amends for the want of joy within. I think I have made this house pretty; there is a large candle in each large payn, and a small lamp in the little ones. . . . The town will be beautiful, for there are more devices than ever I saw. Lord Mansfield's house has 'G.R.' in little lamps . . . outside. . . . Many have . . . a

crown and 'G.R.'; some the word 'Rejoice' . . . there are so many people out
that I dare neither go nor leave my candles at home. Coaches are flying about
at a great rate, and by and by I expect squibs and crackers. . . .[1]

Even the Princes, who had consoled themselves with drink, had
to feign enthusiasm at their father's recovery. But their mother
had no illusions as to their real sentiments, telling the Duke of
York that while he and his brother would be welcome at a
concert at Windsor to celebrate the King's restoration to health,
she thought it fair to let them know that the entertainment was
primarily intended for those who had supported the King and
herself on the late occasion. Portland was furious on hearing of
her comment, writing to Fox on 29 March:

> I own my opinion is clearly for the Princes taking no notice of the offensive
> part of the invitation . . . and for their going to the Concert, that no pretence
> may be taken from their conduct for raising any new difficulty in the way of
> their access to the King, but that they are hurt and offended. . . .[2]

The Queen deeply resented the behaviour of the Prince and the
Duke during their father's illness, and when the Duke of York
fought his duel with Lennox, in which one of his curls was shot
off, she and her husband showed little emotion, the Queen saying
that she believed it was more Frederick's fault than Lennox's.
Fox could not disguise his fury over this incident:

> As to the poor man he is mad, but the Mother seems to me to go beyond
> the worst woman we ever read of . . . Liz would not be such a Mother if she
> had a Son, & with such a Son as the D of Y I do not believe except our Queen
> there is another in the world that would be. . . .[3]

Yet it must be remembered that George III had felt the Duke of
York's desertion to the Whigs so keenly that it contributed to his
mental breakdown, nor had the Prince's behaviour, after the
King had been moved to Kew, been noteworthy for its dignity
and restraint. The King's tribulations as a father had done much
to stimulate public sympathy for him during his madness, and
there was a great outburst of loyalty and affection when the King
and Queen attended the public thanksgiving for his recovery in

St Paul's Cathedral on 23 April 1789. Less than a fortnight later the States-General met at Versailles, and the controversies over the Regency were soon forgotten in the debate which raged over events in France. Before that controversy ended Pitt, Fox, and Burke were all to be in their graves; the Whig party broken; the Prince to become Regent when his father went irredeemably mad in 1810. Ironically the precedent of 1788 was followed; his powers were limited, and his appointment embodied in an Act of Parliament modelled on Pitt's Bill, drafted twenty years earlier.

Yet, whilst the controversies over the French Revolution soon diverted attention from what appeared to be futile discussions over the question of hereditary right and irresistible claim, the Regency Crisis made the break-up of the Whig opposition in the 1790's more likely and more comprehensible. Despite the bold talk of devotion to Rockingham's principles it is difficult to discover precisely what those principles meant to members of the Opposition in 1788—always with the great exception of Edmund Burke. The Opposition depended to an increasing extent on purely personal loyalties, and with no public issue by which to test the political faith of the party, opposition in the 1780's was a fruitless and embittering business. The long succession of disappointments, and the depressing memory of the Coalition, only heightened Fox's inherent opportunism, an opportunism which had easily passed for idealism in the years of the American War. However sincere he was in his devotion to liberty, Fox was principally interested in power, and the longer he had to wait for it the more indifferent he became to the means by which he would attain it. Eventually it became enough for him to oppose Pitt; to emphasise his differences from the Ministry in terms as decisive as possible, without necessarily considering the technicalities of the question in dispute. In the peculiar circumstances of 1788, and the terms on which the Regency controversies were fought, this indifference to technicalities proved fatal.

For Burke, on the other hand, politics were meaningless apart from ideas. Power was necessary for the expression and fulfilment of ideas, not for its own sake. More than interest, more than success, ideas were significant and valuable in themselves, and whenever the constitution was involved they took on an almost religious aura. Thus, whilst for Fox the crisis of 1788 was another episode, although a vitally important one, in the struggle for power, for Burke nothing less than the constitution was at stake. The hereditary principle, fundamental to society and to govern- ment, and duly recognised and sanctified by the Revolutionary Settlement, was being questioned. Whatever one thinks, either of Burke's interpretation of the crisis of 1788, or of his attitude towards the French Revolution, an inner consistency must be recognised here. For Fox no similar consistency can be discerned. Hereditary right was defended in the debate of 10 December merely because it seemed to be the most accessible stick with which to beat the administration of William Pitt. A clear dif- ference, decisive in its magnitude, over the essential nature of politics and government, can be traced between Fox and Burke to the winter of 1788–9. The opportunism of the one and the idealism of the other had united them on the issues raised by the American War and the government of India. Now they were to be thrown further apart. Though they were friends, Burke had never really belonged to the inner circle of Fox's companions. He was not at home in the hearty extravagance of Brooks's, or the brilliant (but brittle) gaiety of Carlton House. The two old campaigners had drifted in divergent directions since Rocking- ham's death, and the crisis over the Regency emphasised how great was the gulf which separated them and how absolute the conflict of ideals which was to sever the most hallowed bonds in 1791. Burke was painfully conscious of the careless attitude of his associates towards hereditary right. He despised the negotia- tions with Thurlow and Northumberland, and the reluctance of his friends to match noble words with brave deeds. Meanwhile

Fox, using ideas as weapons in debate without understanding their significance, gave Pitt his opportunity.

For in the situation created by the King's breakdown men were dimly conscious that there was an 'abstract' issue which was important in determining the correct method of supplying the exigency. Although Burke saw this he was unable to persuade his colleagues to see the crisis in constitutional terms, and he could only tell Windham of his convictions and his frustrations. Only Pitt was equipped with both the political acumen and a sufficiently convincing interpretation of the constitutional aspects of the crisis necessary to withstand the stresses of Parliamentary debate. He was able to exploit and placate the fears of the rank and file member, whose support the Whigs had to gain in order to form a Ministry which had any chance of permanence. Until he was installed in office Fox had nothing to offer those who were the habitual supporters of the Government of the day, and when the two Houses accepted Pitt's restrictions on the powers and patronage of the Regent, he lacked the rewards and blandishments without which negotiation was a feeble artifice. The very nature of the Whig party prevented it from playing any constructive part in the crisis of 1788. It lacked unity; it had no ideas; it was deficient in patronage; its one idealist was regarded by many of his colleagues as a crank. For what made a Whig in 1788? Devotion to the Revolutionary Settlement? How was this to be interpreted? To identify one's interests with the fortunes of Fox and Portland was a miserable incentive to change sides, once doubts were raised about the powers which the Prince would exercise as Regent. Only those dissatisfied with their place or the reward which had been considered appropriate to their merit were likely to go over. Even the 'Armed Neutrality' did not make its change of loyalty apparent from the start, and when Rawdon found himself driven to press for a place in the new Cabinet he had no wish to be thought a convert to the Whigs.

By raising issues which the Whigs were not prepared to face, the crisis intensified the weaknesses which were already destroying the party. Personal devotion soon became warped and twisted in the shallow futilities of opposition. For all his fine words in the Commons about the worth and dignity of opposition Fox was under no illusions. His conduct was more subject to motives of calculation and gain than he either cared—or dared—to admit. Should any crisis arise in which devotion to Fox or to Portland was manifestly inadequate then the party was doomed. The issues precipitated by the French Revolution constituted such a challenge, but so, in a more humble way, did the crisis of 1788. The constitution was under review. Ideas were once more part of the political struggle. The individual member, so distrustful of Fox and his colleagues, would have to be convinced in debate, by a logical interpretation of constitutional principle and practice, as well as by appeals to interest and by the attractions of patronage. For this the Whigs were not equipped. Pitt took time; studied precedent; and finally came to a conclusion which made sense, both as constitutional theory and political practice. No similar attempt was made by his opponents. The policy of negotiation was tried, but without consistency or determination. Even an elementary degree of agreement was lacking. Loughborough argued the case for the Prince's inherent right, and for the Heir Apparent to take the initiative in supplying the exigency. Sheridan and Payne attempted to gain office by negotiation and the deliberate minimising of the abstract issues. Burke favoured a wholehearted stand for the constitution. Grey was preoccupied with his own position in the new Cabinet and inclined to support Sheridan's policy of enlightened self-interest. Portland, the party's nominal leader, floundered ineffectively, failing to take any momentous decisions or to give any definite example to his followers. Fox blundered into a debate on the technicalities of the Regency without any attempt to inform his colleagues of what he intended to do, without any understanding of the issues involved, and without any conception of the effects his action would have upon the political aspects of the crisis. The abstract issues were alternatively ignored and despised, and then assailed with no prior consultation and no unanimity. Burke's hope that the Whigs would prostrate themselves upon a sacrificial altar in order to redeem the constitution made little sense to his friends, who thought his ideas far-fetched, emotional, and not a little ludicrous.

It was, therefore, no accident that the party was even less united in March 1789 than it had been in October 1788. Nothing except the habits acquired during a generation of political conflict and pious sentiments derived from a mythology which had grown up round the years of the American War, held together men who had little confidence in each other. And, even by the indulgent standards by which eighteenth-century parties must be judged, this was inadequate. The price of failure was increasing distrust, bitter suspicion, petty bouts of recrimination. The Whig leaders saw themselves too easily as the helpless victims of a remorseless destiny; or, alternatively, as the innocent dupes of William Pitt's inhuman cunning and diabolical good fortune. They either could not appreciate, or would not admit, their own part in transforming the cheerful prospect of November 1788 into the desolate landscape of March 1789. In their dealings with each other they showed little loyalty; in their conduct in the two Houses, irresponsibility. A curious immaturity coloured their every action. Flippantly approaching the crisis as a happy change in their fortunes they failed to understand its true character. They had no desire to study the nature of Regency, or to prove, by their behaviour during the emergency, that they merited the trust placed in them by the Prince of Wales. Without any clear notion of what the crisis was about they managed the Parliamentary debates badly, seeking in verbal gymnastics a salvation from their own casualness. Burke claimed that his difference with the party turned on no trivial issues; that what separated him from his colleagues was the conviction that some great, decisive, principle was at stake. The greatest divergence of opinion during the controversy over the Regency was that within the Opposition itself—the contrast between sheer opportunism and earnest idealism. The fissures which the French Revolution was to crack wide open already existed, and the Regency Crisis marks the first stage in the disintegration of the old Whig party—the tragic *dénouement* to Edmund Burke's political career.

A BRIEF NOTE ON
THE IRISH CONTROVERSY

Fox and his friends showed little sense of reality in the exaggerated hopes which they entertained of the consequences of Grattan's victory in the Irish Parliament. In fact the controversy in Dublin did not materially influence the course of events in London. When the Irish commissioners arrived to present their address to the Prince of Wales, calling upon him to exercise 'all regal powers, jurisdictions, and prerogatives' the King had already recovered, and they were received with irreverent mirth. Yet the Irish debates throw an interesting sidelight on the controversy, especially if the attitude of Grattan is compared with those of Pitt and Fox.

When the King went mad the Irish Parliament was not in session, and because of the powers vested in the Lord Lieutenant there was no urgency similar to that felt in England over the exigency created by George III's incapacity. But several factors were soon in evidence: the unpopularity of Buckingham, the Lord Lieutenant; the unreliability of the boroughmongers and placemen; the desire of Grattan and Charlemont to assert in no uncertain fashion the independence of the Irish legislature under the constitution of 1782; the connexion between the Irish patriots and the Prince of Wales's circle in London. Buckingham became increasingly gloomy about the chances of controlling the Irish members, and his pessimism was well founded. When Parliament reassembled in Dublin at the beginning of February 1789 a good deal of 'ratting' had taken place: Shannon, Leinster, Tyrone, and the Ponsonbys were all in the Whig camp. On 5 February a Government motion calling for delay until the Regency Bill had been passed in England was defeated by 128 votes to 74; and on

17 February it was decided to proceed by an address to the Prince, modelled on that asking William of Orange to assume the executive government. When Buckingham refused to transmit the address to London he was censured by 115 votes to 83, and, whatever the outcome of the struggle between Pitt and Fox, his days as Lord Lieutenant were numbered.

Yet, though the British Cabinet could take no comfort from the proceedings in Dublin, Grattan's position was far different from that of the Opposition at Westminster. He had been given an assurance by the Prince that if the Whigs took over in London he would be given the opportunity to reform the Irish Parliament. Effective control would be placed in his own hands. Irish Ministers would be accountable to the Irish House of Commons. Official patronage would be used to end the rule of the Castle. Irish self-government would become a reality. It is doubtful whether such a pledge would have been honoured, but the promise made Grattan all the more inclined to resist the proposals of the British Government. But instead of emphasising similarities between the situation in Britain and Ireland he minimised them. Indeed, at times, his language was reminiscent of Pitt. He never affirmed the doctrine of 'inherent right', talking instead of the Prince's 'irresistible claim', and of the responsibility of the two Irish Houses to exercise an undoubted right and indispensable duty in remedying the defect caused by the illness of the King. Grattan was prepared to concede that restrictions might be valid in England—but they could not apply in Ireland without the consent of the Irish Parliament. He saw no difficulty in the Regent exercising different degrees of power in the two countries.

The debates in the Dublin Parliament raged, not over inherent right (although the doctrine had its advocates) and Parliamentary privilege, but over the correct procedure: an address to the Prince? Or a Bill on the English model? Fitzgibbon, the Government's most able apologist, abhorred any suggestion of restrictions on the Irish Regent: on that point he and Grattan were in agreement. But he pleaded for the Prince to be entrusted with the Regency by means of a Bill:

> If you make the Prince of Wales your Regent and grant him the plenitude of power, in God's name let it be done by Bill; otherwise I see such danger that I deprecate the measure proposed . . . I abominate the idea of restraining the Prince Regent in the power of making peers in this country, or in limiting him in the power of making grants on the narrow principles of suspicion and distrust. This is a question which rests upon very different ground in this country from that on which it has been taken up in England. . . .[1]

He reminded the House that without the Great Seal of England no piece of Irish legislation could become law; it was therefore necessary to wait until the British Parliament had reached its decision. It was always wise to concur with the legislature at Westminster, unless there were strong reasons for not doing so. Most of the Irish speakers placed the whole question on a different basis from that which had determined the debates in London. In this way they could ostentatiously display their independence, besides indulging in that opposition to the British executive which formed the staple diet of Irish politics. Yet it is an exaggeration to say (with Mr Steven Watson)[2] that love of a fight was Grattan's main motive. He had an ideal of a free, united, Ireland, and he thought it worth fighting for.

As in England, both sides strained the constitution to some extent. The Irish Parliament could not deny that under Yelverton's Act of 1782 their legislative Bills required the British Great Seal before passing into law; but it was also questionable to create a fictitious means of gaining the royal assent to a Bill. Grattan was overhasty in insisting that the Dublin Parliament should reach its own decision, regardless of events in London, even if this was not, as Lecky maintains, the 'greatest political error of his life'.[3] His conduct becomes more comprehensible when one remembers his determination to vindicate the independent status of the Irish Parliament. Under the constitution of 1782 the Crown was the link between the two kingdoms. There was no technical reason for depending on the British example; and, with the bright prospects opened up by a Whig administration in London, there were valid political reasons for independent action.

But the Irish decision had serious consequences, even if it did not affect the outcome at Westminster. As soon as the King's recovery became known in Dublin those who had gone over to Grattan deserted him: Buckingham's desire for revenge was roused, and Pitt was determined to bring the Irish to heel. More significant still, British faith in the constitution of 1782 was weakened. Pitt saw the need for tighter control. Awkward situations might have arisen, had the Prince been invested with the Irish Regency on terms different from those imposed in England, although, as Professor Harlow has pointed out, current talk about 'separation' was nonsense.[1] Pitt was acutely aware of the dangers inherent in the situation. Grattan had shown restraint and statesmanship in the views he had expounded, but there was no guarantee that this would always be so. There can be little doubt that the Regency Crisis reinforced the melancholy impression which the failure of his Irish resolutions had made upon Pitt. He had now received another reminder of the problem of governing Ireland, and his experience in 1788–9 strengthened the appeal which political union made when the troubles of the 1790's came upon him.

NOTES

PAGE 4

1 *Morning Post*, 31 October 1788.
2 Crawford to the Duchess of Devonshire, 7 November, printed in W. Sichel, *Sheridan* (London, 1909), vol. II, p. 403.
3 Payne to Loughborough, 7 November, printed in Lord Campbell, *Lives of the Lord Chancellors* (London, 1846), vol. VI, p. 189.

PAGE 5

1 R. Huish, *The Public and Private Life of King George III* (London, 1821), p. 500; *Morning Post*, 10 and 11 November 1788.
2 *Morning Post*, 13 November.
3 *Diary and Letters of Madame D'Arblay* (London, 1893), vol. III, p. 52; J. Holland Rose, *William Pitt and National Revival* (London, 1911), p. 408; *A History of the Royal Malady by a Page of the Presence* (London, 1789), p. 21.
4 Sir George Baker's *Diary*, entries for 2, 3, 4, 5, and 6 November 1788.

PAGE 6

1 George III to Pitt, 20 October 1788, printed in the appendix to Earl Stanhope's *Life of Pitt* (London, 1861), vol. II, pp. iii–iv.
2 Baker's *Diary*, 17, 18, and 19 October.
3 *Op. cit.* entry for 22 October.
4 *Op. cit.* entry for 22 October.
5 George III to Pitt, 25 October, Stanhope, *Life of Pitt* (1861), vol. II, p. iv.

PAGE 7

1 Sir Gilbert Elliot to his wife, 27 October, *Life and Letters of Sir Gilbert Elliot, First Earl of Minto* (London, 1874), vol. I, p. 225.
2 *Ibid.*; the report of the violent spasm in the stomach is repeated in *Courts and Cabinets of George III* (London, 1853), vol. I, pp. 428–9: '. . . The King's illness . . . began with a violent spasmodic attack in his stomach; and has continued with more or less violence, and with different symptoms, ever since. We put as good a face as we can upon it . . . but I cannot but . . . think that there is still ground for a good deal of alarm . . .'; Grenville to Buckingham, 22 October 1788.
3 Elliot to his wife, 4 November, *Life and Letters*, vol. I, p. 228; Grenville to Buckingham, 23 October, *Courts and Cabinets*, vol. I, pp. 428–9; also the Same to the Same, 20 November, *op. cit.* vol. II, p. 6.; Holland Rose, *op. cit.* pp. 406–10.

PAGE 8

1 Duchess of Devonshire's *Diary*, 20 November, Sichel, *Sheridan*, vol. II, p. 404; *The Knight of the Cloacina*, a short play printed in *A History of the Royal Malady by a Page of the Presence* (1789); Huish, *op. cit.* pp. 503–4; E. Holt, *Public and Domestic Life of George III* (London, 1820), vol. I, pp. 314–15; Duchess's *Diary*, 23 November, Sichel, *op. cit.* vol. II, p. 406; also Lord Sheffield to Mr Eden, 22 November: 'He fancies London is drowned & orders his yacht to go there. He took Sir George Baker's wig, flung it in his face . . . & told him he might star gaze. Sir George is rather afraid of him . . .' (British Museum Add. MSS. 34428, ff. 308–9, *Auckland Papers*).

PAGE 9

1 Quoted by Sir Lewis Namier in his study of the personality of George III, printed in *Personalities and Powers* (London, 1955), pp. 39–58.
2 For the relationship between George III and the Duke of York, see R. Fulford, *Royal Dukes* (London, 1949), pp. 25–35.

PAGE 10

1 *General Advertiser*, London, 3 November 1788.

PAGE 11

1 Grenville to Buckingham, 7 November 1788, *Courts and Cabinets*, vol. I, pp. 434–5.
2 The Same to the Same, 8 November 1788, *op. cit.* vol. I, p. 439.

PAGE 12

1 *Morning Post*, 15 November 1788.
2 *Op. cit.* 17 November.
3 Public Record Office—*Chatham Papers* P.R.O./30/8/228(3), 247–62.
4 *Chatham Papers*, P.R.O./30/8/228(3), 233–41; *Newcastle Papers*, B.M. Add. MSS. 33052.

PAGE 13

1 Sir W. Holdsworth, *A History of English Law* (1938), vol. X, p. 435.

PAGE 14

1 See W. Stubbs, *Constitutional History of England* (Oxford, 1880), vol. III, p. 103; Holdsworth, *op. cit.* vol. X, p. 436; F. W. Maitland, *Constitutional History of England* (Cambridge, 1950 ed.), p. 201.

2 Stubbs, *op. cit.* vol. III, pp. 104–5: '. . . the protector was empowered to exercise the royal patronage in the administration of the forests, and the gift of smaller ecclesiastical benefices. . . . The members of the council were then named . . . they were to appoint all officers of justice and revenue; they were to have the disposal of wardships, marriages, ferms, and other incidental profits of the crown; nothing at all was to be done without a quorum of six or four at least, nothing great without the presence of the majority. . . .'

PAGE 15

1 Stubbs, *op. cit.* vol. III, p. 115; Maitland, *op. cit.* p. 201.
2 Holdsworth, *op. cit.* vol. X, pp. 437–8; on 1765, see R. Pares, *King George III and the Politicians* (Oxford, 1954), pp. 152–3: 'George III wished to make his ministers responsible in Parliament for the Regency; they seem to have resolved to avoid this responsibility, either because they genuinely thought that a proposal which only concerned the royal family was no business of theirs or because they feared that the King would want power to name his unpopular mother as Regent.' The King's insistence in 1765 on Parliamentary action and Cabinet responsibility gives further justification to Pitt's policy in 1788.

PAGE 16

1 Maitland, *op. cit.* p. 202; also Stubbs, *op. cit.* vol. III, pp. 179–80.
2 Stubbs, *op. cit.* vol. III, p. 187; Holdsworth, *op. cit.* vol. X, p. 439; Maitland, *op. cit.* p. 202.

PAGE 18

1 Holdsworth, *op. cit.* vol. X, p. 445; W. Anson, *The Crown* (4th ed., Oxford, 1935), vol. II, pt. i, p. 274; E. R. Turner, *The Cabinet Council of England in the Seventeenth and Eighteenth Centuries* (Baltimore, 1930), vol. I, pp. 369, 404–5; J. H. Plumb, *The First Four Georges* (London, 1957), pp. 47–8; C. Grant Robertson, *Select Statutes, Cases, and Documents* (1949 ed.), pp. 179–86.
2 Anson, *op. cit.* p. 274; see also an appeal to the people of Great Britain from a Freeholder in the *Public Advertiser*, 23 January 1789: '. . . sometimes the Queen, and sometimes the great Officers of State, were appointed to the Regency' (during George II's absences) 'but the late Prince of Wales, never, though of full age. . . .'
3 Holdsworth, *op. cit.* vol. X, pp. 442–3.

NOTES

PAGE 19

1 Holdsworth, *op. cit.* vol. x, pp. 442–3.

2 *Ibid.*; also *Incepta de Juribus Coronae*:'We have considered the capacity politick and natural of the King; and therein we find that the law doth not invalidate the acts of the King, by reason of those defects, which befall his natural capacity. . . . (T)he Prince as a man is subject to those infirmities and casualties that may befall other men; as Infancy, Sickness, distance from his kingdom and the like. . . . These emergencies . . . are of two kinds. I Accidental . . . II Ordinary. . . .' The accidental were provided for by the appointment of *Custodes Regni* and *Custodes Regis.* The ordinary by 'the King's councils ordinary and extraordinary'. *Chatham Papers,* P.R.O./ 30/8/228(3), 254–6.

3 See the speech of the Solicitor-General (Sir John Scott) in the Commons' debate of 2 February 1789: '. . . a regent could not be appointed but by act of Parliament . . . the consent of the Crown must be obtained to the act; and it was well known that his Majesty could not signify his consent in person, neither could he put his sign manual to a commission. The only mode of obtaining the King's consent was by putting the Great Seal to the commission for passing it, and making it a public act. If it was so authorised, that rendered it a public act; and if, upon the face of it, it expressed that it passed by the consent of the King, Lords, and Commons, the judges of the land could not dispute it. The Great Seal, once put to it, gave it all the authority of law, and no inquiry could be instituted as to the mode of its having been passed. . . . As the Bill was merely to constitute a regent it was quite a matter of indifference whether it was passed by one person or another, so long as it was passed in the name of the King upon the throne. . . .' *Parliamentary History,* vol. xxvii, pp. 1156, 1158.

PAGE 22

1 It was calculated that only 52 members were attached to Pitt: 'Of this party were there to be a new Parliament, and Mr P. no longer Minister, not above twenty would be returned.' The party of the Crown was estimated at 186; the Independent members at 108; several detached parties 'supporting the present Administration' accounted for another 43; Fox's supporters numbered 138; Lord North's 'Remnants' 17; neutrals 14. Circular headed Proposals in the Braybrooke Papers, printed in L. B. Namier, *Monarchy and the Party System* (Oxford, 1952), pp. 22–4.

PAGE 23

1 Despite the unpopularity of the Prince, Pitt was complimented on his restraint: 'To the credit of all parties, the subject Mr Rolle is said to have

205

obtruded upon the House of Commons ... is so generally offensive, that it will probably be ever received with the highest disgust. Mr Pitt is ... too upright a character to need any support of so indelicate and so malevolent a kind ... Mr Rolle ... little understands the nature of Mr Pitt ...', *Morning Post*, 21 January 1789.

PAGE 24

1 *A History of the Late Important Period* (London, 1789), pp. 530–1.
2 Sinclair to Fitzwilliam, 28 December 1788, *Wentworth Woodhouse MSS.* F 34(h); Elliot to his wife, 25 November 1788, *Life and Letters*, vol. I, pp. 238–9.
3 Huish, *op. cit.* p. 502; Holt, *op. cit.* vol. I, p. 313; *A History of the Late Important Period*, pp. 539–40.
4 *Letters to a Prince from a Man of Kent* (London, 1789), p. 25.
5 *Ibid.*

PAGE 25

1 See p. 6, *supra.*
2 See Burke's notes and papers on the Regency question, *Wentworth Woodhouse MSS.* Burke 15.
3 '... If this [the King's illness] lasts beyond a certain time it will produce the most difficult and delicate crisis imaginable in making provision for the government to go on. It must, however, be some weeks before that can require decision but the interval will be a truly anxious one', Pitt to Bishop Pretyman, 10 November; '... our last accounts begin to wear a more favourable aspect though there is not yet ground for very confident hope.... It seems now possible that a total recovery may take place ...', Pitt to Buckingham, 15 November, printed in Holland Rose, *op. cit.* p. 411; even before Willis's intervention Pitt was determined to defend the rights of the King: 'Mr P. thought that any alteration which might make it impossible for the K. to resume the Govt. in such a state as he had left it would be an insuperable objection to any alteration of that nature.' *The Political Memoranda of Francis, Fifth Duke of Leeds* (ed. O. Browning, Camden Society, 1884), p. 119 (26 November 1788).
4 K. Feiling, *The Second Tory Party* (London, 1938), p. 179; see also the entry for 28 November in *The Political Memoranda of Francis, Fifth Duke of Leeds*, pp. 124–5; 'We all seemed perfectly agreed as to the Prince being sole Regent; certain points of limitation would deserve much consideration.... The D. of Richmond thought it not unlikely but some proposal might be made for a coalition, which he thought would be a fortunate circumstance,

as by rejecting any junction with men who were personally obnoxious to the King we should do ourselves honour . . . by not sharing the Govt. with those whose former conduct and principles we had so much reprobated.'

5 Duchess of Devonshire's *Diary*, 20 November, Sichel, *op. cit.* p. 405.
6 Elliot to his wife, 25 November, *Life and Letters*, vol. I, p. 238.

PAGE 26

1 Storer to Eden, 28 November 1788, *The Journal and Correspondence of William Lord Auckland* (London, 1861), vol. II, p. 246; Huish, *op. cit.* p. 505.
2 Willis 'expressed himself very strongly to Pitt as to his hope of the King's recovery, and said that there was no symptom which he saw in him . . . which he had not seen much stronger in other people who have recovered. He has . . . already acquired a complete ascendancy over him. . . .' Grenville to Buckingham, 7 December 1788, *Courts and Cabinets*, vol. II, pp. 35–6.
3 *A Letter from a Country Gentleman to a Member of Parliament* (London, 1789), p. 8.
4 Duchess of Devonshire's *Diary*, 7 November, Sichel, *op. cit.* vol. II, p. 403.
5 *Ibid.* p. 402.

PAGE 27

1 *Alfred, or a Narrative of the Daring and Illegal Measures to Suppress a Pamphlet . . . with the Remarks on the Regency, proving on Principles of Law and Common Sense that a certain Illustrious Person is not Eligible to that Important Trust*, by Philip Withers (London, 1789).
2 *A Solemn Appeal to the Citizens of Great Britain and Ireland upon the Present Emergency* (London, 1788), pp. 31–42.
3 Fox was elected to the House of Commons in March 1768 but he did not take his seat until May of the following year.
4 'A great revolution in patriotic concerns is confidently mentioned, which is no less than the entire secession of Mr Fox from the field of politics. It is said . . . that he had lately won a very considerable sum, which may furnish . . . an ample provision for the rest of his life, and that therefore he has determined to yield to the love of indolent retirement, which . . . is supposed to be the leading wish of his mind . . . [I]f such a relinquishment . . . be really intended by Mr Fox . . . it is probable that the cause will be a conviction of the firm establishment of the present Minister, arising from the wisdom of his measures, the approbation of his Sovereign, and the esteem of the nation . . . and therefore a despair of returning to any official honour and employment, might have been expected long since to urge Mr Fox to peaceable resignation and retirement. . . .' *Morning Post*, 1 November 1788.

PAGE 28

1 Edward Gibbon, *Autobiography* (Everyman Edition, London, 1948), p. 143.
2 *Creevey Papers* (ed. Maxwell, London, 1903), vol. I, p. 22.
3 'Mr Fox rose to reply; but his mind was so much agitated, and his heart so much affected by what had fallen from Mr Burke, that it was some minutes before he could proceed. Tears trickled down his cheeks, and he strove in vain to give utterance to feelings that dignified and exalted his nature. The sensibility of every member of the House appeared uncommonly excited upon the occasion.' *Parliamentary History*, vol. XXIX, p. 388.

PAGE 30

1 'Fox . . . has great difficulty or backwardness in *resolving* as if he had no interest or no judgment in the affairs that are depending, and . . . he lets anybody else decide for him; so measures are often the production of chance instead of wisdom.' Elliot to his wife, 6 January 1789, *Life and Letters*, vol. I, p. 257; Duchess of Devonshire's *Preface* to her *Diary*, Sichel, *op. cit.* vol. II, p. 400.
2 The *Morning Chronicle*, 21 January 1789, contains a poem of six stanzas, entitled *The Political Weathercock* which gives a hostile version of Fox's career from the days when he held office under Lord North in the 1770's.

PAGE 32

1 John Nicholls, *Recollections and Reflections, Personal and Political . . . during the Reign of George III* (London, 1820), pp. 54–6.
2 Lord John Townshend to Lord Holland, 15 June 1830, *Memorials and Correspondence of Charles James Fox* (1853), vol. II, pp. 23–4.
3 Burke to Bullock, 3 March 1783, *Wentworth Woodhouse MSS.* Burke I, No. 1,222.
4 Townshend to Holland, 23 June 1830, *Memorials and Correspondence of C. J. Fox*, vol. II, p. 28.
5 Holland Rose, *op. cit.* pp. 391–405; Duchess of Devonshire's *Diary*, 20 November 1788, Sichel, *op. cit.* vol. II, pp. 404–5; Elliot to his wife, 26 November 1788, *Life and Letters*, vol. I, p. 241.
6 Prince of Wales to Fox, 11 December 1785, *Memorials and Correspondence of C. J. Fox*, vol. II, pp. 283–4.

PAGE 33

1 *Op. cit.* vol. II, pp. 278–84; Holland Rose, *op. cit.* pp. 391–405.

PAGE 34

1 *The Crisis* (1788), p. 3.
2 *A History of the Late Important Period*, p. 535.

3 *The Prospect Before Us* (London, 1788), p. 41.
4 *Op. cit.* p. 42.
5 *Op. cit.* p. 44.
6 *Op. cit.* p. 49.

PAGE 35

1 *Letters to a Prince from a Man of Kent*, p. 45.
2 *Op. cit.* p. 49.

PAGE 36

1 *Alfred*, pp. 9–10.
2 See *A History of the Late Important Period*, p. 531; and Huish, *op. cit.* p. 510.
3 *A Solemn Appeal to the Citizens of Great Britain and Ireland*, pp. 26–7.
4 *Op. cit.* p. 31.
5 *Alfred*, p. 45; *Letters to a Prince from a Man of Kent*, p. 51.

PAGE 37

1 *A History of the Late Important Period*, p. 537.
2 *Remarks on the Regency* (London, 1789), p. 50.
3 *Letters to a Prince from a Man of Kent*, p. 53.
4 D. C. Bryant, *Edmund Burke and His Literary Friends* (Washington Univ. Studies, St Louis, 1939), p. 5.
5 Burke to Fitzwilliam, 4 July 1782, *Wentworth Woodhouse MSS.* F 63(b)— letters of condolence on Rockingham's death.
6 Burke to Bullock, 3 March 1783, *Wentworth Woodhouse MSS.* Burke 1, No. 1,222.

PAGE 38

1 Duchess of Devonshire's *Diary*, 20 November 1788, Sichel, *op. cit.* vol. II, p. 404.
2 Burke to Rockingham, 25 September 1774, *Burke's Correspondence* (ed. Fitzwilliam and Bourke, 1844), vol. I, p. 480.
3 Burke to Loughborough, 17 July 1782, *Wentworth Woodhouse MSS.* Burke 1, No. 1,170; also Burke to Windham, 24 January 1789, *Wentworth Woodhouse MSS.* Burke 1, No. 1,485 + 1, printed in Burke's *Works* (1852 ed.), vol. I, p. 549.

PAGE 39

1 Portland to Burke, 24 July 1788, *Wentworth Woodhouse MSS.* Burke 1, No. 1,467.
2 Burke to Windham, 24 January 1789, *Works* (1852), vol. I, p. 549.

PAGE 40

1 R. Neville to Buckingham, 7 November 1788, *Courts and Cabinets*, vol. I, p. 437.
2 *Op. cit.* vol. I, pp. 444–5.
3 Duchess of Devonshire's *Diary*, Sichel, *op. cit.* vol. II, p. 403.

PAGE 41

1 Grenville to Buckingham, 7 November 1788, *Courts and Cabinets*, vol. I, pp. 435–6; Sichel, *op. cit.* vol. II, pp. 403; *A History of the Late Important Period*, p. 533; also Payne to Sheridan: 'I think the Chancellor might take a good opportunity to break with his colleagues if they propose restriction. The law authority would have great weight with us, as well as preventing even a design of moving the city.' Undated letter printed in Campbell, *Lives of the Lord Chancellors*, vol. V, p. 583.
2 Campbell, *op. cit.* vol. V, p. 583.
3 Holt, *op. cit.* vol. I, p. 313.
4 *Ibid.*
5 *Ibid.*

PAGE 42

1 Nicholls, *op. cit.* pp. 71–2.
2 *Ibid.*

PAGE 43

1 British Museum Add. MSS. 38192, ff. 134–5, *Liverpool Papers*.

PAGE 44

1 Sheridan to the Prince, printed in T. Moore, *Life of Sheridan* (1825), vol. II, pp. 19–20.
2 Fox to Sheridan (undated), printed in Moore, *op. cit.* vol. II, p. 31: 'I have swallowed the pill—a most bitter one it was. . . . I am convinced . . . that the negotiation will not succeed . . .'; see also Campbell, *op. cit.* vol. V, p. 584; vol. VI, p. 199.
3 Nicholls, *op. cit.* pp. 70–2; Campbell, *op. cit.* vol. V, p. 587.
4 Grenville to Buckingham, 7 November 1788, *Courts and Cabinets*, vol. I, p. 435.

PAGE 45

1 The Same to the Same, 7 November, *op. cit.* vol. I, p. 435.
2 The Same to the Same, 9 November, *op. cit.* vol. I, p. 441; also the Doctors Report to Pitt, 8 November, *Chatham Papers*, P.R.O./30/8/228 (1): 'The

dose of James's powder . . . produced a gentle perspiration but no diminution of the delirium; a second dose . . . is now operating in the same manner,
but with as little effect upon the delirium.'

3 Grenville to Buckingham, 9 November 1788, *Courts and Cabinets*, vol, I,
p. 442.

4 *Ibid.*

PAGE 46

1 *Ibid.*

2 Grenville to Buckingham, 13 November 1788, *Courts and Cabinets*, vol. I,
p. 448; also Baker to Pitt, 13 November, 10 a.m.: 'His Majesty's pulse is
nearly quiet this morning, he has eaten his breakfast very well, is not at all
violent in his actions; comprehends when a question is put to him better
than he has done for two days past, but soon relapses into inconsistency.'
Chatham Papers, P.R.O./30/8/228(1).

3 Printed in Holland Rose, *op. cit.* p. 411.

4 Grenville to Buckingham, 13 November, *Courts and Cabinets*, vol. I,
pp. 449–450.

PAGE 47

1 *Ibid.*

2 *Ibid.*

3 *Courts and Cabinets*, vol. I, p. 435.

PAGE 48

1 Buckingham to Grenville, 11 November 1788, *Dropmore Papers*, vol. I,
pp. 362–3 (H.M.C.).

2 *Ibid.*

3 *Ibid.*

4 *Dropmore Papers*, vol. I, pp. 364–6.

PAGE 49

1 'What corner of the globe can Fox be skulking in that the accounts which
have long since visited every quarter of Europe have not been able to reach
him?' Burke to Richard Burke, snr, and jnr (undated), *Wentworth Woodhouse
MSS.* Burke I, No. 1,476+2.

2 Grenville to Buckingham, 13 November 1788, *Courts and Cabinets*, vol. I,
p. 451.

3 The Same to the Same, 13 November, *op. cit.* vol. I, p. 451.

4 The Same to the Same, 15 November, *op. cit.* vol. II, pp. 2–3.

5 *Ibid.*

1 Printed in Holland Rose, *op. cit.* p. 411.
2 *Parliamentary History*, vol. XXVII, p. 685; Grenville to Buckingham, 20 November, *Courts and Cabinets*, vol. II, p. 8.
3 Grenville to Buckingham, 20 November, *op. cit.* vol. II, p. 9.
4 *Ibid.* p. 6.

1 Lord Sheffield to William Eden, 22 November 1788, B.M. Add. MSS. 34428, ff. 308–9, *Auckland Papers*.
2 Yorke to Hardwicke, 24 November, B.M. Add. MSS. 35383, f. 315, *Hardwicke Papers*.
3 Grenville to Buckingham, 23 November, *Courts and Cabinets*, vol. II, p. 12.
4 Duchess of Devonshire's *Diary*, 24 November, Sichel, *op. cit.* vol. II, p. 407; Grenville to Buckingham, 25 November, *Courts and Cabinets*, vol. II, pp. 18–19.

1 Elliot to his wife, 25 November 1788, *Life and Letters*, vol. I, p. 238.
2 Bulkeley to Buckingham, 25 November, *Courts and Cabinets*, vol. II, pp. 14–15; also Young to Buckingham, 30 November, *op. cit.* vol. II, p. 25; Elliot to his wife, 25 November, *Life and Letters*, vol. I, p. 238.
3 Duchess of Devonshire's *Diary*, 20 November, Sichel, *op. cit.* vol. II, p. 404.
4 In 1783; see Loughborough to Fox, Add. MSS. 47568, ff. 170–2, *Fox Papers*.

1 Loughborough to Sheridan (undated) printed in Campbell, *op. cit.* vol. V, pp. 584–5; Loughborough's Paper is printed in Campbell, *op. cit.* vol. VI, p. 195.
2 Burke to Fox, *Wentworth Woodhouse MSS.* Burke I, No. 1,482, printed in Burke's *Works* (1852 ed.), vol. I, pp. 545–7.

1 *Ibid.*
2 Duchess of Devonshire's *Diary*, 22 November, Sichel, *op. cit.* vol. II, p. 405.

1 Duchess's *Diary*, 23 November, Sichel, *op. cit.* vol. II, 406.
2 Duchess's *Diary*, 26 November, Sichel, *op. cit.* vol. II, p. 408.
3 Elliot to his wife, 26 November, *Life and Letters*, vol. I, p. 241.

4 Duchess's *Diary*, 30 November, Sichel, *op. cit.* vol. II, p. 408.

5 *Morning Post*, London, 28 November 1788; Loughborough had accepted the possibility of lower office than the Lord Chancellorship at an early stage in the crisis, if with obvious reluctance. Later, after Thurlow's conduct had thrown the Whigs into disorder, it was necessary to persuade him a second time to let the negotiations go forward. It was on the latter occasion that Fox was asked to help. His rivalry with Thurlow and the knowledge that some of his colleagues were seeking an accommodation with the Chancellor at his own expense helped Loughborough to take up an uncompromising position in favour of the Prince's 'inherent right'. 'I took the liberty of mentioning to the Prince the very liberal accommodation of your conduct in the promotion of his service. He said, "Well, if the C. chooses to remain where he is, Lord L. can have the Privy Seal or President for the present, and settle the other arrangement afterwards, if it is more to his mind". .... I have not yet read to *him* the contents of the transcript enclosed in your last ... but it shall be the first thing I do in the morning. ...' Payne to Loughborough, 9 and 10 November, Campbell, *op. cit.* vol. VI, p. 190.

PAGE 56

1 Unaddressed letter of Windham, 26 November 1788, B.M. Add. MSS. 37873, ff. 159–60, *Windham Papers*.

PAGE 57

1 Duchess of Devonshire's *Diary*, 2 December 1788, and 4 December, Sichel, *op. cit.* vol. II, pp. 410–11.

2 *Ibid.*

3 Elliot to his wife, 26 November 1788, *Life and Letters*, vol. I, p. 240.

4 The Same to the Same, 5 December 1788, *op. cit.* vol. I, p. 244.

5 *Ibid.*

6 *Ibid.*

7 Duchess of Devonshire's *Diary*, 5 December 1788, Sichel, *op. cit.* vol. II, p. 412.

PAGE 58

1 Duchess of Devonshire's *Diary*, 8 December, Sichel, *op. cit.* vol. II, p. 413.

2 Duchess of Devonshire's *Diary*, 5, 8, and 9 December, Sichel, *op. cit.* vol. II, pp. 411–13.

3 *Sheffield Register*, 6 December 1788; Young to Buckingham, 25 November, *Courts and Cabinets*, vol. II, p. 17.

4 Pitt to Grenville, 27 November, *Dropmore Papers*, vol. I, p. 376.

5 Grenville to Buckingham, 28 and 30 November, *Courts and Cabinets*, vol. II, pp. 21, 24.

PAGE 59

1 *Ibid.* For the hat story see Campbell, *op. cit.* vol. V, p. 587; Moore, *op. cit.* vol. II, p. 31; the page's words are reported as 'My Lord, I found it in the closet of his Royal Highness the Prince of Wales'.

2 Grenville to Buckingham, 28 and 30 November, *Courts and Cabinets*, vol. II, pp. 21, 24.

3 Pitt to Grenville, 27 November, *Dropmore Papers*, vol. I, p. 376; Grenville to Buckingham, 28 November, *Courts and Cabinets*, vol. II, p. 21; and 30 November, *op. cit.* vol. II, p. 22; Duchess's *Diary*, 29 November, Sichel, *op. cit.* vol. II, p. 408.

4 Duchess of Devonshire's *Diary*, 27, 29, and 30 November, Sichel, *op. cit.* vol. II, p. 408.

5 Grenville to Buckingham, 30 November, *Courts and Cabinets*, vol. II, p. 22.

6 Duchess of Portland to Burke, August 1786, *Wentworth Woodhouse MSS.* Burke 1, No. 1, 414+2.

7 Grenville to Buckingham, 3 December, *Courts and Cabinets*, vol. II, pp. 30–1.

PAGE 60

1 *Ibid.*

2 *Ibid.*

3 Grenville to Buckingham, 7 December, *Courts and Cabinets*, vol. II, p. 36.

4 The Same to the Same, 4 December, *op. cit.* vol. II, p. 32.

5 Young to Buckingham, 5 December, *op. cit.* vol. II, p. 33.

6 'It is now clear that Mr Pitt's object is entirely delay . . .', *Morning Herald*, 6 December 1788; in the *Morning Post* for 5 December the Opposition is criticised for anticipating 'the complete monopoly of every official appointment'.

PAGE 61

1 *Parliamentary History*, vol. XXVII, pp. 655, 687; Grenville to Buckingham, 6 December, *Courts and Cabinets*, vol. II, p. 34; 'In the evening a meeting of such Members of the House of Commons as have generally supported the measures of the Administration was convened at the Cockpit . . . the Chancellor of the Exchequer . . . informed the gentlemen assembled . . . that he would present the said minute (the examination of the doctors) and move that the same be referred to a Committee, who should be instructed to search for precedents, and make their report thereupon to the House . . .', Postscript to the *General Evening Post*, London, 4 December; also *Sheffield*

Register, 6 December; *The Gazetteer and New Daily Advertiser*, 5 December: 'The Members . . . at the Cockpit were only one hundred and forty three. He (Pitt) has frequently been followed thither by two hundred and fifty . . . this is a dreadful falling off . . .'; see also *The Political Memoranda of Francis, Fifth Duke of Leeds*, p. 128: 'We were unanimously of opinion that the first step to propose to Parlt. upon the indisposition of the K. being laid before them would be for each House to appoint a Committee to examine and report Precedents. . . .'

2 Grenville to Buckingham, 6 December 1788, *Courts and Cabinets*, vol. II, p. 34; 'Dr Willis, the gentleman last directed by the Privy Council to be employed, is of uncommon fame. . . . He was fetched express from Gretford, near Stamford, Lincolnshire . . .', *The World*, London, 8 December; 'Dr Willis . . . has devoted much of his time and attention to persons afflicted in the same manner (as the King). . . . Dr Willis does not profess to treat the disease medically; but to make those . . . subjected to it pass their time as easily . . . and as inoffensively as possible . . .', *General Evening Post*, 8 December; also *Sheffield Register*, 13 December; 'Dr Willis . . . is considered by some as not much better than a mountebank, & not far different from some of those . . . confined in his House. That such a man & Dr Addington shou'd be called in . . . has caused some jealousy . . .', Sheffield to Eden, 12 December, B.M. Add. MSS. 34428, ff. 325–6, *Auckland Papers*.

3 Grenville to Buckingham, 7 December, *Courts and Cabinets*, vol. II, pp. 35–6.

4 *Ibid.*

5 *Ibid.*

PAGE 62

1 Young to Buckingham, 30 November, *Courts and Cabinets*, vol. II, p. 25.

2 Grenville to Buckingham, 7 December, *Courts and Cabinets*, vol. II, p. 37.

3 *Ibid.*

4 *Ibid.*

5 *Ibid.*; also Duchess of Devonshire's *Diary*, 4 December: 'I saw the Prince this evening—he told me he should absolutely refuse any *limited* Regency, so they might do as they will. . . . A meeting at the Duke of York's before the House—the Prince at Brooks's, Sichel, *op. cit.* vol. II, p. 411.

6 Grenville to Buckingham, 7 December, *Courts and Cabinets*, vol. II, p. 37.

PAGE 63

1 The Same to the Same, 9 December, *op. cit.* vol. II, p. 41. Most of the press confidently anticipated that the Queen would play no part in politics —'On Saturday last Mr Pitt had an interview with her Majesty for

upwards of two hours: the result of the conversation was, her Majesty's explicit declaration that she would take no part whatever in any political arrangements of the state' (*Morning Herald*, Monday, 8 December). As late as 27 December the *Sheffield Register* discussed the possible results of a refusal of a limited Regency by the Prince—'The Queen at first seemed rather unwilling to take any share in public concerns, but the Lord Chancellor representing to her . . . the situation . . . the Queen at length gave way.' Lord Sheffield shared the former opinion—'It seems likely that the Queen will not choose in any event to take part in the government', Sheffield to Eden, 22 November, B.M. Add. MSS. 34428, ff. 308–9, *Auckland Papers*.

2 Grenville to Buckingham, 10 December, *Courts and Cabinets*, vol. II, p. 48; '. . . A change of administration will be the consequence of the Prince of Wales's accession to the direction of affairs. It is not a mere speculation, but we announce it confidently as a fact, and that it will take place as soon as the Regency Bill has passed the two Houses of Parliament . . .', *The Times*, 10 December 1788.

3 Grenville to Buckingham, 9 December, *Courts and Cabinets*, vol. II, p. 41; Grenville was too optimistic about Thurlow, but events justified his prediction of Northumberland's conduct; the Opposition press tried to give a sinister explanation of Pitt's policy and popularity: 'The agents of Mr Pitt, who have within these few days been dispersed through every part of the country to solicit addresses . . . are properly instructed what plea they are each to hold forth in their respective routes' (*Morning Herald*, 8 December). To judge by the public's response Pitt's supporters were much more efficient than his opponents in organising and directing public opinion.

PAGE 64

1 Grenville to Buckingham, 9 December, *Courts and Cabinets*, vol. II, p. 41.
2 *Parliamentary History*, vol. XXVII, pp. 690–2.
3 *Morning Herald*, 8 December.
4 Grenville to Buckingham, 10 December, *Courts and Cabinets*, vol. II, p. 47.
5 *Ibid.*
6 *Ibid.*
7 *Ibid.*
8 *Ibid.* Willis's reports were always optimistic, even when the King suffered a slight relapse, e.g. 25 December: 'His Majesty . . . today is quite disturbed . . . his tongue is very white, he is very dry, & his voice is quite hoarse. These changes are constant attendants on such indispositions, & I have no reason to change the opinion I have hitherto held', *Chatham Papers* P.R.O./30/8/228(1), f. 52.

PAGE 65

1 'At Brooks's I found the Prince ... that is to say he was in the House, but I did not see him for he had just retired to a private room with Grey, who ... is a great favourite, & is admitted to all their most private ... councils', Elliot to his wife, 5 December 1788, *Life and Letters*, vol. I, p. 224.

2 Duchess's *Diary*, 7 December, Sichel, *op. cit.* vol. II, p. 412; *The Political Memoranda of Francis, Fifth Duke of Leeds*, p. 133.

PAGE 66

1 Duchess of Devonshire's *Diary*, 7 December, Sichel, *op. cit.* vol. II, p. 412.

2 Duchess's *Preface* to her *Diary*, Sichel, *op. cit.* vol. II, p. 400.

PAGE 67

1 Sir John Eden to William Eden, 11 December 1788, *The Journal and Correspondence of William, Lord Auckland* (London, 1861), vol. II, p. 252.

2 E.g. *A Solemn Appeal to the Citizens of Great Britain and Ireland* (London, 1788); *Three Letters on the Question of Regency*, by Capel Lofft (London, 1788); *A Short View of the Present Great Question* (London, 1788); *Considerations on the Establishment of a Regency* (London, 1788); *The Prospect Before Us* (London, 1788); *Answer to the Considerations on the Establishment of a Regency* (London, 1788).

PAGE 68

1 *Parliamentary History*, vol. XXVII, pp. 704–5; the examination of the physicians by the Commons' committee is printed in the same volume, pp. 692–704.

2 *Op. cit.* vol. XXVII, p. 706.

PAGE 69

1 *Op. cit.* vol. XXVII, p. 707.

PAGE 71

1 *Op. cit.* vol. XXVII, pp. 709–10.

PAGE 72

1 *Op. cit.* vol. XXVII, pp. 712–13.

PAGE 73

1 'I think His Majesty has been more composed today ... & his mind has been less confused & agitated & he has taken his medicines very readily & his meals very regularly', F. Willis to Pitt, 8 December 1788, P.R.O./30/8/228(1),

f. 44, *Chatham Papers*; 'I am more & more confirmed in the opinion . . .
that I have not the least doubt whatever of his Majesty's compleat recovery',
T. Willis to Pitt, 18 December, P.R.O./30/8/228(1), f. 50, *Chatham Papers*.

PAGE 74

1 *Parliamentary History*, vol. XXVII, p. 713.
2 *A Letter from an Irish Gentleman in London to the People of Ireland on the
Limitation of the Regency* (London, 1789), p. 7; 'A loose expression falling un-
premeditated from Mr Fox was seized upon with avidity and pursued with
rancour by his opponents. . . .'
3 *Parliamentary History*, vol. XXVII, pp. 714-15.

PAGE 75

1 *Op. cit.* vol. XXVII, p. 716.

PAGE 76

1 Duchess of Devonshire's *Diary*, 10 December 1788, Sichel, *op. cit.* vol. II,
p. 414.
2 Campbell, *op. cit.* vol. VI, p. 195.

PAGE 77

1 *Ibid.*
2 Campbell, *op. cit.* vol. VI, p. 197.
3 *Ibid.*

PAGE 78

1 Campbell, *op. cit.* vol. VI, p. 198.

PAGE 79

1 Young to Buckingham, 11 December, *Courts and Cabinets*, vol. II, pp. 49-50.
2 Bulkeley to Buckingham, 11 December, *op. cit.* vol. II, p. 51.
3 *Op. cit.* vol. II, p. 52.
4 Grenville to Buckingham, 11 December, *Courts and Cabinets*, vol. II, pp. 53-4.
5 Charlemont to Forbes, 18 December 1788, *Manuscripts and Correspondence
of James, 1st Earl of Charlemont*, vol. II, p. 84 (H.M.C. 13th Report, appendix
viii).
6 Sheffield to Eden, 12 December, B.M. Add. MSS. 34428, ff., 325-6, printed
in *The Journal and Correspondence of William, Lord Auckland*, vol. II, p. 257.

PAGE 80

1 *The Times*, 11 December 1788; *General Advertiser*, 12 December; *Morning Herald*, 12 December.
2 *Preface* to the Duchess of Devonshire's *Diary*, Sichel, *op. cit.* vol. II, p. 401.
3 *Parliamentary History*, vol. XXVII, p. 668.
4 *Op. cit.* vol. XXVII, pp. 670–1.

PAGE 81

1 *Op. cit.* vol. XXVII, p. 674. Thurlow's argument denying the distinction between the natural and political capacities of the King was to be used in favour of the means proposed by the Government for fixing the royal assent to the Regency Bill.
2 *Op. cit.* vol. XXVII, p. 675.
3 *Ibid.*
4 *Ibid.*

PAGE 82

1 *Op. cit.* vol. XXVII, pp. 718–19.

PAGE 83

1 *Op. cit.* vol. XXVII, p. 721.
2 *Op. cit.* vol. XXVII, p. 723.

PAGE 85

1 *Op. cit.* vol. XXVII, p. 726.
2 *Op. cit.* vol. XXVII, p. 727.
3 *Op. cit.* vol. XXVII, p. 730.

PAGE 86

1 *Ibid.*
2 *Ibid.*
3 'I never remember such an uproar as was raised by his [Sheridan's] threatening us with the danger of provoking the Prince to assert his right', Grenville to Buckingham, 13 December, *Courts and Cabinets*, vol. II, p. 56.

PAGE 87

1 *Parliamentary History*, vol. XXVII, p. 731.
2 Duchess's *Diary*, 11 and 12 December 1788, Sichel, *op. cit.* vol. II, pp. 414–16; also Elliot to his wife, 13 December, *Life and Letters*, vol. I, p. 245.

PAGE 88

1 Duchess of Devonshire's *Diary*, 12 December, Sichel, *op. cit.* vol. II, pp. 415–16.
2 *Ibid.*
3 Duchess's *Diary*, 14 December, Sichel, *op. cit.* vol. II, p. 416.

PAGE 89

1 Fox to Mrs Armistead, 15 December 1788, B.M. Add. MSS. 47570, ff. 180–1, *Fox Papers.*

PAGE 90

1 Grenville to Buckingham, 17 December, *Courts and Cabinets*, vol. II, p. 64.
2 Campbell, *op. cit.* vol. VI, pp. 199–200.
3 Campbell, *op. cit.* vol. VI, p. 201.

PAGE 91

1 *Parliamentary History*, vol. XXVII, p. 677.
2 *Ibid.*
3 *Op. cit.* vol. XXVII, p. 678.
4 *Ibid.*

PAGE 92

1 *Op. cit.* vol. XXVII, p. 679.
2 Duchess of Devonshire's *Diary*, 15 and 16 December 1788, Sichel, *op. cit.* vol. II, pp. 417–18.
3 *Parliamentary History*, vol. XXVII, p. 681.

PAGE 93

1 *Op. cit.* vol. XXVII, p. 682.
2 *Op. cit.* vol. XXVII, p. 684.
3 Elliot to his wife, 16 December 1788, *Life and Letters*, vol. I, p. 246.
4 Sir John Eden to William Eden, 15 December 1788, B.M. Add. MSS. 34428, ff. 349–50, *Auckland Papers.*
5 Pitt to Lonsdale, 13 December 1788; Prince to Lonsdale, 13 and 14 December; Pitt to Lonsdale, 16 and 31 December; Payne to Lonsdale, 6 January 1789, *Lonsdale Papers* (H.M.C. 13th Report, Appendix vii), pp. 141–5.

PAGE 94

1 Sir John Eden to William Eden, 15 December 1788, B.M. Add. MSS. 34428, ff. 349–50, *Auckland Papers.*

2 Grenville to Buckingham, 9 December, *Courts and Cabinets*, vol. II, p. 41; see also p. 63, *supra*.

3 *Parliamentary History*, vol. XXVII, p. 733.

PAGE 95

1 *Op. cit.* vol. XXVII, p. 737.

2 *Op. cit.* vol. XXVII, p. 738.

PAGE 96

1 *Op. cit.* vol. XXVII, p. 738.

2 *Op. cit.* vol. XXVII, p. 740.

3 *Op. cit.* vol. XXVII, p. 742.

PAGE 97

1 *Op. cit.* vol. XXVII, pp. 746-7.

2 *Op. cit.* vol. XXVII, p. 747.

3 *Op. cit.* vol. XXVII, p. 748.

4 *Op. cit.* vol. XXVII, p. 749.

PAGE 98

1 W. B. Pemberton, *Lord North* (London, 1938); Grenville to Buckingham, 23 November, *Courts and Cabinets*, vol. II, p. 13: 'He has not five votes in this Parliament'; see also I. R. Christie, *The End of North's Ministry* (London, 1958), p. 375; '. . . The North papers include part of an analysis of the House as at 1 May 1788. This provides lists of 108 out of the 139 members identified as usually acting with Charles Fox and of the seventeen members described as Lord North's party' (*Guilford MSS.* Kent R. O.); see also p. 22 n. 1, *supra*.

2 *Parliamentary History*, vol. XXVII, p. 751.

PAGE 99

1 *Op. cit.* vol. XXVII, pp. 752-3.

2 *Op. cit.* vol. XXVII, p. 754.

3 *Op. cit.* vol. XXVII, p. 755.

PAGE 100

1 *Op. cit.* vol. XXVII, p. 757.

2 *Op. cit.* vol. XXVII, p. 766.

3 *Op. cit.* vol. XXVII, p. 768.

PAGE 101

1 *Op. cit.* vol. XXVII, p. 772; also discussed in D. G. Barnes, *George III and William Pitt, 1783-1806* (Stanford University, California, 1939), pp. 189-92.

PAGE 102

1 *Parliamentary History*, vol. XXVII, p. 773.

PAGE 103

1 *Op. cit.* vol. XXVII, p. 775.
2 *Op. cit.* vol. XXVII, pp. 777–8.
3 *Ibid.*
4 Sheffield to Eden, 17 December 1788, B.M. Add. MSS. 34428, f. 326, *Auckland Papers*.
5 Duchess of Devonshire's *Diary*, 17 December, Sichel, *op. cit.* vol. II, p. 418.

PAGE 104

1 Elliot to his wife, 18 December, *Life and Letters*, vol. I, p. 248.
2 *Ibid.*
3 *The Times*, 15 December; *Morning Chronicle*, 15 December; *The World*, 17 December; *The Times*, 18 December.
4 *The Times*, 18 December.

PAGE 105

1 Fox to Loughborough, 26 December 1788, Campbell, *op. cit.* vol. VI, p. 206; see also the Duchess of Devonshire's *Diary*, 15 and 17 December, Sichel, *op. cit.* vol. II, pp. 417–18.
2 Elliot to his wife, 27 December, *Life and Letters*, vol. I, p. 250; *Sheffield Register*, 3 January 1789.
3 Grenville to Buckingham, 13 December, *Courts and Cabinets*, vol. II, p. 56.

PAGE 106

1 Young to Buckingham, 13 December 1788, *op. cit.* vol. II, p. 58.
2 Grenville to Buckingham, 17 December 1788, *op. cit.* vol. II, p. 64.
3 Palmerston to his wife, 17 December 1788, B. Connell, *Portrait of a Whig Peer* (London, 1957), p. 191.
4 Sir John Eden to William Eden, 19 December 1788, B.M. Add. MSS. 34428, f. 351, *Auckland Papers*; see also Elliot to his wife, 20 December, *Life and Letters*, vol. I, p. 249.

PAGE 107

1 *Parliamentary History*, vol. XXVII, p. 783.
2 *Op. cit.* vol. XXVII, pp. 789–97.
3 *Op. cit.* vol. XXVII, p. 797.

PAGE 108

1 *Op. cit.* vol. XXVII, pp. 814–15.
2 *Op. cit.* vol. XXVII, p. 819.
3 Duchess of Devonshire's *Diary*, 20 December 1788, Sichel, *op. cit.* vol. II, p. 419.
4 Duchess's *Diary*, 21 December, Sichel, *op. cit.* vol. II, p. 419.

PAGE 109

1 *Parliamentary History*, vol. XXVII, p. 819.
2 *Op. cit.* vol. XXVII, p. 823.

PAGE 110

1 *Op. cit.* vol. XXVII, p. 825.
2 Young to Buckingham, 22 and 23 December 1788, *Courts and Cabinets*, vol. II, pp. 71, 73.
3 *Parliamentary History*, vol. XXVII, p. 827.
4 *Op. cit.* vol. XXVII, p. 830.

PAGE 111

1 *Op. cit.* vol. XXVII, p. 833.
2 *Op. cit.* vol. XXVII, p. 838.
3 *Op. cit.* vol. XXVII, pp. 838–44.

PAGE 112

1 *Op. cit.* vol. XXVII, p. 845.
2 Sir William Young to Buckingham, 23 December 1788, *Courts and Cabinets*, vol. II, p. 72.
3 *Parliamentary History*, vol. XXVII, p. 884.

PAGE 113

1 *Op. cit.* vol. XXVII, p. 881.
2 *Op. cit.* vol. XXVII, p. 886.
3 *Op. cit.* vol. XXVII, p. 889.

PAGE 114

1 The Protest is printed in *Parliamentary History*, vol. XXVII, pp. 901–3.

PAGE 115

1 P.R.O. 30/8/228(1), ff. 50, 52, *Chatham Papers*; a Whig view of the same period is found in Palmerston's letter to his wife, dated 17 December: '. . . The King is just the same. When exhausted and reduced by physic and want of

sleep he is quiet, when recruited he is outrageous. When in his calmest state he was suffered to see the Queen and one of the Princesses, which threw him into such an outrageous frenzy as might have been attended with fatal consequences and they were obliged to put on the strait waistcoat. Most people think Willis a great quack, whose judgement is little to be trusted and whose knowledge extends no further than to the means of keeping his patients in order and treating them in the common method which is known to all who have the care of persons in that situation . . .', Connell, *op. cit.* pp. 190–1.

PAGE 116

1 *The Times*, Monday, 22 December 1788.
2 *Morning Chronicle*, 27 December; *Sheffield Register*, 3 January 1789.
3 Robert Sinclair to Fitzwilliam, 20 December 1788, *Wentworth Woodhouse MSS*. F 34(h).

PAGE 117

1 Sinclair to Fitzwilliam, 21 December, *Wentworth Woodhouse MSS*. F. 34(h).
2 John Dixon to Fitzwilliam, 24 December 1788, *Wentworth Woodhouse MSS*. F. 34(h).
3 P. Wentworth to Fitzwilliam, 25 December, *Wentworth Woodhouse MSS*. F 34(h).

PAGE 118

1 Sinclair to Fitzwilliam, 28 December, *Wentworth Woodhouse MSS*. F 34 (h).
2 *Sheffield Register*, 3 January, gives the division of the Yorkshire members in the debate of 16 December. For the question: Henry Duncombe and William Wilberforce (county); R. S. Milnes (York); Sir R. Pepper Arden and J. Galley (Aldborough); Sir J. Pennyman (Beverley); Sir R. Sutton (Borough-bridge); L. Darell (Headon); S. Thornton and W. S. Stanhope (Hull); H. Pierce and E. Lascelles (Northallerton); J. Smith and W. Southerton (Pontefract); Sir G. Page (Thirsk); Earl Tyrconnell and G. Osbaldeston (Scarborough). Against the question: Lord Galway (York); Viscount Palmerston (Boroughbridge); Edmund Burke and W. Weddell (Malton); Earl of Inchquin and Sir Grey Cooper (Richmond); W. Laurence (Ripon); R. Vyner (Thirsk); Viscount Duncannon (Knaresborough).
3 Burke to Windham, 25 December 1788, B.M. Add. MSS. 37843, ff. 13–14, *Windham Papers*; also Elliot to his wife, 27 December, *Life and Letters*, vol. I, .p. 249.
4 *Sheffield Register*, 3 January 1789.

PAGE 119

1 George Cavendish to Mrs Ponsonby, 31 December: 'Yesterday Pitt condescended to let the Prince know the Shackles he had prepared for him', *Grey Papers*, Box 70; Grenville to Buckingham, 4 January 1789, *Courts and Cabinets*, vol. II, p. 86; also W. Adam to Burke, 29 December, *Wentworth Woodhouse MSS.* Burke 1, No. 1,481.

2 *Grey Papers*, Box 70.

PAGE 121

1 Palmerston to his wife, 5 January 1789, Connell, *op. cit.* pp. 193–4.

PAGE 122

1 Liston to Eden, 6 January 1789, B.M. Add. MSS. 34428, ff. 393–4, *Auckland Papers*; Elliot to his wife, 6 January, *Life and Letters*, vol. I, pp. 257–8; Duchess's *Diary*, 5 January, Sichel, *op. cit.* vol. II, p. 423; Pelham to Foljambe, 5 January, *Savile-Foljambe MSS.* (H.M.C.) 158; *Parliamentary History*, vol. XXVII, p. 907.

2 *Parliamentary History*, vol. XXVII, p. 907.

3 *Op. cit.* vol. XXVII, p. 908.

4 *Op. cit.* vol. XXVII, p. 914.

PAGE 123

1 *Op. cit.* vol. XXVII, pp. 915–16.

PAGE 124

1 *Op. cit.* vol. XXVII, p. 919; the report of the Lords' Committee is printed in the same volume, pp. 659–66.

2 *Op. cit.* vol. XXVII, p. 921.

3 *Op. cit.* vol. XXVII, p. 922.

4 *Op. cit.* vol. XXVII, 924.

5 *Op. cit.* vol. XXVII, p. 925.

6 *Op. cit.* vol. XXVII, p. 928.

PAGE 125

1 Lord John Cavendish to Mrs Ponsonby, 9 January 1789, *Grey Papers*, Box 70.

PAGE 126

1 *Ibid.*

2 Elliot to his wife, 10 January 1789, *Life and Letters*, vol. I, pp. 260–1.

3 The Same to the Same, 10 January, *op. cit.* vol. I, pp. 261–3.

4 The Same to the Same, 10 January, *op. cit.* vol. I, pp. 261–3.

PAGE 127

1 The Same to the Same, 10 January, *op. cit.* vol. I, pp. 260–1.
2 Duchess's *Diary*, 10 and 11 January 1789, Sichel, *op. cit.* vol. II, pp. 424–5.
3 Duchess's *Diary*, 13 January, Sichel, *op. cit.* vol. II, p. 425.
4 Armytage to Fitzwilliam, 7 January 1789; also Beckett to Fitzwilliam, 5 January, *Wentworth Woodhouse MSS.* F 34(h).

PAGE 128

1 Beckett to Fitzwilliam, 12 January 1789, *Wentworth Woodhouse MSS.* F 34(h).
2 The Same to the Same 15 January 1789, *Wentworth Woodhouse MSS.* F 34(h).
3 *Sheffield Register*, 17 January 1789.
4 *Op. cit.* 10 January 1789.

PAGE 129

1 *Op. cit.* 17 January; *The Times*, 19 January; *Morning Chronicle*, 19 January; *The World*, 19 January; though the *Morning Chronicle* prints an account of the tumultuous meeting at the London Tavern on 7 January no similar account appears in *The Times*, which contents itself with the ministerial interpretation of the event.
2 *The Times*, 19 January 1789.
3 *Birmingham Gazette*, 19 January.
4 *The World*, 19 January; *The Times*, 20 January; the addresses were from the following towns and boroughs: Aberdeen, Gateshead, Leicester, Nairn, Chichester, Durham City, Dunfermline, Leominster, Newcastle upon Tyne, Oxford, Glasgow, Bridport, Southwark, Henley, Selkirk, Dumbarton, City of London, Canterbury, Tiverton, Stirling, Haddington, Woodstock, Reading, Leeds, Andover, Hull, Worcester, Sunderland, Taunton, Manchester, Windsor, Cambridge, Edinburgh, Southampton, Perth, Halifax, Maidstone; in several instances there were two addresses from the same place: e.g. the magistrates and Town Council of Glasgow sent one address, the merchants another; the Corporation of Hull sent one address, the clergy and merchants another; the Provost, Magistrates, and Town Council of Stirling sent one address, the Guildry another.
5 *Morning Chronicle*, 20 January; *The Times*, 22 January; Sir John Chichester opened the proceedings, the motion being proposed and seconded by Sir Thomas Acland and Sir Boucher Wrey, and received with 'bursts of applause'. His constituents took seriously Bastard's contention that he favoured the Prince as Regent, and Pitt as Minister.

PAGE 130

1 *Morning Herald*, 20 January 1789.
2 *Ibid.*
3 *The Times*, 20 January 1789.

PAGE 131

1 Thomas Buck to Fitzwilliam, 24 January 1789, *Wentworth Woodhouse MSS.* F 34(h). After two attempts the Pittites gave up the struggle—'Mr Danser thinks an Address from the Corporation to the Prince . . . after he accepts the Regency might easily be carried.' Danser was the leader of the Whig interest within the Corporation.
2 *Sheffield Register*, 31 January; *The World*, 19 January, contains accounts of the meetings in Montgomeryshire and Denbighshire.

PAGE 133

1 'This conviction of the evils which may arise to the King's interests, to the peace & happiness of the Royal Family, & to the safety and welfare of the nation, from the government of the country remaining longer in its present maimed & debilitated state, outweighs, in the Prince's mind, every other consideration, & will determine him to undertake the painful trust reposed upon him by the present melancholy necessity . . .', *Parliamentary History*, vol. XXVII, pp. 909–11, where both Pitt's letter of 30 December and the Prince's reply of 2 January are printed.
2 Buckingham to Grenville, 15 January 1789, *Dropmore Papers*, vol. I, p. 400.
3 *The World*, 19 January: 'When the apparent disagreements in the evidence of the physicians may strike the public, they should recollect how seldom it will be found that even two Apothecaries can join in one opinion; even when they have no politics to inflame them and no party to set them on.'

PAGE 134

1 *Parliamentary History*, vol. XXVII, p. 934; *Report from the Committee appointed to examine the Physicians who have attended His Majesty during his Illness* (London, 1789).
2 Canterbury to Eden, 16 January, B.M. Add. MSS. 34428, ff. 404–5, *Auckland Papers*.

PAGE 135

1 Storer to Eden, 16 January, B.M. Add. MSS. 34428, ff. 408–9, *Auckland Papers*.
2 Willis's Bulletins to Pitt, 1, 2, 3, 4, 5, & 6 January, P.R.O. 30/8/228(1), Nos. 54, 56, 57, 61, 62, *Chatham Papers*.
3 *Physicians' Bulletin*, 18 January, printed in *the Morning Herald*, 19 January.

PAGE 136

1 Unidentified correspondent to Eden, 16 January, B.M. Add. MSS. 34428, f. 206, *Auckland Papers*.
2 *The Times*, 19 January 1789.
3 *Ibid.*; *Sheffield Register*, 24 January (London news dated 17 January).

PAGE 137

1 Sheffield to Eden, 14 January 1789, B.M. Add. MSS. 34428, ff. 400–1, *Auckland Papers*.
2 Canterbury to Eden, 16 January 1789, B.M. Add. MSS. 34428, ff. 404–5: '. . . it is thought that things are not yet ripe enough for the manager of Drury Lane to be manager of the House of Commons', *Auckland Papers*.

PAGE 138

1 *Ibid.*

PAGE 139

1 *Parliamentary History*, vol. XXVII, pp. 946–7.
2 *Op. cit.* vol. XXVII, p. 950.
3 *Op. cit.* vol. XXVII, pp. 951–9.

PAGE 140

1 *Parliamentary History* vol. XXVII, p. 961.

PAGE 141

1 *Parliamentary History*, vol. XXVII, p. 964.
2 *Op. cit.* vol. XXVII, p. 966.
3 *Op. cit.* vol. XXVII, p. 966.
4 *Op. cit.* vol. XXVII, p. 970.

PAGE 142

1 'Nothing could be more beautiful than that part of Mr Sheridan's speech . . . where he paid a just tribute of liberal & elegant eulogium to the transcendent merits of Mr Fox. . . . After this full & honourable testimony . . . will it now be said . . . that an invidious competition has ever subsisted between these two great characters . . . ?' *Morning Herald*, 21 January 1789.

PAGE 143

1 *Parliamentary History*, vol. XXVII, pp. 974–87.
2 *Op. cit.* vol. XXVII, pp. 995–1003.

PAGE 144

1 *Op. cit.* vol. XXVII, pp. 1004–8.
2 *Op. cit.* vol. XXVII, pp. 1009–14.
3 *Op. cit.* vol. XXVII, p. 1014.
4 *Op. cit.* vol. XXVII, p. 1014.
5 *Op. cit.* vol. XXVII, p. 1015.

PAGE 145

1 *Op. cit.* vol. XXVII, pp. 1017–20.
2 *Op. cit.* vol. XXVII, pp. 1020–3.
3 *Op. cit.* vol. XXVII, p. 1023.
4 *Op. cit.* vol. XXVII, pp. 1024–6.

PAGE 146

1 *Op. cit.* vol. XXVII, p. 1034.
2 *Op. cit.* vol. XXVII, p. 1037.
3 *Op. cit.* vol. XXVII, p. 1039.
4 *Op. cit.* vol. XXVII, p. 1039.

PAGE 148

1 *Op. cit.* vol. XXVII, p. 1039; Pitt's restraint earned him compliments in the press, e.g. *Morning Post*, 21 January: 'Mr Pitt is . . . too upright . . . to need any support of so indelicate & so malevolent a kind as that brought forward with such rancorous perseverance . . . & has expressed himself in terms of strong disapprobation on this disgusting topic.'
2 *Parliamentary History*, vol. XXVII, pp. 1040–93.

PAGE 149

1 Fox to Portland, 21 January 1789, B.M. Add. MSS. 47561, ff. 91–2, *Fox Papers*.

PAGE 150

1 Fox to Portland (from Bath), 6 February 1789, B.M. Add. MSS. 47561, f. 102, *Fox Papers*.
2 Dorset to Hawkesbury, 5 February, Add. MSS. 38224, ff. 1–2, *Liverpool Papers*.

PAGE 151

1 Dorset to Hawkesbury, 24 February 1789, B.M. Add. MSS. 38224, f. 19, *Liverpool Papers*.
2 Fox to Adam, 2 February 1789 (from Bath), B.M. Add. MSS. 47568, ff. 238–9, *Fox Papers*.

NOTES

PAGE 153

1 *Bath Chronicle*, Thursday, 29 January 1789.

PAGE 154

1 G. Pellew, *The Life and Correspondence of the Right Honourable Henry Addington, First Viscount Sidmouth* (London, 1847), vol. I, p. 60.
2 *The Journals and Correspondence of William, Lord Auckland*, vol. II, p. 291.
3 George Selwyn to Lady Carlisle, 5 December 1788, *Carlisle MSS.* (H.M.C.) 660.
4 *A History of the Late Important Period*, p. 537.
5 *Parliamentary History*, vol. XXVII, p. 1199.
6 *Op. cit.* vol. XXVII, pp. 714 (10 December), 1171 (6 February), 1213 (9 February), 1248 (11 February).
7 *History of England in the Eighteenth Century*, vol. V, pp. 422–3.

PAGE 155

1 *Wentworth Woodhouse MSS.* Burke 15 (Papers on the Regency Question).
2 *Parliamentary History*, vol. XXVII, p. 713.

PAGE 156

1 *Op. cit.* vol. XXVII, pp. 1171–2.
2 Burke to Flood, 18 May 1765, Burke's *Correspondence* (1844 ed.), vol. I, pp. 79–80.
3 Burke to Fitzwilliam, 5 June 1791, *Wentworth Woodhouse MSS.* F 115(a).

PAGE 157

1 *Wentworth Woodhouse MSS.* Burke 15.

PAGE 158

1 *Ibid.*
2 *Ibid.*
3 *Ibid.*

PAGE 159

1 *Parliamentary History*, vol. XXVII, p. 715.
2 *Wentworth Woodhouse MSS.* Burke 15.
3 *Ibid.*
4 *Ibid.*
5 *Ibid.*
6 *Ibid.*
7 *Ibid.*

PAGE 160

1 *Ibid.*
2 *Ibid.*

PAGE 161

1 *Ibid.*
2 *Ibid.*
3 *Parliamentary History*, vol. XXVII, pp. 819–20.
4 *Op. cit.* vol. XXVII, pp. 819–20.

PAGE 162

1 *Op. cit.* vol. XXVII, p. 823.
2 *Wentworth Woodhouse MSS.* Burke 15.
3 *Ibid.*
4 *Ibid.*

PAGE 163

1 *Ibid.*
2 *Ibid.*
3 *Parliamentary History*, vol. XXVII, p. 714.
4 *Wentworth Woodhouse MSS.* Burke 15.

PAGE 164

1 *Works* (1852 ed.), vol. I, pp. 549–55; *Wentworth Woodhouse MSS.* Burke I,
No. 1,485 + 1.
2 *Ibid.*
3 *Ibid.*

PAGE 165

1 See pp. 52 and 76 above for Loughborough's paper advising the Prince and
his advice to Fox; and p. 53 for Burke's advice to Fox. Loughborough
wanted the Prince to take the initiative in the Privy Council; Burke wanted
him to take the lead by notifying the two Houses; otherwise there was an
almost direct parallel in their points of view.
2 I.e. that the Prince ought to take the lead in informing the two Houses of
the King's condition.
3 *Works* (1852), vol. I, pp. 549–55; *Wentworth Woodhouse MSS.* Burke I,
No. 1,485 + 1.
4 *Parliamentary History*, vol. XXVII, p. 819.
5 The Prince to Burke, 8 February 1789, *Wentworth Woodhouse MSS.* Burke I,
No. 1,487.

6 *Works* (1852), vol. I, pp. 549–55; *Wentworth Woodhouse MSS.* Burke I, No. 1,485+1.
7 *Ibid.*

PAGE 166

1 *Ibid.*
2 Duchess's *Diary*, Sichel, *op. cit.* vol. II, p. 401.
3 *Wentworth Woodhouse MSS.* Burke I, No. 1,485+1.
4 *Ibid.*

PAGE 167

1 *Works* (1852), vol. I, pp. 549–55; *Wentworth Woodhouse MSS.* Burke I, No. 1,485+1.
2 *Ibid.*
3 *Ibid.*

PAGE 168

1 I.e. the moderate style of debate upon which Pitt had congratulated Fox.
2 *Works* (1852), vol. I, pp. 549–55; *Wentworth Woodhouse MSS.* Burke I, No. 1,485+1.

PAGE 169

1 *Ibid.*
2 *Ibid.*
3 *Ibid.*

PAGE 170

1 *Ibid.*

PAGE 171

1 Burke to William Weddell, 31 January 1792, printed in *The Correspondence of Edmund Burke* (ed. Fitzwilliam and Bourke, 1844), vol. III, pp. 383–409.

PAGE 173

1 Wilberforce to Lord Kenyon, 12 February 1789: 'You cannot imagine how insipid and vapid our debates are without Fox. They serve us up the same tasteless mess day after day, till one loathes the very sight of it', *Kenyon MSS.* (H.M.C.) No. 1346, p. 527.
2 Report signed by Willis, Pepys, and Warren, Kew, 5 February, printed in *The Times*, 6 February; Willis to Pitt, 10 February, P.R.O. 30/8/228(1), 65, *Chatham Papers.*
3 *The World*, 10 February; *The Times*, 10 February.

PAGE 174

1 *The Times*, 12 February; also reports from Kew 9, 10, and 11 February, printed in *The Times*, 10 February, *Morning Herald*, 11 February, *Morning Chronicle*, 12 February; F. Willis to Pitt, 10 February; T. Willis to Pitt, 14 February, P.R.O. 30/8/228(1), 65–6, *Chatham Papers*; Warren Hastings's *Diary*, B.M. Add. MSS. 39881, f. 67, *Warren Hastings Papers*, entries for 6, 8, 10, and 11 February; J. Reeves to Hawkesbury, 9 February, B.M. Add. MSS. 38224, f. 3, *Liverpool Papers*.

2 Canterbury to Eden, 12 February 1789, B.M. Add. MSS. 34428, ff. 431–2, *Auckland Papers*.

PAGE 175

1 W. Fraser to Eden, 13 February, B.M. Add. MSS. 34428, ff, 433–4, *Auckland Papers*.

2 Grenville to Buckingham, 2 February, *Courts and Cabinets of George III*, vol. II, p. 103.

3 Grenville to Buckingham, 14 February, *op. cit.* vol. II, pp. 106–7.

PAGE 176

1 Elliot to his wife, 12 February, *Life and Letters*, vol. I, p. 271.

2 Grenville to Buckingham, 7 February, *Courts and Cabinets*, vol. II, p. 106; also Elliot to his wife, 18 February, *Life and Letters*, vol. I, p. 274.

PAGE 177

1 *British Gazette and Sunday Monitor*, 1 February; *The London Recorder or Sunday Gazette*, 1 February; *The Times*, 4, 10, and 11 February; *The World*, 4 February; *Morning Herald*, 11 February; *Morning Chronicle*, 13 February; *Bath Chronicle*, 19 February; 'Mr Fox seems to me to be offended at Sheridan's violent passions; his Journey to Bath is not for health only . . .', M. Huber to Eden, 3 February, B.M. Add. MSS. 34428, f. 418, *Auckland Papers*; *Sheffield Register*, 7 and 14 February.

PAGE 178

1 Fox to Portland, 6 and 11 February, B.M. Add. MSS. 47561, ff. 102–3, 104, 105–6, *Fox Papers*.

2 Lord John Cavendish to Mrs Ponsonby, 9 February, *Grey Papers*, Box 70.

PAGE 179

1 See Appendix—A Brief Note on the Irish Controversy.

2 Fox to Portland, 12 February, B.M. Add. MSS. 47561, ff. 107–8, *Fox Papers*.

3 Fox to Portland, 16 February, B.M. Add. MSS. 47561, f. 109, *Fox Papers.*
4 Fox to Fitzpatrick, 17 February, B.M. Add. MSS. 47580, ff. 139–40, *Fox Papers.*

PAGE 180

1 'Westminster has done very well . . .', Fox to Adam, 15 February, B.M. Add. MSS. 47568, f. 250, *Fox Papers*; *Morning Herald*, 16 February; *Sheffield Register*, 21 February.

PAGE 181

1 *Parliamentary History*, vol. XXVII, p. 822.
2 *Op. cit.* vol. XXVII, p. 1153.

PAGE 182

1 *Op. cit.* vol. XXVII, p. 1156.
2 Holdsworth, *History of English Law*, vol. X, p. 444.

PAGE 183

1 *Parliamentary History*, vol. XXVII, p. 1171.

PAGE 184

1 *Op. cit.* vol. XXVII, p. 1176.
2 *Op. cit.* vol. XXVII, p. 1178.
3 *Op. cit.* vol. XXVII, pp. 1182–3.

PAGE 185

1 *Op. cit.* vol. XXVII, pp. 1186, 1187, 1188, 1191.
2 *Op. cit.* vol. XXVII, p. 1215.
3 *Op. cit.* vol. XXVII, p. 1213.

PAGE 186

1 *Op. cit.* vol. XXVII, p. 1215.
2 *Op. cit.* vol. XXVII, p. 1239.
3 *Op. cit.* vol. XXVII, p. 1248.
4 *Ibid.*
5 *Op. cit.* vol. XXVII, p. 1249.

PAGE 187

1 *Op. cit.* vol. XXVII, pp. 1250–5.
2 *Op. cit.* vol. XXVII, p. 1258.
3 *Op. cit.* vol. XXVII, pp. 1273–93.

PAGE 188

1 George III to Pitt, 23 February 1789, Stanhope, *Life of Pitt* (1861), vol. II, Appendix vi–vii.

PAGE 189

1 Lord Sydney to Cornwallis, 21 February 1789, *Correspondence of Charles, First Marquis Cornwallis* (1859), vol. I, pp. 406–7.

PAGE 190

1 Rawdon to Cornwallis, 28 February 1789, *Cornwallis Correspondence*, vol. I, pp. 408–9.
2 Storer to Eden, 24 February, B.M. Add. MSS. 34428, ff. 456–7, *Auckland Papers*.

PAGE 191

1 *Kenyon MSS.* (H.M.C.) 526–7.
2 Portland to Fox, 29 March, B.M. Add. MSS. 47560, f. 33, *Fox Papers*.
3 Fox to Mrs Armistead, undated, B.M. Add. MSS. 47560, f. 182, *Fox Papers*.

PAGE 200

1 *Irish Parliamentary Debates*, vol. IX, pp. 53, 54.
2 *The Reign of George III* (Oxford, 1960), p. 391.
3 *History of Ireland in the Eighteenth Century* (1913), vol. II, p. 481.

PAGE 201

1 V. T. Harlow, *The Founding of the Second British Empire* (1952), pp. 616–27.

SELECT BIBLIOGRAPHY

I. ORIGINAL SOURCES

British Museum

Fox Papers, especially Add. MSS. 47560, 47561, 47568, 47570, 47571, 47580.
Auckland Papers, especially Add. MSS. 34428.
Warren Hastings Papers, especially Add. MSS. 39881.
Liverpool Papers, especially Add. MSS. 38192, 38223, 38224, 38310, 38471.
Windham Papers, especially Add. MSS. 37843.
Hardwicke Papers, especially Add. MSS. 35383, 36525.
Newcastle Papers, especially Add. MSS. 33052.

Public Record Office

Chatham Papers, especially P.R.O./30/8/228(1), Doctors' Correspondence with Pitt; P.R.O./30/8/228(3), Papers relating to the King.

Sheffield Central Library

Wentworth Woodhouse MSS. Papers on the Regency Question (Burke 15); Burke Correspondence (Burke 1); Fitzwilliam Correspondence (F 115a); Letters to Earl Fitzwilliam from Yorkshire during the Regency Crisis (F 34h); Letters of Condolence on Rockingham's death (F 63b).

The Prior's Kitchen, Durham

Grey Papers, Box 70.

The Royal College of Physicians Library

The Diary of Sir George Baker, F.R.C.P., relating to the illness of George III in 1788, together with some correspondence. (Typescript and facsimiles from the originals in the possession of Sir Randle Baker Wilbraham, of Rode Hall, Stoke-on-Trent.)
Letters and Bulletins relating to George III's illness. (Warren-Munro correspondence.)

II. PRINTED SOURCES

Historical Manuscripts Commission

Lonsdale MSS; Savile-Foljambe MSS; Kenyon MSS; Carlisle MSS; Charlemont MSS; Dropmore Papers.
The Parliamentary History (ed. Cobbett), XXVII and XXIX.
E. Burke: Works (1852 edition).

III. PAMPHLETS

A Short View of the Present Great Question. London, 1788.

Three Letters on the Question of Regency, by Capel Lofft. London, 1788.

The Prospect Before Us. London, 1788.

A Solemn Appeal to the Citizens of Great Britain and Ireland Upon the Present Emergency. London, 1788.

Considerations on the Establishment of a Regency. London, 1788.

Answer to the Considerations on the Establishment of a Regency. London, 1788.

The Crisis, or Remarks on a Letter to His Royal Highness the Prince of Wales, London, 1788.

An Address to His Royal Highness the Prince of Wales on the Report of His Intentions to Refuse the Regency, by a Member of Parliament. London, 1789.

Letters to a Prince from a Man of Kent. London, 1789.

A Letter from an Irish Gentleman in London to the People of Ireland on the Limitation of the Regency. London, 1789.

The Death, Dissection, Will, and Funeral Procession of Mrs Regency. London, 1789.

Observations upon the National Embarrassment and the Proceedings in Parliament relative to the Same, by John Lewis de Lolme, LL.D. London, 1789.

Copy of a Declaration and Articles Subscribed by Members of the Administration. London, 1789.

Constitutional Doubts on the Pretensions of the Two Houses of Parliament. London, 1789.

An Impartial View of the Present Great Question. London, 1789.

Regency and the Uses and Abuses of the Great Seal. London, 1789.

A Letter from a Country Gentleman to a Member of Parliament on the Present State of Public Affairs. London, 1789.

Seven Letters to the People of Great Britain by a Whig. London, 1789.

Alfred, or a Narrative of the Daring and Illegal Measures to Suppress a Pamphlet ... with Remarks on the Regency, proving on Principles of Law and Common Sense, that a Certain Illustrious Personage is not Eligible to that Important Trust, by Philip Withers. London, 1789.

A History of the Royal Malady by a Page of the Presence. London, 1789.

Report from the Committee appointed to examine the Physicians who have attended His Majesty during his Illness. London, 1789, ordered to be printed 13 January.

IV. NEWSPAPERS

E. Johnson's British Gazette and Sunday Monitor (especially for 1 February 1789).

The London Recorder or Sunday Gazette (especially for 1 February 1789).

The Times (especially for 29 October 1788; 10, 11, 12, 15, 18, 22, 26 December 1788; 19, 20, 22, 24, 26, 27, 29, 30, 31 January 1789; 2, 3, 4, 5, 6, 10, 11, 12, 13, 14, 16, 18 February 1789).

The World (especially for 30 and 31 October 1788; 1 and 3 November 1788; 5, 6, 8, 9, 17 December 1788; 19, 22, 26, 27, 28, 29, 30 January 1788; 4 and 10 February 1789).

Morning Herald (especially for 29, 30, 31 October 1788; 1 November 1788; 6, 8, 12 December 1788; 19, 20, 21, 23 January 1789; 11, 13, 16 February 1789).

Morning Chronicle and London Advertiser (especially 10, 15, 27 December 1788; 19, 20, 21 January 1789; 12 and 13 February 1789).

Bath Chronicle (especially for 29 January 1789; 12 and 19 February 1789).

General Evening Post (especially for 24 and 25 October 1788; 1 November 1788; 4 and 8 December 1788).

The Gazetteer and New Daily Advertiser (especially for 5 December 1788 and 29 January 1789).

Morning Post (especially for 29 and 31 October 1788; 1, 3, 6, 8, 10, 11, 13, 15, 17, 18, 19, 28 November 1788; 5 December 1788; 21 January 1789).

The Star (especially for 27 October, 31 October 1788; 9 December 1788; 30 January 1789).

General Advertiser (especially for 28 and 30 October 1788; 3 November 1788; 12 December 1788).

London Gazette (especially for 17 January 1789).

Daily Advertiser (especially for 23 January 1789).

Public Advertiser (especially for 23 January 1789).

St James's Chronicle (especially for 24 January 1789).

Whitehall Evening Post (especially for 30 October 1788).

London Packet (especially for 31 October 1788).

Sheffield Register (especially for 15, 22, 29 November 1788; 6, 13, 20, 27 December 1788; 3, 10, 17, 24, 31 January 1789; 7, 14, 21 February 1789).

Birmingham Gazette (especially for 12, 19, 26 January 1789).

V. CORRESPONDENCE, DIARIES, AND BIOGRAPHIES INCORPORATING PRIMARY MATERIAL

The Diary and Letters of Madam D'Arblay (ed. C. Barrett). London, 1893.

The Journal and Correspondence of William, Lord Auckland. London, 1861.

The Correspondence of Edmund Burke (ed. Fitzwilliam and Bourke). London, 1844.

Lord Campbell: *Lives of the Lord Chancellors and Keepers of the Great Seal of England*, vols. v and vi. London, 1846.

SELECT BIBLIOGRAPHY

B. Connell: *Portrait of a Whig Peer, compiled from the papers of the Second Viscount Palmerston, 1739–1802.* London, 1957.

The Correspondence of Charles, First Marquis Cornwallis (ed. C. Ross). London, 1859.

The Creevey Papers (ed. H. Maxwell). London, 1903.

The Diary of Georgiana, Duchess of Devonshire, printed in W. Sichel's *Sheridan*, vol. II, pp. 399–426. London, 1909.

Memorials and Correspondence of Charles James Fox (ed. Lord John Russell). London, 1853.

Lord Fitzmaurice: *Life of William, Earl of Shelburne.* London, 1912.

Courts & Cabinets of George III (ed. Buckingham). London, 1853.

E. Gibbon: *Autobiography* (Everyman Edition). London, 1948.

J. Holland Rose: *William Pitt and National Revival.* London, 1911.

The Political Memoranda of Francis, Fifth Duke of Leeds (ed. O. Browning). Camden Society, 1884.

The Diaries and Correspondence of James Harris, First Earl of Malmesbury. London, 1844.

The Life and Letters of Sir Gilbert Elliot, First Earl of Minto. London, 1874.

T. Moore: *Memoirs of the Life of the Right Honourable Richard Brinsley Sheridan.* London, 1825.

J. Nicholls: *Recollections and Reflections, Personal and Political, as connected with Public Affairs during the reign of George III.*

G. Pellew: *The Life and Correspondence of the Right Honourable Henry Addington, First Viscount Sidmouth.* London, 1847.

Memoirs of the Marquis of Rockingham and His Contemporaries (ed. Albemarle). London, 1852.

The Diaries and Correspondence of the Right Honourable George Rose. London, 1860.

Lord John Russell: *The Life and Times of Charles James Fox.* London, 1859–66.

Earl Stanhope: *Life of the Right Honourable William Pitt.* London, 1861.

H. Twiss: *Public and Private Life of Lord Chancellor Eldon.* London, 1844.

The Windham Papers. London, 1913.

VI. SECONDARY WORKS REFERRED TO IN THE TEXT

W. Anson: *The Crown*, Fourth Edition. Oxford, 1935.

W. Baring Pemberton: *Lord North.* London, 1938.

D. G. Barnes: *George III and William Pitt, 1783–1806, a new interpretation based upon a study of their unpublished correspondence.* Stanford University, California, 1939.

D. C. Bryant: *Edmund Burke and His Literary Friends.* Washington University Studies, St Louis, 1939.

I. R. Christie: *The End of North's Ministry*, 1780–2. London, 1958.

T. Erskine May: *The Constitutional History of England*. London, 1912.

K. Feiling: *The Second Tory Party*, 1714–1832. London, 1938.

R. Fulford: *Royal Dukes*. London, 1949.

V. T. Harlow: *The Founding of the Second British Empire*. London, 1952.

W. Holdsworth: *History of English Law*, vol. x. London, 1938.

E. Holt: *The Public and Domestic Life of George III*. London, 1820.

R. Huish: *The Public and Private Life of King George III*. London, 1821.

A History of the Late Important Period. London, 1789.

W. E. H. Lecky: *A History of England in the Eighteenth Century*, vol. v. London, 1913.

W. E. H. Lecky: *A History of Ireland in the Eighteenth Century*, vol. II. London, 1913.

F. W. Maitland: *Constitutional History of England*. Cambridge, 1950.

L. B. Namier: *Monarchy and the Party System*. Oxford, 1952.

L. B. Namier: *Personalities and Powers*. London, 1955.

R. Pares: *King George III and the Politicians*. Oxford, 1954.

J. H. Plumb: *The First Four Georges*. London, 1957.

W. Stubbs: *Constitutional History of England*. Oxford, 1880.

E. R. Turner: *The Cabinet Council of England in the Seventeenth and Eighteenth Centuries*. Baltimore, 1930–2.

J. Steven Watson: *The Reign of George III*, 1760–1815. Oxford, 1960.

INDEX